Personal Salvation and Filial Piety

CLASSICS IN EAST ASIAN BUDDHISM

Personal Salvation and Filial Piety

Two Precious Scroll Narratives of Guanyin and Her Acolytes

Translated and with an introduction
by
WILT L. IDEMA

A KURODA INSTITUTE BOOK
University of Hawai'i Press
Honolulu

Paperback edition 2022
Printed in the United States of America

Library of Congress Cataloging-in-Publication Data
Personal salvation and filial piety : two precious scroll narratives of Guanyin and her acolytes / translated and with an introduction by Wilt L. Idema.
p. cm.—(Classics in East Asian Buddhism)
Uniform title not available.
Includes bibliographical references
ISBN 978-0-8248-3215-5 (alk. paper)
1. Avalokitesvara (Buddhist deity) I. Idema, W. L. (Wilt L.)
BQ4710.A8P42 2008
294.3′422—dc22
2007043306

ISBN: 978-0-8248-9242-5 (paperback)

The Kuroda Institute for the Study of Buddhism and Human Values is a nonprofit, educational corporation founded in 1976. One of its primary objectives is to promote scholarship on the historical, philosophical, and cultural ramifications of Buddhism. In association with the University of Hawai'i Press, the Institute also publishes Studies in East Asian Buddhism, a series of scholarly investigations of significant themes and topics in the East Asian Buddhist tradition.

The Kuroda Institute gratefully acknowledges a generous subsidy from the Harvard University Asia Center toward the publication costs of this book.

University of Hawai'i Press books are printed on acid-free paper and meet the guidelines for permanence and durability of the Council on Library Resources.

Designed by Santos Barbasa Jr.

Kuroda Institute
Classics in East Asian Buddhism

The Record of Tung-Shan
William F. Powell

Tracing Back the Radiance: Chinul's Korean Way of Zen
Robert E. Buswell Jr.

The Great Calming and Contemplation:
A Study and Annotated Translation of the First Chapter of
Chih-i's Mo-ho chih-kuan
Neal Donner and Daniel Stevenson

Inquiry into the Origin of Humanity:
An Annotated Translation of Tsung-mi's Yüan jen lun
with a Modern Commentary
Peter N. Gregory

Zen in Medieval Vietnam:
A Study and Translation of the Thiền Uyển Tập Anh
Cuong Tu Nguyen

Hōnen's Senchakushū:
Passages on the Selection of the Nembutsu in the Original Vow
Senchakushū English Translation Project

The Origins of Buddhist Monastic Codes in China:
An Annotated Translation and Study of the Chanyuan qinggui
Yifa

The Scriptures of Won Buddhism:
A Translation of Wŏnbulgyo kyojŏn *with Introduction*
Bongkil Chung

Contents

Acknowledgments

My interest in the rich vernacular literature on the bodhisattva Guanyin was first aroused by the publications of Glen Dudbridge, but I only started to pursue this topic in more detail when Mark Meulenbeld decided to devote his MA thesis to a novel on Guanyin from the early years of the twentieth century. Because of our discussions I was stimulated first to read and then to translate *The Precious Scroll of Incense Mountain*, first into Dutch, and later into English.

After I moved from Leiden to Harvard, I twice co-taught a class on Buddhist *bianwen* with Robert Gimello. I learned a lot from him in this way, and I hope that my enhanced understanding of Buddhism is reflected in the current translations. Beata Grant kindly read through the draft of the complete manuscript, which was greatly improved by her many suggestions on matters of style and content. I also benefited from detailed suggestions by Stephen Teiser and Dan Stevenson. William Bodiford supplied me with the computer font to insert all the diacritics required by publications on Buddhist subjects.

I am very grateful to Peter Gregory and the Board of the Kuroda Institute for their decision to publish this work in their prestigious series. The comments and corrections of the two anonymous readers were very helpful. It is also a pleasure to acknowledge the efficient production of this book by University of Hawai'i Press. A special word of thanks is due Joanne Sandstrom for her meticulous copyediting.

Needless to say, all remaining defects of this monograph are purely my own.

Introduction

Even while the stern and majestic image of the Śākyamuni Buddha occupies the place of honor in every Buddhist temple throughout East Asia, among lay believers the veneration he receives pales in comparison to that offered to the bodhisattva Guanyin. If the Buddha holds out the elusive promise of nirvana to those who have chosen a monastic career, the bodhisattva is eager to come to the rescue of all those in need who appeal to her. The bodhisattva's almost universal veneration is testified to both by the ubiquitous small statues on domestic altars and by the colossal images erected in the open air, wherever the public manifestation of this veneration is allowed. Guanyin—the Chinese translation of Avalokiteśvara—has enjoyed this popular veneration almost from the very moment his/her name was introduced into East Asia a little less than two thousand years ago. Initially Guanyin was venerated in the form of a handsome young prince, whose male gender was underlined by his thin moustache. In later centuries he/she was also venerated in various esoteric manifestations, the most popular of which was the Guanyin with a Thousand Arms and a Thousand Eyes. From the tenth century onward, however, Guanyin was increasingly venerated in the shape of a woman, initially a dazzlingly beautiful young girl, later more often a stately matron.[1]

Modern scholarship continues to debate the question of Guanyin's change of gender.[2] But from the ninth century, the popular imagination came up with various legends that related, often in great detail, the history of Guanyin's female manifestations. The most popular of these legends focuses on her mortal life as the Princess Miaoshan (Marvelous Goodness). The beginning of the development of this legend can be traced to the very first years of the twelfth century. As the legend was taken up in various genres of literature, from formal biographies to plays and novels, it adapted itself to the changing demands of place and time.[3] The most popular version of the legend of the miraculous life of the saintly Princess Miaoshan, however, was a version titled *The Precious Scroll of Incense Mountain* (*Xiangshan baojuan*). Intended for performance, the story in this version is told in an alternation of prose and verse. While the earliest external reference to this text dates only from the early sixteenth century, and its earliest preserved printing only to 1773, its history may perhaps be traced back as far as the twelfth century.[4] The text circulated both in a more elaborate version and in a later, shorter version. This monograph offers an annotated translation of *The Precious Scroll of Incense Mountain* based on this later, shorter version of the text, which circulated widely among Guanyin's devotees in the second part of the nineteenth and the first half of the twentieth century and is known through many printings. *The Precious Scroll of Incense Mountain* is both an important document in the history of Chinese popular Buddhism that provides important insights into images of the religious experience of women and also a powerful and moving work of literature that merits wider exposure.

On the frontispiece of the 1773 edition of *The Precious Scroll of Incense Mountain*, however, Guanyin is not portrayed as Princess Miaoshan. While her legend was the most popular tale explaining Guanyin's female nature, Miaoshan as such did not become an important subject in Buddhist religious art.[5] The female Guanyin was more widely venerated in the forms of the White-robed Guanyin or the Guanyin of the Southern Sea, and in later popular iconography these images became fused. Accordingly, the frontispiece depicts a White-robed Guanyin, seated on Potalaka Rock. She is placed in front of a bamboo grove, which is depicted in the upper right-hand corner. Above her, to the left, flies her white parrot, while Good-in-Talent (Shancai, Sudhana) and Dragon Girl (Longnü, Nāgakanyā) are shown in the lower left and right corners respectively.[6] The story of how the bodhisattva Guanyin acquired these three disciples is narrated in the second text translated here, *The Precious Scroll of Good-in-Talent and Dragon Girl* (*Shancai longnü baojuan*), a relatively short prosimetric text that may date from the eighteenth or nineteenth century.

The Precious Scroll of Incense Mountain is very much concerned with the conflicting demands of religious salvation and filial piety. Religious salvation requires the individual to break with all social bonds and obligations in order to achieve his or her personal liberation, while the demands of filial piety insist on the subordination of the child to the family because of all the grace and favors the parents bestow on a child by raising it. *The Precious Scroll of Good-in-Talent and Dragon Girl,* borrowing from popular lore and legend, pokes fun at the common tendency of people to forget the favors they have received and at the fact that their greatest desire is not for religious salvation, but rather for personal gain and satisfaction. But as *The Precious Scroll of Incense Mountain* shows, the desire for religious salvation, which appears initially as utterly selfish and antisocial, proves in the end to be the most filial act of all, as it results not only in the salvation of a single individual, but also the salvation of her parents, when Princess Miaoshan donates her eyes and arms to rescue her father from a wasting disease.

In presenting these translations of *The Precious Scroll of Incense Mountain* and *The Precious Scroll of Good-in-Talent and Dragon Girl,* I hope to make a contribution to the study of both Chinese Buddhism and Chinese literature. Through my discussions in this Introduction, I also hope to point out some aspects in which these texts may be of interest to students of comparative studies. While *The Precious Scroll of Incense Mountain* and *The Precious Scroll of Good-in-Talent and Dragon Girl* are clearly set in a Chinese world, and grapple with problems phrased in Chinese terms, some of the motifs underlying these narratives would appear to be far more widespread, if not universal.

Avalokiteśvara and Guanyin

Guanyin is only one of the several common translations of the Sanskrit name Avalokiteśvara. The precise meaning of the name Avalokiteśvara is not clear; most modern scholars suggest the name means roughly "the lord who looks down." The early Chinese translators of Buddhist scriptures apparently based themselves on the alternative form Avalokatasvara (He who sees sounds), and accordingly translated the name as Guanyin (He who contemplates the sounds) or Guanshiyin (He who contemplates the sounds of the world). The famous seventh-century monk and translator Xuanzang (600–664) strongly argued that the correct translation should be

Guanzizai (The lord who contemplates), but despite his scholarly authority this rendering never displaced the earlier translation.[7] Very little is known about the early veneration of Avalokiteśvara in India before his cult was introduced into China. One theory holds that Avalokiteśvara started out as a protective deity of horses, a theory that would explain the existence of later images in which Avalokiteśvara is crowned with a horse head.[8]

When Buddhism was introduced into China by way of Central Asia from the first century CE onward, it arrived largely in its Mahayana Buddhist form, which had come into being in northern India in the second and first centuries BCE.[9] Buddhism of earlier centuries may have focused on the historical Buddha Śākyamuni (sixth century BCE?) and his teaching of a method to liberate oneself from suffering by one's own efforts. Buddhism accepted the ancient Indian worldview that every living being is subject to *saṁsāra*, the endless cycle of reincarnation and retribution. According to this belief, one's life as a demon or a god, an animal or a human being, a man or a woman, on earth or in one of the many heavens and hells is determined by one's deeds (karma) in an earlier existence.[10] Buddhism stressed that each and every existence, even a life as one of the gods, is marked by suffering. The cause of suffering is the attachment to the impermanent phenomenal world by our "ego" or self, which believes itself to be permanent but actually is as impermanent and empty as all other phenomena, as it is only a temporary bundle of elements (dharmas). Once the ephemerality of all phenomena is realized, one is freed from attachment, liberated from suffering, and enters into nirvana (extinction/annihilation), never again to be reborn. Those who followed the Buddha's teaching (Dharma) and achieved this superior insight were called arhats. Early Buddhism taught that, if one was truly serious about achieving enlightenment, one had to cut off all social ties to one's family by "leaving the household" and joining the *saṅgha*, the monastic community of monks and nuns (tradition held that the Buddha had only reluctantly agreed to the establishment of the order of nuns). Although the Buddha condemned extreme forms of ascetic behavior, monks and nuns were expected to relinquish all worldly possessions, adhere to a strict code of moral conduct and physical behavior, and engage in meditation and other religious exercises. Pious laymen and laywomen were encouraged to lead a moral life so as to achieve a better rebirth, in which they might join the monastic community and achieve enlightenment too. No deed promised more merit than donations to the monks and nuns, who were forbidden to engage in either agriculture or commerce and had to survive by begging.

The biographies of the historical Buddha Śākyamuni tell how he prepared himself for his final life of teaching and liberation over the course of innumerable lifetimes, during which he performed many meritorious deeds of self-sacrifice.[11] At one stage in this process toward becoming a buddha, he had received the promise of his future buddhahood from the preceding buddha, Ratnagarbha. As he pursued his pious career through many reincarnations he was called a "bodhisattva," one who is destined to become a buddha. If early Buddhism focused on this single buddha and bodhisattva, Mahayana taught that in this cosmos, which is made up of innumerable worlds, there exists not just one buddha, but innumerable buddhas, and that, by the same token, innumerable bodhisattvas are preparing themselves for a future buddhahood. Mahayana commends the bodhisattva-path and its goal of future buddhahood as an ideal that all beings should embrace, a goal that is in fact deemed superior to that of an arhat. Eventually Mahayana thinkers would teach that all living beings share the same Buddha-nature and that each has the potential to become a buddha.

Mahayana also taught that some of these innumerable buddhas had dedicated their hard earned merit to the creation of a Pure Land or a world of heavenly bliss. In China none of these Buddha-worlds became more popular than the Pure Land of the Buddha Amitābha, the buddha of the west, who held out the promise of a rebirth in his paradise to each and every believer who called on his name with complete sincerity, even if only once.[12] The cult of Amitābha was often paired with that of Maitreya, the future buddha. Maitreya was believed to be residing in the Tuṣita Heaven, preparing for his descent to the human world, from which he would lead all who had faith in him to final liberation.[13]

Mahayana not only turned buddhas from human teachers into supernatural deities, it turned the buddhas-to-be or bodhisattvas into compassionate saviors, as Mahayana bodhisattvas have taken a vow to put off their final exit from *saṁsāra* until they have saved each and every sentient being. As a result, Mahayana Buddhism introduced into China a large pantheon of buddhas and bodhisattvas, all eager to deliver pious men and women.[14] One of the most popular of these bodhisattvas introduced into China in the early centuries of the first millennium was Avalokiteśvara, although the images of Avalokiteśvara that were introduced into China in the early centuries of the first millennium were far from uniform.

One important and influential early image of Avalokiteśvara was as one of the two assistants of the Buddha Amitābha (the other being Mahāsthāmaprāpta or, in Chinese translation, Dashizhi). The two assistants were often depicted together with Amitābha and shared in his widespread veneration; Avalokiteśvara was often depicted wearing a crown that featured an image of Amitābha.[15] Avalokiteśvara also plays a prominent role in the final section of the *Avatamsaka* or *Flower Garland Sutra* (*Huayan jing*), which narrates the pilgrimage of the young student Sudhana (Shancai, Good-in-Talent), who in his quest for wisdom visits fifty-four teachers. One of the "good friends" who is consulted by Sudhana is the bodhisattva Avalokiteśvara, who is portrayed as seated atop the Potalaka Rock at the edge of the world.[16] The pilgrimage of Sudhana became a popular subject in Buddhist iconography and popular literature from an early date.[17] In China for the last thousand years or so, Avalokiteśvara's Potalaka has been traditionally identified with Mt. Putuo (Putuoshan), a little island in the Zhousan archipelago off the Zhejiang coast near Ningbo. During the Ming and Qing dynasties, Mt. Putuo was a major pilgrimage center, and Guanyin was believed to occasionally manifest herself there to ardent believers. Many paintings show "Guanyin of the Southern Sea" seated on her favorite rock, shaded by a willow tree, and contemplating the reflection of the moon in the waves.[18]

By far the most influential literary portrait of Avalokiteśvara introduced into China in the early centuries of the first millennium was the one provided by the *Lotus Sutra*.[19] This enormously influential sutra devotes an entire chapter (which also circulated separately as the *Pumen jing* [Sutra on the gate of universal salvation] or *Guanyin jing* [Guanyin sutra]) to the Buddha's glowing praise of the salvific powers of Avalokiteśvara. According to the Buddha, Avalokiteśvara will come to the rescue of anyone who appeals to him for his aid, whatever the nature of his or her distress. Moreover, the Buddha credits Avalokiteśvara with the ability to manifest himself in whatever shape, male or female, is best for accomplishing his salvific miracles. The *Lotus Sutra* mentions twelve perils from which the bodhisattva will rescue those who call on his name: being threatened by falling into a great fire or into swift river currents, being shipwrecked on the island of giantesses, being executed by the sword, being attacked by goblins, being locked in manacles or fetters, being assaulted by brigands, being tempted by lust, being in a state of delusion, being threatened by thunderbolts or snakes.[20] Aside from these, the bodhisattva was also ready to come to the rescue of those who desired a male or female child, or great wealth.[21] This portrait of Avalokiteśvara greatly contributed to the popularization of his cult, and from the fifth century onward collections appeared that chronicled the miraculous rescues and cures said to have been effected by the bodhisattva. These miracle accounts only increased in number as time went by.[22] To invoke the aid of the bodhisattva people could simply invoke his name, but even better results might be obtained by the repeated devout recitation of the *Pumen jing* or, better still, the complete (and quite long) *Lotus Sutra*. Many sutras would follow in which even greater powers were ascribed to Avalokiteśvara, and which often included magical formulas (*dhāraṇī*) and elaborate rituals designed to ensure his aid.[23]

Avalokiteśvara was a popular subject of Buddhist iconography of the first millennium. Usually the bodhisattva was depicted as a richly arrayed, handsome (Indian) prince. Despite the rather feminine curves of his two- or three-dimensional body, the male sex of the bodhisattva is often clearly indicated by a thin moustache. Tantric Buddhism of the Tang dynasty (617–906) resulted in popular images of Avalokiteśvara with numerous heads and hands, symbolic of his omnipresent readiness to come to the aid of his devotees. The most magnificent iconographical type of Avalokiteśvara shows the bodhisattva with "a thousand arms": the standing bodhisattva is surrounded by "a thousand arms," each with an open eye in the palm of its hand.[24]

From the tenth century onward, however, images increasingly depicted Avalokiteśvara in female form, and it is in this female manifestation that the bodhisattva has attained greatest popularity in late-imperial China.[25] The female Guanyin was venerated by men, but especially by women. Her power is seen as practically unlimited; while she is nominally subject to the highest deities, whether the Buddha or the Jade Emperor, these never refuse her requests on behalf of her protégés. Modern scholars have been greatly puzzled by the gender change of Avalokiteśvara/Guanyin. But while the *Lotus Sutra* is clear in stating that Avalokiteśvara may manifest himself as a woman (and so provides scriptural support for depictions of Guanyin in female form), it is a more likely explanation that as Buddhism spread across China and became more and more a truly popular religion, its deities came to replace generic local divinities, including "dragon ladies and rain maidens,"[26] often assuming their characteristics. Where Buddhism replaced local cults of goddesses, Avalokiteśvara would be the logical replacement of the local female deity.[27] Whereas modern mythology holds that some goddesses are born from a drop of blood of Guanyin,[28] it is more likely the other way around: that local goddesses lend their form to Guanyin, whereupon legends sprang up to explain the background of Guanyin's female transformation. We should not forget that Avalokiteśvara continued to be venerated in his male manifestation too.

One group of legends focuses on Guanyin's use of her physical charms to convert men to the emptiness of all existence. Buddhism teaches that we can achieve enlightenment through any of the senses, and touch is one of those senses. According to early legends Guanyin manifested herself as a loose woman, willing to give herself to any man if doing so would convert him to the Dharma. In later legends she promises herself in marriage to any man who can meet her demands (for instance, memorizing the *Lotus Sutra*), but as soon as such a man successfully completes the task and happily goes to fetch the young wife he has won for himself, he finds the bridal sedan empty, the sight of which awakens him to the emptiness of all phenomena. One such legend tells of a certain village fated to be destroyed with all its inhabitants because of their accumulated sins. Guanyin obtains permission from the Jade Emperor to make one final attempt to get inhabitants to change their ways.[29] She then appears to them as an ugly old fishwife. In this form, she is ignored by all. But in the shape of a pretty young girl, she is immediately surrounded by the men of the village, eager to meet her ever-increasing demands in order to possess her. In the end, a young Mr. Ma succeeds in doing just that, only to discover that his bride has disappeared, leaving Mr. Ma and all the men of the village to realize the illusory nature of all striving and convert to Buddhism. Versions of this legend can be found in a number of literary genres, and Guanyin Carrying a Fish Basket (*Tilan Guanyin*) or The Wife of Mr. Ma (*Malang fu*) became a popular motif in Chinese religious art as well.[30] Another common female manifestation of Guanyin was the White-robed Guanyin (*Baiyi Guanyin*). Images of the White-robed Guanyin started to appear from the tenth century onward in Sichuan and Hangzhou. In Hangzhou it was especially the Upper Tianzhu Monastery that was linked to the cult of the White-robed Guanyin. The monastery would in later centuries develop into a major site of Guanyin pilgrimage.[31] In prints of the Ming and Qing dynasties the Guanyin of the Southern Sea (*Nanhai Guanyin*) is also usually depicted as being dressed in white.[32]

The most popular legend to explain the female appearance of the bodhisattva was, however, that of Princess Miaoshan. We can trace the origin of this legend to a very precise time and place. In 1100, Jiang Zhiqi, the prefect of Ruzhou (in modern Henan province), visited the local Incense Mountain Monastery (Xiangshan si). This monastery was famous for its grand statue of Avalokiteśvara with a Thousand Arms and a Thousand Eyes. While Jiang was there, the abbot Huaizhou recounted to him the tale of Princess Miaoshan, which he claimed to have heard from a mysterious monk who had recently visited his monastery. This monk, the abbot claimed, had shown him a book that had been revealed to the monk Daoxuan (596–667), who was famous for his visions. According to this tale, Princess Miaoshan is the youngest daughter of King Miaozhuang of the country of Raised Forest (Xinglin) in the far west (that is, a mythical India). As the king has no sons, he wants his daughters to marry and bear him grandsons to succeed him on the throne. While her two elder sisters are only too eager to marry, Miaoshan stubbornly refuses as she wants to devote herself to spiritual cultivation and escape from *saṁsāra*. When even the physical hardships she has to endure as a novice at the nearby White Sparrow Convent fail to change her mind, her father has her executed, but she is miraculously saved to pursue a life of religious austerities on Incense Mountain. After this, the king falls ill, afflicted by a foul disease that none of his doctors is able to cure. He is then informed that only the arms and eyes of someone without anger will cure him. When his two eldest daughters refuse to donate their limbs, the king is informed that only the hermit of Incense Mountain would be willing to make such an extreme donation. The king thereupon eats these body parts and is subsequently cured. He then visits Incense Mountain to express his gratitude to the hermit, only to discover that she is none other than his youngest daughter. Overcome by remorse, he falls to her feet, whereupon she manifests herself as the Avalokiteśvara with a Thousand Arms and a Thousand Eyes, whose statue is venerated in this very monastery. Upon his return, Jiang Zhiqi wrote an account of his visit to the monastery, including a lengthy account of the legend as told to him by the abbot. This account was subsequently inscribed in stone and erected at the monastery.[33]

Glen Dudbridge sees this story as a ploy on the part of the local abbot to revive the fortune of his monastery as a pilgrimage site (which may well have suffered from a growing popularity of the cult of the female Guanyin). If that was the abbot's intention, his ploy was successful: the monastery has survived all the vicissitudes of nearly a thousand years and is still in existence, although in an ironic twist of events, it has been taken over by the nuns of the White Sparrow Convent and turned into a convent. While the abbot invoked the authority of the early-Tang monk Daoxuan, we have no reference whatsoever to the tale of Miaoshan from the eleventh century or earlier. The tale would appear to have been concocted from whole cloth by the abbot, who drew heavily from the *Lotus Sutra* for names and motifs.[34]

When Jiang Zhiqi was appointed as prefect of Hangzhou in 1102, he also had his account inscribed in stone at the local Upper Tianzhu Monastery (famous for its White-robed Guanyin statue), contributing further to the rapid popularization of this legend over many areas of China. Soon the legend was enriched with a description of a visit of Guanyin to the hells following her own execution.[35] From later centuries we have many adaptations for the stage and as novels. However, by far the most popular adaptation was *The Precious Scroll of Incense Mountain*.

The Precious Scroll of Incense Mountain: Authorship and Editions

The first reference to *The Precious Scroll of Incense Mountain* probably is found in an early-sixteenth-century list of precious scrolls, which mentions a *Scroll of Incense Mountain* (*Xiangshan zhuan*).[36] The text must have been in circulation in some form or another by the middle of the sixteenth century as it would appear that the adaptation of the legend as a short vernacular novel of the late sixteenth century was based on the precious scroll version. The earliest surviving printed version, however, dates only from 1773. This edition is representative of the more elaborate version of the text and has as its formal title *Sutra of the Original Life of the Bodhisattva Guanshiyin* (*Guanshiyin pusa benxing jing*).[37] The editions of the text that date from the second half of the nineteenth century on usually offer a somewhat shorter version of the text and carry the title *Abbreviated Collection of the Sutra of the Original Life of the Bodhisattva Guanshiyin* (*Guanshiyin pusa benxing jing jianji*).[38]

Both the elaborate version and the abbreviated version of the text come with a preface that credits the authorship of the text to the monk Puming of the Upper Tianzhu Monastery near Hangzhou, who, it is said, composed the text after having had a vision of the bodhisattva Guanyin on the night of the fifteenth of the eighth month of the second year of the Chongning reign-period, which corresponds to the year 1103. This would mean that Puming had been inspired to write a prosimetric version of the legend of Miaoshan only a few weeks after Jiang Zhiqi's first visit to Upper Tianzhu Monastery! This coincidence is almost too good to be true. However, research has shown that a monk by the name of Puming was living at the Uppper Tianzhu Monastery at the time and that he later rose to the position of abbot there, which suggests that he must have been a man of at least some learning.[39] However, he is not a well-known name in the history of Chinese Buddhism, and it is difficult to imagine that a later author or publisher would have tried to enhance the attractiveness of this precious scroll by associating it with such an obscure monk.

Another argument for a relatively early date for *The Precious Scroll of Incense Mountain* is that, despite its popular title, there is no reference to itself as a precious scroll within the text itself. The term "precious scroll" (*baojuan*; also translated as "precious volumes") would appear to have become the general designation of Buddhist prosimetric narratives (and of the prosimetric canonical texts of the many new religions of the Ming and Qing dynasties) only from the fifteenth century onward.[40] On the three occasions when *The Precious Scroll of Incense Mountain* refers to itself, however, it calls itself a "[tale of] cause and conditions" (*yinyuan*) or a "long [tale of] cause and conditions" (*da yinyuan*). As we know from the manuscripts discovered at Dunhuang, so-called *yinyuan* (*nidāna*) texts represent a well-established genre in the Buddhist prosimetric literature of the ninth and tenth centuries. These Dunhuang *yinyuan* are relatively short texts, composed in alternating passages in prose and verse (both rhymed seven-syllable verse and unrhymed six-syllable verse). A specific feature of the performance of a *yinyuan* text was that at regular intervals the performer would recite the name of a buddha or bodhisattva and then invite his (or her) audience to join in, repeating the invocation. Some of the Dunhuang *yinyuan* deal with the life of the Buddha, but others recount pious legends, often featuring a female protagonist, and there are indications that these texts were written with a primarily female audience in mind.[41] *Yinyuan* texts survived as a genre of Buddhist storytelling into the Southern Song and the Yuan. *Tanchang yinyuan* (strumming and singing tales of cause and conditions) is listed as a variety of Hangzhou storytelling by Zhou Mi in his *Old Things about Hangzhou* (*Wulin jiushi*) of about 1275;[42] and in chapter 5 of the early novel *The Story of Water Margin* (*Shuihu zhuan*), one of the main protagonists, the large and violence-prone hero Lu Zhishen, claims at one point that while hiding in a monastery at Mt. Wutai, he "learned to narrate tales of cause and condition."[43]

The Precious Scroll of Incense Mountain is not only much longer than the average Dunhuang *yinyuan* text; it also does not make any use of unrhymed six-syllable verse. It does, however, retain the regular invocation of the name of a bodhisattva, and it features a female protagonist. The main body of *The Precious Scroll of Incense Mountain* is divided into segments, each of which consists of a passage in rhyming seven-syllable verse followed by a passage in prose; the prose passage then ends with two lines of seven-syllable verse that draw a lesson from the preceding narrative, often couched in religious metaphors, and the segment as a whole is brought to a conclusion by the congregational invocation of the name of the bodhisattva Guanyin.

Whereas the main body of *The Precious Scroll of Incense Mountain* shows great similarity to Dunhuang *yinyuan* in formal matters, the text opens and begins with long passages that show characteristics of the *shihua* (tale with poems) format, as we know it from the *Tale of the Reverend Huiyuan of Mt. Lu* (*Lushan Yuangong hua*) discovered at Dunhuang and the *Tale with Poems of Tripitaka of the Great Tang Fetching Sutras* (*Da Tang Sanzang qujing shihua*), which was printed at Hangzhou in the late thirteenth century. Both of these texts are primarily in prose, with the close of each paragraph or major segment marked by a *gātha* (here meaning a four-line poem on a Buddhist theme) spoken by one of the characters in the text. We find the same arrangement in the opening pages of *The Precious Scroll of Incense Mountain*, which narrate the miraculous birth of Princess Miaoshan, and then again in the final section, which recounts her apotheosis.[44]

The story as told in *The Precious Scroll of Incense Mountain* contains a number of episodes that are absent from the earliest known versions of the legend. It also includes some passages that seem to echo ideas associated with Quanzhen Daoism,[45] and one of the arguments of King Miaozhuang against Buddhism closely echoes a late-fourteenth-century diatribe against Buddhist monks by the Hongwu emperor (r. 1368–1398). These various facts would seem to support Dudbridge's conclusion that the text as we have it substantially dates from the fifteenth century. Even if it were the case that a twelfth-century monk of the Upper Tianzhu Monastery may have been the author of a prosimetric account of the legend of Miaoshan,[46] a comparison between the elaborate version and shorter version shows that the text was continuously updated and revised throughout the following centuries, in response to the needs and interests of different groups of users.

The textual changes apparent in the shorter version are decidedly minor for the first one-third of the text. For the most part they are limited to the judicious suppression of verbiage in the verse sections. However, following the arrival of Princess Miaoshan at the White Sparrow Convent, they become more extensive. Following her return from the Underworld, the abbreviations also increasingly start to affect the prose passages. Once King Miaozhuang has arrived at Incense Mountain and has recognized his daughter in the mutilated hermit, the cuts of the editor of the *Abbreviated Collection* become even more drastic. He has very little patience with the many sermons that are found in the elaborate version at this point (although he does retain a long diatribe against sectarian teachings) and makes short shrift of the long (but isolated) description of the association of the bodhisattva Guanyin with Mt. Putuo.

The elaborate version of *The Precious Scroll of Incense Mountain*, which may have been related to the Putuo pilgrimage, also contains a number of quite explicit anti-clerical passages. When Princess Miaoshan arrives at the White Sparrow Convent, for example, she berates the abbess at length for her luxurious lifestyle. This passage is considerably toned down in the shorter version, which also omits a detailed description of the panicked reaction of the nuns when the troops sent by King Miaozhuang surround the convent. The shorter version of *The Precious Scroll of Incense Mountain* has been edited (perhaps by a local monk or nun connected with the Hangzhou pilgrimage?)[47] for performance on the birthday of the bodhisattva on the nineteenth of the second month and makes an effort to emphasize the scriptural authority of the text by including at its very beginning a long quote from the *Lotus Sutra* on Guanyin's powers. An interesting aspect of the shorter version is that it includes instructions on how to perform the text (printed in smaller characters in the woodblock editions, and in italics in this translation).[48]

Female Saint and Female Bodhisattva

Scholars have noted that the legend of Miaoshan draws heavily on the *Lotus Sutra* for many names and incidents. As the *Lotus Sutra* is a primary canonical source for the veneration of Avalokiteśvara, this is only to be expected.[49] Scholars have also noted the folktale motif of the three sisters and the correspondences between the legend of Miaoshan and the story of King Lear.[50] *The Precious Scroll of Incense Mountain* also exhibits many other folktale motifs. To bring out some until now neglected characteristics of the legend of Miaoshan as retold in *The Precious Scroll of Incense Mountain* it may, however, be especially instructive to compare our text to the roughly contemporary European genre of the vernacular verse hagiographies of virgin saints.[51] For practical purposes I shall limit myself here primarily to a comparison of *The Precious Scroll of Incense Mountain* with the texts translated and studied by Brigitte Cazelles in *The Lady as Saint: A Collection of French Hagiographic Romances of the Thirteenth Century*.[52]

In the introduction to her translations, Cazelles concludes that "the saints celebrated in hagiographic romance are the product of a predominantly male discourse that elaborates an idealized representation of female greatness."[53] The same holds true, it may be stressed, for *The Precious Scroll of Incense Mountain*: while it is conventional wisdom that women have constituted its main audience, all people known or believed to have been involved in the production of the text as author or editor were male. Cazelles also notes that the medieval French poets, when dealing with female saints, showed a "remarkable preference for legends whose storylines involve the disrobing, torturing, cross-dressing, or physical transformations of mute and powerless heroines."[54] As not only *The Precious Scroll of Incense Mountain* but many other precious scrolls recounting the lives of pious women demonstrate, their male colleagues from China shared these interests to a large degree.

Cazelles points out that most of her thirteenth-century tales are set in a faraway land and in a distant past. The same is true of *The Precious Scroll of Incense Mountain*: the action takes place in the mythical country of Raised Forest, somewhere to the far west of China in a time long past. In the case of the medieval French hagiographies one might argue that this setting is historically required inasmuch as many texts describe the confrontation of a virgin saint and a pagan tyrant. This situation does not apply, however, to *The Precious Scroll of Incense Mountain*: our heroine is not shown in opposition to a long since displaced superstitious creed; rather, she refuses to submit to the demands of a commonly accepted social ideology that, very generally speaking, might be called popular Confucianism. More important may be the consideration that the heroines in hagiographic romances are not intended as direct models for emulation in daily life: "the audiences of vernacular hagiographic texts . . . were not asked to imitate the saint."[55] The texts were rather intended to deepen the popular expression of piety toward the saint.

"To be a saint, one must be born noble, handsome, courteous, wise and devout."[56] Virgin saints tend to be of aristocratic birth, to be exceedingly beautiful and precociously intelligent, and to display a remarkable piety from a very early age. The Chinese Miaoshan is no exception: she is the third daughter of a king, exceptionally gifted, and from birth inclined toward a religious lifestyle. "The basic saintly storyline revolves around the encounter between the heroine and a male protagonist, the result of which is an emphasis on the relation between genders."[57] In the French hagiographic romances studied by Cazelles, the male protagonist may be a suitor, a father, a tyrant, or the devil in person. While the heroine prefers to remain a virgin as the bride of Christ, the male protagonists often urge her to marry, and promise her great riches. In the case of *The Precious Scroll of Incense Mountain*, all these different male roles are exemplified by the figure of the king, who combines in a single person the highest parental, political, and ideological authority.

While he does not go so far as to set himself up as her suitor, his insistence that she marry a husband who will live with her at home in the palace brings him dangerously close to filling that role as well.

In many French hagiographic romances the male protagonist is portrayed as a hated tyrant while the virgin saint enjoys the sympathy of everyone else; this is not the case in *The Precious Scroll of Incense Mountain*. Miaoshan does not have the outspoken or silent support of her surroundings in her fight against the male protagonist. As her father is the representative of authority and as such represents (Confucian) common sense, he can draw upon the support of all segments of the court.[58] When his promises and threats are unable to sway his stubborn daughter, others who appeal to her common sense replace him. Miaoshan finds herself confronted at one time or another by her mother, her elder sisters, all of the palace ladies, the prioress of the White Sparrow Convent, and the assembled civil and military officials. Only the common folk who live in the city consistently sympathize with her.[59] This may well be an indication of the intended audience of *The Precious Scroll of Incense Mountain*.

Cazelles stresses at various points the silence of the victims, despite including in her corpus of texts the story of St. Catherine, whose eloquent words were said to have left dumbfounded fifty philosophers. In fact, many of the other virgin saints she describes are quite outspoken in their declarations of faith. They are of course not great theologians, but then theological nitpicking is not always an indication of deep faith. Still, when compared to the French hagiographic romances, *The Precious Scroll of Incense Mountain* allows much more space for debates between the representatives of common sense and the representative of religious aspiration, Miaoshan. "In the first half of the story, ending with Miao-shan's execution, the effect is a series of incidents (the refusal to marry—the punishment in the palace garden—the entry to the threatened monastery—the return to the palace) punctuating an endless, agonized dialogue between Miao-shan and her baffled family."[60] In these dialogues, all the well-known arguments in favor of a married life and against a religious career and a monastic existence are paraded out, as Miaoshan's dialogue partners alternately stress the joys of palace life, appeal to classical authority, describe the sufferings of a monastic existence, and bring out all the conventional Chinese arguments against Buddhism.

The author of *The Precious Scroll of Incense Mountain* does not for a moment assume that Miaoshan's choice will have the automatic support of either her kith and kin or of his audience. Miaoshan has a lot of explaining to do. While her opponents sing the praises of a life of luxury and indulgence, Miaoshan counters by stressing the transience of human life and the inevitability of death and the karmic punishments that will inevitably follow. While the virgin saints look forward to the blessings of heaven where they will be united with their heavenly groom (blessings that are often described in titillating physical detail), Miaoshan's positive motivation is highly abstract. Nevertheless, one finds references to a heavenly marriage, if only in an ironic way. When her father orders her to marry and asks her what kind of husband she would prefer, she replies that she will not marry unless he can find her a physician who can cure all the ills of the world—the Buddha. Miaoshan may ask for such a husband, but it is clear that nowhere in the world will her father be able to find him. And when, after her return from the Underworld, the god of the Morning Star in the guise of a Daoist hermit jokingly suggests to her that they devote themselves to religious exercises as a couple, she indignantly rejects his proposal. Miaoshan does not aspire to be the Buddha's bride, and she certainly does not want to preserve her virginity merely for his sake: she rejects all physical comforts, including the pleasures of the flesh. Rather, Miaoshan asserts her (near) equality with the Buddha as his younger sister.[61]

Although it is true that the dialogues between Miaoshan and her interlocutors take up much of the text, one should note that the author has taken care to include speakers of both sexes and from different social classes. While Miaoshan usually remains respectful when she replies to her parents, she is much more direct when she counters the arguments of her sisters and the other palace ladies, and she is downright sarcastic when she addresses her social inferiors, such as the prioress and her father's officials. These contrasting attitudes adopted by Miaoshan may have provided a skilled narrator ample opportunity to enliven his performance. One of the very first instructions to the performer in the shorter version reads "It is essential to imitate the sounds of suffering, joy, and sadness" (*kule aiyin xuyao xiangxiang*), although this could also be translated as "It is essential to imitate suffering and joy, sadness and accents."[62] It also may be noted in passing that while the editor of the shorter version considerably softened Miaoshan's harsh castigation of the prioress of the White Sparrow Convent, he apparently felt no qualms about retaining the full text of the sarcastic put-down of the officials.

When the massive social pressure of all the appeals to common sense, all the promises, and all the threats are still not enough to make Miaoshan give in to her father, action has to follow. "Suffering," writes Cazelles, "is presented as a prerequisite for the attainment of sainthood. Forced exposure, forced enclosure, accusation, tortures, and death at the stake are integral components of our narratives."[63] *The Precious Scroll of Incense Mountain* exhibits all these elements. First Miaoshan is locked up in the flower garden behind the palace. Next, when Miaoshan is allowed to take up residence at the White Sparrow Convent, she is burdened with the impossible task of taking care of all the physical needs of the five hundred nuns in the convent. She does not for a moment shrink from her duties, and immediately animals and gods come to her rescue. When the king is informed of these miracles, he decides to have the convent burned down. This time Miaoshan intervenes with a miracle of her own: stabbing her palate with a hairpin, she spits out blood, which turns into a red rain that quenches the fire. The king, convinced now that his daughter is a witch, condemns her to death, and orders her execution.

Elizabeth Robertson in her 1991 article "The Corporeality of Female Sanctity in *The Life of Saint Margaret*,"[64] treating a medieval English hagiography, reaches many of the same conclusions as Cazelles. She places an even stronger emphasis on the centrality of sexual temptation in the female saint's experience and is more explicit in spelling out the sexual symbolism of some of the images in her text. She notes her author's "obsessive interest in the physical torture of the female saint" and argues that his "interest may be linked...to his focus on female sexual temptation."[65] She further notes that "the focus on female blood seems to reflect a male fascination with and horror of female blood."[66] While in other precious scrolls on devout Buddhist women, for instance the many retellings of the legend of Woman Huang, the inherent impurity of sexually active women because of their menstrual bleedings and loss of blood during childbirth is often stressed,[67] this issue is not explicitly raised in *The Precious Scroll of Incense Mountain*. This may well be because Miaoshan remains a (presumably prepubescent) virgin, whereas Woman Huang is depicted as a married woman and a mother of two children, who renounces all sexual intercourse as soon as she learns about the pollution she involuntarily but inescapably causes. When Miaoshan does shed blood, she does so with a self-inflicted and inverted "defloration," which turns her (potentially polluting) blood into a life-saving rain.[68]

In the earliest known versions of the legend of Miaoshan, the burning of the White Sparrow Convent brings about the death (and subsequent resurrection) of the protagonist. In a following phase in the development of the legend, represented by the *Life of the Mahāsattva Guanyin* (*Guanyin dashi zhuan*), a text associated with the name of Guan Daosheng (1262–1319), Miaoshan visits purgatory and the hells before coming back to life.[69] The introduction of this element has attracted the attention of scholars, many of whom regard it as closely connected to the function of Guanyin in the Pudu festival of feeding the hungry ghosts (there are also precious scrolls of a later date solely devoted to the description of Guanyin's visit to the Underworld).[70] However, the introduction of a separate scene devoted to her execution in that text may well be equally meaningful. The scene of the execution of Miaoshan and the events leading up to it are greatly developed in *The Precious Scroll of Incense Mountain*. In a final attempt to change Miaoshan's mind, in *The Precious Scroll of Incense Mountain* the king (at the suggestion of the queen!) decides to have her brought back to the capital and led through its streets as a condemned criminal, naked and in shackles, while her parents and relatives watch from specially erected decorated grandstands, in a conspicuous display of luxury and enjoyment. In this scene we encounter the stress on corporeality and visibility that Cazelles sees as one of the most important elements of her hagiographic romances.[71] Miaoshan's public humiliation perfectly illustrates the following characterization by Cazelles of the medieval French verse hagiographies: "Exposure of the female martyr, therefore, implies an involuntary projection onto center stage. Revelation . . . implicates the concrete disrobing of the heroine."[72] Cazelles notes that such a forced exposure and public disrobing is endured by every one of the female martyrs in her study and so may be seen as an essential episode in their legends. In the description of Miaoshan's humiliation in *The Precious Scroll of Incense Mountain*, it is clear that although Miaoshan herself hardly pays any attention to the displays of worldly pleasures, she is very much the object of the gaze of the whole population of the capital, from emperor to common citizen.

At the very last moment, however, the execution of Miaoshan is postponed for one day, and she is once again locked up in the garden of the palace. After a series of visits by the queen, her sisters, and the palace ladies, none of whom succeed in changing her mind, her father comes to visit her at midnight in her prison cell, where he appeals to her one last time. Cazelles describes the function of forced enclosure in her texts in the following terms: "The narrowing of space experienced by the women martyrs... serves to stress the intimate, and therefore dangerous, dimension of the encounter between heroines and tormentors. Temporary imprisonment... is a narrative device that amplifies the erotic element inherent in these stories." And she adds, "In Passions devoted to persecuted daughters (Christina and Barbara), enclosure is an ordeal imposed by incest-minded fathers who become tyrants out of sexual frustration."[73] Many of these elements have their counterpart in *The Precious Scroll of Incense Mountain*. Miaoshan's father is described as a typical tyrant who flies into a rage if his orders are not immediately obeyed. He can also be said to suffer sexual frustration as he has been unable to sire a son, despite the number of his concubines; his behavior toward Miaoshan is certainly overly possessive, and it is not difficult to detect incestuous motives in his behavior and language—his repeated reference, for example, to his daughter as "a slut" (*dizi*) and "a she-devil" (*yaojing*). During his nighttime visit to his naked and shackled daughter in her cell, he describes to her the pleasures of the flesh in great detail. And even if we grant that the father himself may not be aware of the full implications of his complex and strong emotions toward his daughter, his daughter is fully aware of her father's unconscious intentions and repulses his advances in the terms that leave little room for doubt:

> When Marvelous Goodness heard this, she replied: "My father the emperor, dear daddy, you are misled and deluded and unenlightened, and your perverse heart is all ablaze. This is not the behavior of a lord and emperor in possession of the Way! Daddy, you are the ruler of the myriads of people, the lord of the whole nation. If you cannot control your family, how can you control the nation? If you are a

> Son of Heaven and an emperor of men, in possession of the Way, how would you, a father, ever think of entering this side palace at midnight, in the third watch,[74] and urge your daughter to marry a husband? How would it look if the world came to know of this?"[75]

On the surface the legend of Miaoshan tells a Buddhist moral romance of filial piety, the tale of a girl who eventually sacrifices herself for the sake of her father, even to the point of allowing him to eat her flesh.[76] Underlying *The Precious Scroll of Incense Mountain*, however, is the hidden horror story of the patriarchal family, the tale of the father who tries to impose his will on his daughter. When Miaoshan's father appeals to her sense of duty and filial piety in order to convince her to take a husband who will live with them in the palace, he is making an extraordinary demand. The normal behavior of a father as head of the family is to sire a son who as his heir will continue the ancestral sacrifices, and to allow his daughters to leave the family so they may bear children to other patrilines. So when the king fails in his own filial duty to sire a son (a failure that, according to *The Precious Scroll of Incense Mountain*, is a punishment for his inordinate attachment to hunting), he experiences this as a great sorrow and falls into a deep depression. He does not immediately conclude that the problem can be solved by having his daughters marry an in-living son-in-law who will give him a grandson. As adoption is considered to be unnatural and therefore fraught with danger,[77] the king has to be persuaded to pursue this course of action by his officials. But as soon as the king as father makes this unnatural demand on the bodies of his three daughters, he is confronted by one daughter who not only wants to leave the family but, equally unnaturally, wants to do so not in order to marry into another patriline, but to pursue her own individual salvation. She refuses to allow her father to dispose of her person.[78] If the king can be seen to impose an extraordinary and therefore unnatural degree of control on his daughter, the daughter displays an equally extraordinary and uncommon desire to free herself from such familial constraints. As such, both become extremes of male and female will and desire. While the father goes to the extreme of symbolic rape (torching the convent) and seduction (the midnight visit to his daughter's cell), the daughter counters with her unnatural auto-defloration. And while her father is unable to have her killed by the sword, she allows herself to be suffocated. The introduction of the execution episode into the legend of Miaoshan and its lengthy development in *The Precious Scroll of Incense Mountain*, therefore, serve to make explicit the issues of gender and sexuality, which are only implied in the earliest version of the legend. The emphasis on the contrast between the king and the princess as male and female is strengthened in *The Precious Scroll of Incense Mountain* by the frequent use of the word "dragon" (*long*) as an adjective for the king and by the association of Miaoshan with the tiger: on two occasions Miaoshan is shown to ride that symbol of death and female sexuality.

Miaoshan is not only a martyr; she claims near equality with the Buddha as his younger sister, and her story therefore goes beyond that of a virgin martyr. As she is a savior, her birth is miraculous, and her death only a stage in her spiritual career. Her death as a martyr, however, is not yet self-sacrifice on behalf of others. It may be followed by a harrowing of hell and a resurrection (as her soul reenters her dead body and brings it back to life), but the self-sacrifice by feeding her own flesh to the worst sinner still has to take place. So when her father is punished for his evildoing by a terrible disease (inspiring one of the most gruesome descriptions of illness in all of Chinese literature)[79] and all his servants and relatives have forsaken him (with the exception of his wife), Guanyin offers up her own eyes and arms to him to consume as medicine.[80] This act of self-sacrifice is again explained by a reference to filial piety, but it is followed by a lengthy exposition by Miaoshan on her father's many sins. Only after she has sacrificed her eyes and limbs for the worst sinner of them all (who happens to be her father) and has been reduced to a blind and bloody trunk can her apotheosis finally take place.

This extensive comparison of *The Precious Scroll of Incense Mountain* and the medieval hagiographic romance has shown some remarkable parallels. While *The Precious Scroll of Incense Mountain* puts more emphasis on social pressure and less on virginity as such than the female saints' lives, it shares with them to a large extent the basic outline of the story and its emphasis on the corporeality of the heroine, culminating in a scene of forced public disrobing of the aristocratic virgin. *The Precious Scroll of Incense Mountain* also shares with its medieval European counterparts an emphasis on issues of gender and sexuality, pitting male lust against a female desire to be the sole mistress of her own body. But while the Christian saint was pitted against a long since displaced pagan religion, Miaoshan had to deal with a conventional morality that was very much alive and had the full backing of society and the state. Further, while the role of the saints was constrained by a centralized Christian theology, Miaoshan had the room to develop into a universal savior. In fact, her story also acquired elements that in the Christian tradition are associated with Christ, such as the harrowing of hell, the resurrection, and the sacrifice of the body for the sake of others. While it is tempting to discern signs of cross-cultural influence, there is no clear evidence of any direct influence in either direction.

Filial Daughter and Filial Son

The comparison between *The Precious Scroll of Incense Mountain* and medieval hagiographies of female saints has helped to highlight the sexual tension between father and daughter in this text. The romance of filial piety turned upon closer reading into the horror story of the patriarchal family. As a story of the sexually loaded tension between father and daughter we might classify the legend of Miaoshan as a Chinese representative of a universal family-complex tale. Recognizing the legend of Miaoshan as an instance of the family-complex tale would go a long way in filling the almost total absence of Chinese examples in *Oedipus Ubiquitous: The Family Complex in World Folk Literature* by Allen W. Johnson and Douglass Price-Williams.[81] As the authors claim that the family-complex tales are universal, the fact that Chinese culture is represented in their study by a single obscure joke should at least have given them occasion for thought.[82] While the authors argue that the expression of the incestuous desires within the family tends to be more hidden in more complex societies, our examples from both ends of the Eurasian continent should go a long way to show that in the case of the father-daughter relationship this euphemistic veneer is very thin indeed.

We might therefore be tempted to read the legend of Miaoshan as an ahistorical reflection of the tensions inherent in the patriarchal family in China. Furthermore, when looking for a Chinese parallel for the Oedipus tale of incestuous desire between mother and son, we might be inspired by Alan Cole's monograph *Mothers and*

Sons in Chinese Buddhism and identify the legend of Mulian as such.[83] "Buddhists in China developed a style of filial piety that was preoccupied with the mother.... The Buddhists aimed their filial piety discourse at sons and not at daughters.... A mother-son dyad came to headline Buddhist family values."[84] The legend of Mulian presents us with a family in which the father is absent and in which the relationship between mother and son is extremely close. In the fully developed version of the legend, the mother's sin is her sexuality as such, and the son realizes that by being born he is implicated in his mother's sexuality (if she had not given in to sinful desire, he would not have been born in the first place). "Mu Lian is a living evidence of his mother's sexuality."[85] This is why even to this day in at least some areas of China, sons are required by tradition to atone for their deceased mother's sinful sexuality by drinking the (ritual equivalent of) her menstrual blood as part of the funerary ritual.[86]

But whereas the patriarchal family would appear to have been a permanent fixture of Chinese civilization, the legend of Mulian took a longer time to develop.[87] As the study of Alan Cole makes clear, in order to develop it first had to establish the sinfulness of female sexuality. Whereas male sexuality continued to be seen as pure, female sexuality was increasingly viewed as inherently sinful.

> A man is not really to blame for his desires because he is the victim of sexual predation. It is the goblinesses, themselves consumed by desire, who try to lure men away from their duties as well as from their parents and the obligations owed to them.... Buddhist men are again cast as pure, upright types who are in charge of culture, while women are dangerous non-human beings who are outside the system and intent on ruining both it and the men who dominate it.[88]

Their sinfulness is reified by their uterine blood, which is a defilement of the gods. Because of her menstrual bleeding and the pains of parturition, a woman is considered to be a denizen of hell not only after her death, but even while she is still alive. Cole traces the developments of these conceptions in popular Chinese Buddhism from the medieval period to the Song, culminating in the composition of the *Blood-Bowl Sutra* (*Xuepen jing*) by the twelfth century.[89] I would argue that the legend of Miaoshan could only have emerged once the notion of the sinfulness of female sexuality had been firmly established. I read Miaoshan's repeatedly expressed fear of death and of the punishments of hell as well as her refusal to marry as an expression of her fear of her own female, and therefore sinful, sexuality.[90]

The patriarchal family is confronted with a dilemma. To ensure its survival, it needs fertile women from outside the family, but at the same time it fears the potentially disruptive power of these women's sexuality. To obtain daughters from outside for his own sons, the father has to give away his own daughters. So to obtain a grandson and fulfill his own duty to the patriline, a father must force his daughters to give up their virginity and engage in sexuality, or in other words, to sin.[91] This is basically the situation that is presented in *The Precious Scroll of Incense Mountain*: to assure himself of an heir, the king insists on the marriage of his daughters. But by causing his daughter to sin, the father commits a sin for which he must suffer the karmic consequences, in this case the rotting away of his diseased body.

Some women, fired by desire, eagerly agree to sin—and thereby assure themselves of the sufferings of hell. If a woman refuses to sin by denying her sexuality, she is by that very act freed from hell—the powers of the Underworld have no hold over her (this applies even when a married woman decides to forgo sex, as demonstrated in the case of Woman Huang)—and she may be said to have subverted hell itself. The sinning father can be saved only if a daughter is willing to selflessly, without anger or desire, give her body away, as in the case of the hermit.

The legend of Princess Miaoshan has often been interpreted as a charter for opposing marriage. There is no doubt that it was used as such.[92] I would argue, however, that it may also be read as a guide to marriage under the conditions of the sinfulness of female sexuality: a woman behaves without sin and virtuously, as a filial daughter, not if she agrees to marriage because of her own lustful desire, but rather if she agrees of her own free will to make a sacrifice of her own body for the sake of her father's well-being and the continuity of his patriline. By this act of hers, her father is retroactively freed from the sin of forcing her to sin, and the patriline can be vigorously continued. In this respect, the final healing of her father's illness is indeed the crowning episode in *The Precious Scroll of Incense Mountain*; from that moment both father and daughter may ascend to heaven.[93] *The Precious Scroll of Incense Mountain* may therefore also be seen, despite its surface narrative, as a tract designed to persuade daughters to accept marriage, to accept being sacrificed for the sake of the patriarchal family. It is for this reason, I would suggest, that the virgin Guanyin can also be a bestower of sons.[94]

The existence and widespread popularity of the legend of Mulian and the legend of Princess Miaoshan might be taken as proofs of the universality of the family-complex tale. However, the origin and development of these two legends during a specific period in Chinese history may also be taken as arguments against the universality of the family-complex tale. I would argue that only after the establishment of the patriarchal family at all levels of Chinese society could these tales have acquired their massive importance. In this respect one could easily point to developments in Song-dynasty (960–1278) society (such as the strengthening of lineage organization and the rise of neo-Confucianism) as explanations for the rise of these legends. On the other hand, one could also cite the spread of these legends as proof of the growing importance of the patriarchal family outside elite circles. In any case, the historicity of the development of these legends is an undeniable fact and so would seem to deny the universality of the family romance.

The development of the Mulian legend (and the subsequent development of the legend of Miaoshan), in accordance with historical changes from the Tang to the Song, has a close parallel in the development of the legend of Shun, China's primordial filial son. The various early versions of the legend of Shun have recently been revisited by Robert G. Henricks in "The Three-bodied Shun and the Completion of Creation."[95] In this article, Henricks argues that the legend of the filial son Shun may be interpreted as a reworking of an ancient creation myth, in which first the fire of heaven has to be dominated by elevating heaven, and next the waters of the earth have to be regulated. Only after these two feats have been successfully carried out can the third feat—agriculture—be instituted. Henricks sees a parallel between Shun's escape from the top of a burning barn by floating down by means of two winnowing baskets and legends of men who become birds and elevate the sky. In passing, Henricks remarks that in the early versions of the tale he studies, Shun's stepmother plays only a minor role in the machinations against Shun.[96]

Henricks has not included in his consideration of variants of the legend of Shun the most extensive treatment of these materials, the *Tale of the Son Shun* (*Shunzi bian*), one of the texts discovered among the Dunhuang manuscripts together with the *Tale of Maudgalyāyana Saving His Mother from the Dark Realm* (*Da Muqianlian mingjian jiumu bianwen*) and most likely of roughly the same date.[97] In this version of the tale of Shun, the stepmother plays a very prominent part indeed. While she is said to hate Shun, she also attempts to seduce him during her husband's absence (or at least she tries to create the impression that he is flirting with her when she asks him to remove a thorn from her foot). Later she accuses Shun of having tried to rape her.[98] Once she has convinced her husband of Shun's sins, she first hatches the plots to burn Shun while he is repairing the barn and then to kill him with stones when he is down in the well. In this way, the unnaturally close relationship between heaven and earth in the reconstructed early myth is, in this Tang-dynasty version of the tale, replaced by the equally unnatural desire of a (step)mother for her son. It seems a safe assumption that in this version the burning barn no longer represents the scorching heat of a heaven that lies too close to the earth, but rather the unnatural desire of the stepmother. After all, fire as a symbol for desire is one of the oldest tropes in Chinese literature. The basic configuration of characters in the *Tale of the Son Shun* now is very close to the one in the fully developed Mulian legend: an absent husband, a filial son, and a sinful (step)mother.

If the growth and spread of the Mulian legend may have been a precondition for the rise of the legend of Miaoshan, the narrative of the *Tale of the Son Shun* offers a remarkable structural parallel to the legend of Miaoshan as told in *The Precious Scroll of Incense Mountain*. Whereas Shun is pursued by his (step)mother, Miaoshan must live in fear of her father's desires. Whereas Shun escapes from a burning barn, Miaoshan is almost engulfed by flames when her father torches the White Sparrow Convent. When Shun is trapped in the family well, a dragon bores a tunnel for him to the well of a neighbor's house, a journey below the surface of the earth, which may be said to be equivalent to Miaoshan's visit to the Yellow Springs.[99] Both then retire to the wilds of a mountain, where they enjoy the help of animals and achieve supernatural powers (Shun establishes his unique qualifications as king by being the only one to reap a bountiful harvest; Miaoshan through her religious exercises achieves buddhahood). Once they have acquired these powers, they return to the world to secretly assist their families, who are being punished for their former evil deeds by sickness and poverty. By feeding their families with the products of their achievement, Shun and Miaoshan show their magnanimity and manifest their power in all its glory.

I do not intend to suggest that *The Precious Scroll of Incense Mountain* at any stage modeled itself on the *Tale of the Son Shun*. *The Precious Scroll of Incense Mountain* is a much more developed story than the occasionally clumsy *Tale of the Son Shun*. Moreover, the ideological orientation of these two texts is diametrically opposed: if Miaoshan is the epitome of Buddhism, Shun as the future emperor is the exemplar of Confucianism: as soon as he has a chance, he retreats to his room to study the *Analects* and the *Classic of Filial Piety*. But a few incidents in *The Precious Scroll of Incense Mountain* do seem to echo some in the *Tale of the Son Shun*. For instance, the dragon that digs a tunnel for Shun reappears in *The Precious Scroll of Incense Mountain*, where he bores a well for Miaoshan after she is ordered to do all the kitchen work in the White Sparrow Convent. But it is especially the structural parallels that I find striking. One wonders to what extent this common pattern may reflect an ancient tradition of shamanistic initiation (domination of desire, of fire and water, voluntary death, and solitary retirement to a mountain).

The legend of Mulian incorporates some of these same structural elements: searching for his mother Mulian three times ascends to heaven and three times descends into hell, acquiring greater powers with each journey. We reencounter the fires of passion in the thirst and fire Mulian's mother has to suffer as a hungry ghost. But Mulian's final descent into hell is not followed by a period of seclusion in the wilds—although one might argue that it has been removed to the beginning of the story, when Mulian leaves home for a long business trip, thus unwittingly providing his mother with an opportunity to sin. However, while the basic configuration of characters in the Mulian legend closely resembles that of the *Tale of the Son Shun*, the development of the story may well show a greater structural parallel to the narrative "The Count of Zheng Defeats Duan in Yan" (Zhengbo ke Duan yu Yan) from the *Zuozhuan* (Duke Yin, year 1). As part of the *Zuozhuan* this story is usually treated as sober historiography, but perhaps it is better treated as myth. This story held a strange fascination for traditional (male) Chinese readers; in later ages it figured as the first selection of the *Epitome of Ancient Prose* (*Guwen guanzhi*), though it could hardly function as a model for prose essays.

"The Count of Zheng Defeats Duan in Yan" tells the story of a man who is willing to go down to the Underworld to be reunited with his sinful mother, whom he had imprisoned. Although the sin of the mother is not explicitly identified as sexual in nature, it clearly has sexual overtones. She is said to hate her eldest son because of the pain he caused her at birth and to love her younger son because his birth was much easier. When later the younger son rebels against his elder brother, his mother promises to open the gates of the capital for him. In this way, her transgressive love for her (younger) son threatens the proper order of both the family and the state. After the rebellion has been suppressed, her elder son has her locked up and swears that he will not see her again unless it is at the Yellow Springs (i.e., after death). When later one of his dinner guests refuses to eat the best part of his food because he wants to take it home to his mother, the count is filled with regret and with longing for his own mother. At the suggestion of his guest, he has a deep tunnel dug and meets with his mother below the earth. If the artificiality of the tunnel suggests a ritual scenario, the contemporary southern Chinese ritual of the smashing of the City of Hell by the filial son as part of the burial rites for a mother may well have a very long history indeed.[100]

The Count of Zheng did not rely on a higher instance, secular or divine, to punish his mother; he ordered her imprisonment on his own authority. Cole argues that deep down it is Mulian himself who punishes his mother for her sin of sexuality.[101] In the same way, one may well wonder whether Miaoshan isn't responsible for causing her father's disease: it is her memories of the White Sparrow Convent that cause the Buddha to punish the king by his disease. The Count of Zheng needs the example of a filial son to change his mind and forgive his mother. In *The Precious Scroll of Incense Mountain* the queen facilitates the reconciliation between father and daughter. The queen, who is given a prominent role in *The Precious Scroll of Incense Mountain*, is both the only one to stay with her husband during his foul illness and the first to suspect that the "hermit of Incense Mountain" may be her own daughter. Later, although Miaoshan refuses to disclose her identity to her father, despite his formal display of gratitude, she reveals her identity to her mother, when the latter washes her wounds. But whereas Miaoshan may demonstrate her exceptional character as a saint by her willingness to donate her limbs to a father she will go on to berate at length for his moral turpitude, her mother shows herself to be a truly compassionate human being. Miaoshan may show what one may be capable of if, transcending all attachments, one frees oneself of all anger, but her mother demonstrates the strength of a love that grows from attachment. That may be why *The Precious Scroll of Incense Mountain* in its final pages devotes quite some space to the king's future buddhahood but has nothing further to say about the queen.

Guanyin's Acolytes: *The Precious Scroll of Good-in-Talent and Dragon Girl*

In popular iconography of the Ming and Qing dynasties the White-robed Guanyin is often accompanied by two young acolytes, one male and one female. While triads of deities are common in medieval Chinese Buddhist iconography, it is not usual to find a buddha or bodhisattva accompanied by both a male and a female disciple. For instance, on a Northern Song–dynasty painting from Dunhuang, now in the Boston Museum of Fine Arts, Avalokiteśvara is still accompanied by a *shan tongzi* (youth [keeping track] of good deeds) and an *e tongzi* (youth [keeping track] of evil deeds).[102] Many scholars therefore assume that the representation of Guanyin with one male and one female acolyte was inspired by the iconography of the Jade Emperor, the highest deity in the traditional Chinese pantheon, who is often accompanied by the Golden Lad and the Jade Maiden. However, irrespective of their ultimate origin, Guanyin's acolytes soon became identified as Shancai (Good-in-Talent, Sudhana) and Longnü (Nāgakanyā, Dragon Daughter).[103]

Both Shancai and Longnü have a well-established scriptural pedigree. The same *Lotus Sutra* that in chapter 25 elaborates on the miraculous powers of Avalokiteśvara devotes a large part of chapter 12 to a description of the precocious wisdom of Dragon Girl. She is there described as the eight-year-old daughter of the Dragon King Sāgara; she achieves instantaneous enlightenment and offers a pearl to the Buddha.[104] While the *Lotus Sutra* does not explicitly connect her to Guanyin, other sutras have her offer her pearl to Avalokiteśvara.

The adventures of Sudhana fill the final chapter of the *Flower Garland Sutra*: in search of enlightenment the young Sudhana visits fifty-four teachers. The story of his pilgrimage originally constituted an independent work, known as the *Gandavyūha*. In the twenty-eighth episode of his pilgrimage, Sudhana visits Avalokiteśvara at Potalaka.[105] The story of the pilgrimage of Sudhana became very popular in China during the Song dynasty, when it was adapted and circulated in small and amply illustrated devotional booklets, one page devoted to each of Sudhana's "good friends."[106]

Shancai and Longnü make a nice contrasting couple. Whereas his long pilgrimage makes him a perfect example of gradual enlightenment, she (a female child with an animal nature) dramatically represents sudden enlightenment. However, no canonical scriptural source connects both of them at the same time to Guanyin. The first work to explain how the two of them became disciples of Guanyin is the short sixteenth-century "novel" *Complete Tale of Guanyin of the Southern Seas* (*Nanhai Guanyin quanzhuan*), itself a rewriting of *The Precious Scroll of Incense Mountain*.[107] In chapter 18 of the novel, after Princess Miaoshan/the bodhisattva Guanyin has achieved enlightenment and retired to Mt. Putuo, she needs disciples. Shancai, in his search for enlightenment, presents himself. To test his resolve, Guanyin has the trees and plants on Mt. Putuo turn into brigands who threaten to kill them. When she jumps from a cliff to escape them, Shancai immediately follows her example. When they have reascended the cliff, she tells him to look down, and at the foot of the cliff Shancai sees his mortal remains.

When next Guanyin learns that the third son of the Dragon King of the Eastern Ocean while swimming about as a carp has been captured by fishermen, she orders Shancai to go and buy the prince in order to set him free again. When the Dragon King orders his son to take a pearl to Guanyin as a token of gratitude, the prince's daughter steps forward and volunteers to go in place of her father; after she has offered the pearl to Guanyin, she stays with the bodhisattva as her disciple.[108] Only a few elements of the scriptural sources have been retained by the novel, in which the legends have been reduced to a minimum.[109]

In the *Complete Tale of Guanyin of the Southern Seas* the legend of Shancai and Longnü occupies only a single chapter. From a later (eighteenth- or nineteenth-century?) date, however, we also have a short precious scroll that is completely devoted to their legend and that provides a new and much more developed story. This text, *The Precious Scroll of Good-in-Talent and Dragon Girl,* is known in a woodblock edition of 1912. It has been mentioned in passing in a number of studies on the popular veneration of Guanyin,[110] but it merits a more extended discussion in its own right. Within its genre it is a well-crafted work, and the story it tells shows many and unexpected ramifications to other popular legends.

The text of *The Precious Scroll of Good-in-Talent and Dragon Girl* occupies twenty-nine folios, each single page consisting of nine columns of twenty characters each.[111] The text opens with a conventional four-line poem in which the audience of believers is admonished to attend to the performance of the precious scroll that is about to begin with utmost reverence, as such an attitude will confer great blessings. The story is then told in alternating prose and verse. Both the prose and the verse sections vary considerably in length. The verse passages are written almost exclusively in seven-syllable verse, the staple of prosimetric literature. Occasionally, a seven-syllable line may be preceded by a three-character extrametrical phrase. Only in one short passage, in which Guanyin provides a description of meditation techniques to Sudhana/Shancai/Good-in-Talent, does the text make use of an alternation of lines of six syllables (two times three) and of seven syllables (pp. 22a–23a).

The story of *The Precious Scroll of Good-in-Talent and Dragon Girl* is set in the Qianfu reign-period (874–879) of the Tang dynasty. The virtuous minister Chen Debao and his wife, lady Han, are still childless and are getting older with each passing year. When Chen refuses his wife's suggestion to take a concubine, she then suggests that they pray to Guanyin. Guanyin, who knows that the couple is destined to remain without descendants, nevertheless orders a Boy Who Brings Wealth (Zhaocai tongzi) to be born into the family, so he may save his parents by his example. Lady Han thereupon becomes pregnant and eventually gives birth to a boy, who is named Chen Lian, but she dies when he is only five years old.

Even as a child, Chen Lian is interested not in the study of civil or military affairs, but only in the pursuit of religious truth. When he is seven, his father gives in to his pleas and allows him to study under the Yellow Dragon Immortal (Huang Long zhenren) at the Hemp Lady Grotto-Heaven (Magu dongtian).[112] Here Chen Lian, now called Shancai/Good-in-Talent, gladly accepts all the tasks assigned to him by his master, but whenever his father invites him to return home for a visit, Shancai, who has left the household, refuses to go.

When the sixtieth birthday of his father approaches, Chen Lian is invited home once again. His teacher leaves on some business, and in his loneliness Chen Lian decides to visit his father just this once since it is very special occasion. As soon as he starts down the mountain, he hears a voice crying out for help; the voice turns out to be that of a snake that has been locked up in a bottle for eighteen years. Shancai releases the snake from the bottle, but as soon as he does so, it turns into a huge monster that threatens to devour him. When Shancai protests at this unseemly behavior, the snake makes the argument that it is the way of the world that a favor is repaid by a feud. However, it agrees to submit their disagreement to the judgment of three persons.

Shancai first comes across an old man who is an incarnation of the Golden Buffalo Star, who sides with the snake in view of his own experiences at the hands of man. They next meet with an old Daoist priest, who also sides with the snake. This Daoist priest turns out to be Master Zhuang (Zhuangzi), who once brought a skeleton back to life—but as soon as the skeleton had been revived, he took Master Zhuang to court for stealing his money. They next meet a young girl, and the snake begins to salivate in anticipation of a tasty dessert. The girl promises the snake that it may eat her too, provided it can worm its way back into the bottle from which Shancai had earlier released it. As soon as the snake has wormed its way into the bottle, it finds itself trapped inside. The girl then reveals her true form, which is the bodhisattva Guanyin.[113] When the snake begs for her mercy, Guanyin says that in order to be saved it must first engage in religious exercises for seven years in the Grotto of the Sounds of the Flood at Mt. Putuo.

Inserted at this point in the precious scroll is a potted version of the legend of the filial parrot, who in popular iconography is often depicted with Guanyin. This short account provides a summary of *The Precious Scroll of the Parrot* (*Yingge baojuan*), itself a sectarian reworking of the fifteenth-century *Tale of the Filial Parrot* (*Yingge xiaoyi zhuan*), a prosimetric adaptation of a well-known *jātaka* tale.[114] The little parrot is an emblem of filial piety: it is captured when it is looking for its mother's favorite food. When it finally manages to escape, its mother has already died. It then mourns its mother and provides her with a fitting funeral before becoming Guanyin's disciple.

The story then skips ahead to three years later, when Guanyin returns to Mt. Putuo and appears to Shancai in the middle of the ocean, standing on the head of a huge tortoise (*ao*). Shancai joins her, walking across the waves. "To this very day, this picture remains in the world" (p. 27a–b). Following this confirmation of the sincerity of his faith, his parents are reborn in heaven. After the snake has submitted itself to austerities for seven years, it has rid itself of all its poison and created a pearl. It is now transformed into the Dragon Girl and joins Guanyin, Shancai, and the filial parrot at Mt. Putuo.[115] The text concludes with an eight-line poem in which the members of the audience are once against urged to persist in their devotions.

The Precious Scroll of Good-in-Talent and Dragon Girl tells its pious tale efficiently and not without touches of humor. The Buffalo Star, for instance, relates how he never wanted to descend to earth but was pushed out of the Gate of Heaven by the bodhisattva Kṣitigarbha (Dizang), who had taken pity on the toiling masses and had vowed to the Buffalo Star that his eyes would fall out on the ground if humans would not repay a favor with a favor. Because of his fall from heaven, the buffalo had lost the teeth in his upper jaw, and because of the bad treatment the buffalo subsequently suffered at the hand of man, Kṣitigarbha's eyes had indeed fallen to the ground, where they turned into the snails that are trampled by the buffalo when plowing the fields.

If we take *The Precious Scroll of Good-in-Talent and Dragon Girl* first of all as the religious biography of Shancai, as seems to be suggested by the text, the story reads very much like a minor mirror image of *The Precious Scroll of Incense Mountain*. This mirroring even extends to the matter of names: Miaoshan's mother is called Baode; Chen Lian's father is named Debao. But whereas Chen Debao allows his son to pursue a religious career, Miaoshan's father is fiercely opposed to his daughter's wish to become a nun. And whereas Miaoshan is brought back from the White Sparrow Convent in shackles, Shancai returns to his father's home on his own initiative. Miaoshan stubbornly frustrates all attempts to persuade her to marry, but Shancai is immediately seduced by the voice of the snake. Miaoshan, following her execution, frees all the suffering beings in hell; Shancai frees a snake from its bottle. And whereas Miaoshan happily donates her arms and eyes to serve as a medicine for her cruel father, Shancai refuses to become a meal for the hungry snake he has liberated. Miaoshan is continuously in control; Shancai soon finds himself at the mercy of his antagonist.

Both *The Precious Scroll of Good-in-Talent and Dragon Girl* and *The Precious Scroll of Incense Mountain* deal extensively with the issue of *en* (favor, grace, care, kindness) and the need to repay it. Whereas a filial Miaoshan, following her enlightenment, freely repays her parents' *en*, the refractious snake refuses to repay Shancai's *en* and even argues that ingratitude is the way of the world. So perhaps we should have a closer look at Shancai's crafty adversary. After all, she shares equal billing with the male protagonist in the title of this precious scroll.

The ingratitude of a creature that has been saved from danger is a well-known motif. All over the world this ungrateful animal usually is a snake, but in China the best-known representative of this ungrateful creature is the wolf in the tale of the Wolf of Zhongshan.[116] The tale of the Wolf of Zhongshan also introduces the three judges to whom the wolf and his savior appeal in order to settle their quarrel. The three unlikely judges (animals, trees, objects) have their counterparts in other parts of Eurasia, too, wherever the story of the ungrateful animal is told.[117]

The story of the Wolf of Zhongshan first appeared in print when it was included in the *Ocean of Stories from Past and Present* (*Gujin shuohai*) of 1544 as an anonymous tale in the classical language, entitled *Tale of the Wolf of Zhongshan* (*Zhongshan lang zhuan*). The contents of this tale may be briefly summarized as follows.[118] When Lord Jian of Zhao goes out hunting, he comes across a wolf that raises itself on its hind legs like a human being. He shoots at it, but the beast escapes and runs away. The wolf then meets with a traveling Mohist scholar, Master Dongguo, whom he implores for help, appealing to the Mohist teaching of universal love. The scholar takes pity on the animal and hides it in one of the book chests strapped on his donkey. He then meets up with the hunters, who ask him whether he has seen the wolf. The scholar denies any knowledge of the animal's whereabouts, and after the hunters have gone, he lets the wolf out of the chest. However, the hungry wolf now wants to eat him: only by serving as his food, the wolf claims, will Master Dongguo complete the act of saving his life. Master Dongguo protests, and they decide to submit their quarrel to the judgment of three elders. The first, a withered apricot tree about to be chopped down, and the second, an old buffalo about to be slaughtered, both side with the wolf, but the third, an old man, feigns disbelief and first wants proof that the wolf could really have fitted into the chest. The wolf climbs into the chest to demonstrate, but as soon as he has done so, the old man takes the scholar's sword, and together they put an end to the ungrateful creature.

In classical Chinese literature, the *Tale of the Wolf of Zhongshan* is an unusual text in that it is a rare example of a fully developed animal fable. While texts in which animals are described as imbued with human emotions are not uncommon, we only seldom encounter a prose fable or a poem in which animals as such, without first having to be transformed into human beings, are allowed to speak.[119] In this tale not only are a wolf and a buffalo allowed to speak, but so is a tree. This latter phenomenon may be due to a possible Indian origin of the tale. In his 1826 rendition of the Indian fable-collection *Pañcatantra* on the basis of versions from South India, J. A. Dubois included a fable in which a brahmin carries a crocodile at the latter's request from a small creek to the river Ganges; when they arrive there a few days later, the hungry crocodile wants to eat his benefactor, and they put their quarrel before a mango tree, a buffalo, and a jackal.[120] One may also discern the influence of fifteenth-century Chinese drama in the figure of the complaining apricot tree, as the plays of Zhu Youdun (1379–1439) feature a large number of quite talkative plants and trees.[121] The disgruntled old (but still alive) buffalo has his direct predecessor in the slaughtered animal that in a long song suite by Yao Shouzhong (second half of the thirteenth century) pleads his case in the underworld before King Yama.[122]

Despite its obvious roots in international folklore, the *Zhongshan lang zhuan* is anything but a popular legend when it first appears in print. Its many classical allusions mark it as a learned fable on ingratitude. The authorship of this text is a matter of dispute. Both Kang Hai (1475–1541) and Ma Zhongxi (1446–1512) have been mentioned as author, and both are said to have written this text as an attack on an ungrateful former friend. Later the text was also credited to a Song-dynasty author, and even a Tang-dynasty poet. The story was very popular with playwrights as well: in addition to a four-act play commonly ascribed to Kang Hai, there is also a one-act adaptation ascribed to Wang Jiusi (1468–1551).[123]

A more detailed comparison between *Tale of the Wolf of Zhongshan* and *The Precious Scroll of Good-in-Talent and Dragon Girl* may be useful to highlight the underlying themes of the latter work as a popular legend. When we first turn our attention to the judges, we notice that the apricot tree has been dropped from the panel, perhaps for a variety of reasons. The simplest explanation may be that a talking tree was regarded as being simply too fantastic to be believable. The precious scroll also tries to provide a rationale for the miracle of a speaking buffalo by turning the animal into an old man who is a manifestation of the Heavenly Star of the Golden Buffalo (*Tianshang jin niuxing*, p. 13b). On the other hand, the suppression of the apricot tree may also be related to the Buddhist background of the legend of Shancai and Longnü as told in our precious scroll.

Traditional Chinese thought, whether Confucian or Daoist, is very much concerned with life. In this worldview, life is shared by human beings, animals, and plants alike, and demands respect in all its manifestations.[124] The *zouyu*, a mythical white tiger that appears during the reign of a holy ruler, not only refrains from eating any meat but also is careful not to tread on a single blade of living grass. Daoist immortals eat no grain; a special subgroup of Daoist deliverance plays even feature trees that achieve immortality. Chinese Buddhism, on the other hand, ended up being much more concerned with souls and their transmigrations. Although the tiniest insect is credited with a soul that once may have been human, plants were not regarded as having souls. Thus, it was considered a sin to eat meat but a virtue to be a vegetarian. From a Buddhist perspective, the complaint of the tree and the complaint of the buffalo in the tale of the Wolf of Zhongshan are of a completely different order. The buffalo, a harmless and useful creature, accuses man of a sin when he complains about his many years of servitude without reward and his master's desire to have it slaughtered to be eaten. But what can a soulless tree complain about if its fruit and its timber are used by men?

If one regards the disappearance of the apricot tree from the panel of judges in *The Precious Scroll of Incense Mountain* as related to the Buddhist orientation of the genre, one can only be surprised to see the tree replaced by the figure of Master Zhuang, the main hero of the competing genre of *daoqing* (Daoist ballads). The story of the meeting of Master Zhuang with a skeleton has a long pedigree.[125] The *Zhuangzi* itself already contains an anecdote of Master Zhuang coming across a skull, and this theme was later taken up by poets in the second and third centuries CE, in works such as *Rhapsody on a Skull* (*Dulou fu*) by Zhang Heng (78–139). The theme became popular again in the twelfth and thirteenth centuries with the founding fathers of Quanzhen Daoism. Their obsession with skulls and skeletons as objects of meditation may well have been due to Buddhist influence. In the writings of these early Quanzhen masters we encounter two related themes. First, all persons who have not been reborn into the light are characterized as living corpses or running skeletons.[126] This theme was later also taken up by both sectarian and Buddhist precious scrolls, such as *The Precious Scroll of Incense Mountain*.[127] A second theme is the encounter with an unburied skeleton by the side of the road; texts on this theme stress the transience of our earthly existence. Such laments eventually found their way into both Buddhist and Daoist funeral liturgies.[128] The theme also found a more narrative development in the story of Master Zhuang's meeting with a skeleton. This story was already in circulation in the Yuan dynasty (1260–1368), and by the Ming had become the favorite subject of Daoist storytelling, although it would appear to have been largely forgotten by the eighteenth century.

According to this story, Master Zhuang in the course of his travels comes across an unburied skeleton. After wondering what kind of person the skeleton might have been during his lifetime, Master Zhuang takes pity on him and decides to bring him back to life. As three pieces of bone in his shoulder are missing, Master Zhuang replaces them with willow twigs. When the skeleton has been brought back to life, he turns out to have been a traveling merchant, and when he cannot find the money he was carrying with him, he immediately accuses Master Zhuang of robbing him and hauls him before the local magistrate. To prove his innocence, Master Zhuang has no choice but to turn his accuser into a skeleton again, the willow twigs serving as proof of the truth of his version of the story. (*The Precious Scroll of Good-in-Talent and Dragon Girl* has Master Zhuang replace a missing thigh bone with the branch of a mulberry tree.) But Master Zhuang makes use of more extraneous matter in resurrecting the skeleton. In an obvious echo of the story of the Wolf of Zhongshan, he makes use of "a wolf's heart and a dog's innards" (p. 17b) to fill out the corpse. The ingratitude of the resurrected skeleton now is perhaps only to be expected, and Master Zhuang is finally led to conclude that "in this world all people are evil skeletons!" (p. 18b).

In contrast to the story of the Wolf of Zhongshan, the major change in *The Precious Scroll of Good-in-Talent and Dragon Girl* is of course that the wolf is replaced by the snake as the ungrateful protagonist. The snake can be regarded as the embodiment of female sexuality, and as such as a tempting and destructive power. In many other legends and tales the snake has the same function: it may present itself in the guise of a young and alluring woman ready at any moment to devour the man it has seduced.[129] One only has to think of the famous Hangzhou legend of the White Snake. That the dangers to a young man of sexual passion are very much on the mind of the anonymous author of the precious scroll is shown by the following passage, which appears right before Chen Lian's departure from his parental home for the hermitage of his master:

> Let's talk about the mahāsattva Guanyin. "Seven years have passed since I sent that lad down to the mortal world. He was given the name of Chen Lian and was born into the realm of dust. He does not eat any pungent food: his root in the Way has not yet been obscured, and his single-minded heart is still undivided. If I do not provide him guidance along with the Way and its Virtue, I fear he will end up taking the wrong road. 'By practice people grow distant.' Availing myself of the opportunity that 'his hole of passion has not yet been opened,' I will lead him into the Way, so he will avoid stumbling into the domain of misty flowers."[130]

By "leaving the household" a man puts himself outside the ties of marriage (and sexuality). But as soon as he entertains the thought of even a temporary "return to the household," he opens himself up to temptation. This is what happens to Shancai. While the bodhisattva (who herself succeeded in evading marriage) may wish to safeguard Shancai from experiencing passion, the author of *The Precious Scroll of Good-in-Talent and Dragon Girl* shares with the author of the famous eighteenth-century novel *Dream in the Red*

Chamber (*Honglou meng*) the insight that passion can be transcended only after it has been experienced to the fullest degree. The danger implied in passion, as it is spelled out in *The Precious Scroll of Good-in-Talent and Dragon Girl*, is annihilation: the snake threatens to devour Shancai.[131] Shancai's meeting with the buffalo and Master Zhuang may also hint at a message that was spelled out in more detail in the writings of the early Quanzhen masters: a man who is induced by passion to marry is only a beast of burden to his wife and children, a running corpse pulling a cart filled with his dependants, a walking skeleton engendering ungrateful skeletons.[132] It is also important to note that the man is incapable of killing the snake. Nor are the old buffalo and Master Zhuang of any use either. The snake has to be subdued by the intervention of a young girl, who tricks the snake into returning to its bottle.

While the intervention of the three judges in *The Precious Scroll of Good-in-Talent and Dragon Girl* seems to be inspired by the story of the Wolf of Zhongshan, the victory of a young girl over a snake echoes much older legends and seems to reflect more general anxieties about female sexuality (at least in the southeastern coastal areas). Let us have a look at the story of Li Ji as told in the fourth-century *In Search of the Supernatural* (*Soushen ji*). A man-eating snake that lives in a cave in the wilds of Fujian has the power to bring either prosperity or disaster to the surrounding area, depending on whether or not it is supplied with its annual offering of a young virgin. The officials, the male representatives of the community, find themselves unable to subdue the monster. A young girl, Li Ji, against her parents' wishes, volunteers to be sacrificed. She tricks the monster and succeeds in killing it with the help of a dog and a sword; the snake dies as it crawls back into its cave. When Li Ji enters the monster's cave, she finds all the skulls of its earlier victims. The story ends with the marriage of Li Ji to the local king.[133] In this tale we can already see the various motifs we encountered in *The Precious Scroll of Good-in-Talent and Dragon Girl*: a devouring snake, ineffective males, skulls and skeletons, and a victorious maiden.

The tale of Li Ji may be read in many different ways. It may be read as a reflection of the many dangers the first settlers of the southeastern coastal region encountered while clearing the snake-infested jungle. It may also be read as a reflection of the development of yet another local cult in which an animal is replaced as object of veneration by a deity in human form who incorporates the full range of powers of his or her predecessor. Another way to read the tale is as a paean to the daring and inventiveness of women. I would suggest, however, that one may also read the tale as a myth about the incorporation of female fertility from outside into the patriarchal family. As stated before, the patriarchal family cannot reproduce itself and needs outside female fertility for its very survival. However, women from outside the family also constitute a danger to its survival as they may not fully commit themselves to their new family by marriage, but continue to prefer their natal family and seek ways to transfer wealth from their new home to their old one. This dangerous power of fertility/female sexuality is represented in this tale by the monstrous snake in its grotto. Men are shown to be ineffective against this danger. Only when a woman is willing to act against the instructions of her own parents and slay the monster is a full integration into her new family by marriage possible. If not, even a virgin is turned into the very image of death—a skull.

The Precious Scroll of Good-in-Talent and Dragon Girl is not simply a retelling of an old myth. After all, its main theme is not the continuation of the family but rather leaving the family. However, many motifs are still clearly recognizable. The nature of the snake as an embodiment of female sexuality is made clear from the very start in the precious scroll. The grotto has been replaced by a bottle, which is described as a *huangsha ping* (yellow earth bottle). While the term *huangsha* is used to refer to the grave, the bottle may stand for the gourd, which in Daoism represents the inexhaustible container or womb. Shancai, by showing himself susceptible to female charms, is defenseless as soon as the snake wants to devour him, and it is now he who is in danger of being turned into a skeleton instead of the hapless virgins in the tale of Li Ji. Again, the savior is a young girl who tricks the snake, in this story by getting it to crawl back into the bottle from which it had emerged. Both tales, although centuries apart, in this way credit the victory over the snake to virtuous female cunning. In the tale of Li Ji, the heroine finally marries the king, for whom, one assumes, she will bear many sons. In *The Precious Scroll of Good-in-Talent and Dragon-Girl* it is the snake that is turned into a dragon daughter, who in turn produces a pearl of wisdom, while Shancai pursues his religious career.[134]

Conclusion

The bodhisattva Avalokiteśvara enjoyed wide and fervent veneration almost from the very moment of his introduction into China. The bodhisattva's popularity only increased after he was, from the tenth century on, increasingly worshipped in female form. This new manifestation gave rise to many legends, the most popular of which was that of Princess Miaoshan, who refused to marry and give her father a grandson, but who was willing to give her limbs to him to use as medicine when he was wasted by a terrible disease. The most powerful version of this legend is *The Precious Scroll of Incense Mountain*, which may go back to a composition by the monk Puming of 1103 but has reached us only in the heavily revised versions of later centuries.

The Precious Scroll of Incense Mountain presents a powerful and gripping account of the problems and opposition facing a young woman in a Confucian society if she is determined to pursue her own individual religious salvation, even as it holds out the promise that her personal salvation may benefit her entire family, including the father who wanted her dead. The text has traditionally been read both as a charter for opposing marriage and a paean to filial piety. A comparison with the hagiographies of Christian female saints from medieval France shows many structural parallels and also draws attention to some of the sexual tensions in the patriarchal family that help to give the narrative in the precious scroll its particular tension and dynamism.

The Precious Scroll of Good-in-Talent and Dragon Girl, which probably dates from the eighteenth or nineteenth century, is an original and charming account of how Shancai and Longnü (and the white parrot) became the acolytes of Guanyin. This enjoyable, fairy-tale-like narrative returns to many of the same themes as those of *The Precious Scroll of Incense Mountain*, such as the tension between the duties toward the family and society and the yearning for individual salvation, the dangers posed by female sexual hunger, and the need to repay the favors one has received.

The overwhelming majority of Buddhist texts were written by monks for monks. Both these precious scrolls, however, offer us texts that, although most likely written by monks, were intended for an audience of laypeople, for they spoke to the issues confronting laymen and, especially, laywomen. In this respect, the precious scrolls continued the tradition of the transformation texts and other genres of Buddhist prosimetric storytelling known from the manuscripts discovered at Dunhuang. The continuing popularity of *The Precious Scroll of Incense Mountain* over many centuries serves as the best proof of how well it succeeded in speaking to the yearnings and needs of its largely female audience and helped them give meaning to their existence.

Translator's Note

Longer passages in verse tend to be constructed of building blocks of four lines. To help the reader, the beginning of a new group of four lines is marked by an indentation. I have made no attempt to rhyme the verse passages, but I have tried to keep the lines of verse roughly of equal length within each verse passage. At times I have been rather successful in this, at other times not. In six-syllable lines that are made up of two three-syllable half-lines, the division between the half-lines is marked by a slash. The same slash is also used to separate lines of verse that are quoted inside prose passages. Occasional three-character phrases that precede seven-syllable lines are printed in smaller format in the original text; here they follow a double indentation.

The "stage-directions" in *The Precious Scroll of Incense Mountain* are printed in smaller size too in the original, but in the translation they are printed in italic. Passages in the main body of the text that are preceded by honorific empty spaces are printed in capitals.

I have translated more personal names than is usual nowadays, but many of these names are "speaking names," so I felt justified in doing so. On the other hand, I have left the formula *Namo Guanshiyin pusa* (Hail, Bodhisattva Guanshiyin) untranslated.

The Precious Scroll of Incense Mountain
Part 1

Anonymous

Preface to *The Precious Scroll of Incense Mountain*

On the fifteenth day of the eighth month of the second year of the Chongning reign-period (1103), Chan master Puming of the Song dynasty (960–1278) was sitting alone in meditation in the Penance Hall at the Upper Tianzhu Monastery of Hangzhou.[1] In the light of the full moon he suddenly saw an old monk, who said to him: "You merely cultivate the Way of the Absolute Truth of the Unsurpassable Vehicle, forging connection solely with [those persons] of superior capacity. But how are you able to be of universal assistance? You should practice preaching on behalf of the Buddha. When the Three Vehicles are preached and glorified, and when the Sudden and Gradual [approaches] are both practiced, one can widely deliver sentient beings of the middle and lower [capacities].[2] Only by acting in this manner will you be able to repay the grace of the Buddha!"

The master asked the monk: "By what method should I deliver the people?" The monk replied: "I notice that the people of this land have a karmic affinity to the bodhisattva Guanshiyin. Tell them in brief the outline of the career of the bodhisattva so it will circulate throughout the world. The blessing of those who venerate her[3] and recite her name will be unassailable." This monk thereupon fully expounded her origin, and once he had finished speaking, he disappeared. Chan master Puming had heard it only once, but he fully understood, and thereupon composed the scroll.

All of a sudden he saw the bodhisattva Guanshiyin, who personally manifested her purple-gold form. Holding in her hands her pure vase and willow wand, she appeared riding a cloud, and only after a long while did she return to the void. Everyone who saw her was filled with respect. When afterward people heard about this, they further increased their vigorous zeal. In this way [the scroll] has circulated throughout the wide world as a warning mirror for all eternity.

The First Scroll of the New Printing of the Short Version of the *Sutra of the Original Life of the Bodhisattva Guanshiyin*

THE OPENING DISCOURSE ON ASCENDING THE PLATFORM

(*The one charged with this task should purify and bathe and change into a fresh set of clothes, because then a reverential attitude will come naturally. To enhance respect toward the bodhisattva, that person should first offer incense and praise her, then pronounce the opening discourse, and only then should he enter into the main story.*)

On the nineteenth day of the second month of the year with the cyclical characters XX we respectfully celebrate the good occasion of the descent and birth of the GREATLY COMPASSIONATE BODHISATTVA GUANSHIYIN. I now ascend the platform to pronounce and expand upon the *Precious Scroll of Guanyin*. Congregation, you should sit up straight with an attentive mind, and show respectful reverence by your correct attitude. You are not allowed to talk and joke, and it is strictly forbidden to make any kind of noise. (*Sound the ruler.*[4]) You must listen carefully to the recitation of the text; when you have heard it with clear and pure ears, you should then ponder it and cultivate the indivisible unity of the sacred and the profane.

The SUTRA reads: "For what reason is the bodhisattva Guanshiyin called the One Who Contemplates the Cries of the World? If there are living beings who are subjected to all kinds of suffering and distress and who hear the name of this Bodhisattva Who Contemplates the Cries of the World, and with all their mind call upon that name, the Bodhisattva Who Contemplates the Cries of the World will instantly regard their cries, and all of them will be delivered. If there be any who keep to the name of the Bodhisattva Who Contemplates the Cries of the World, though they fall into a great fire, the fire will not be able to burn them. Yes, even if they are carried away by a large flood and call upon that name, they will instantly arrive at a shallow spot. It is for this reason that the bodhisattva is called the One Who Contemplates the Cries of the World."[5] A *gātha* reads: (*Sound the ruler.*)

Guanyin's original home is the old Numinous Terrace,
Because of her compassion she descends to the world.
It doesn't matter whether you are a Turk or a Tartar—
Upon hearing your voice the bodhisattva is all smiles.

The Text of the *Sutra of the Original Life*

(*The intonations of suffering, joy, and pity should all be imitated.*)

Respectfully I have heard that in the times of the buddha Kāśyapa there was to the west of Mt. Sumeru a world, the capital of which was called Raised Forest, and which used the reign-period Marvelous Splendor (Miaozhuang). The human ruler of that land was called Po Qie. When he was just twenty, the masses praised him as the most honored of men, and beseeched him to establish himself as emperor. With propriety he ruled the domain within the borders, an area of one hundred eight thousand miles square. The wall of the imperial city had twelve gates, and encircled an area of three thousand miles square. The palace halls were high and wide, and gold and emerald glimmered in profusion. He was respectfully served by four chancellors, and guarded and protected by three dukes. The nine barbarians and the seventy-two countries maintained constant communication; the myriad clans all submitted, and each and every person kowtowed, filled with awe. The emperor always loved to go out hunting, and his concubines shared in his sport.[6] Their unsurpassed pleasure was out of this world! His only sorrow was that none of the women of the Six Palaces had borne him a crown prince.[7] Time and again he prayed to Blue Heaven, and then composed the following *gātha*:

I, Po Qie, emperor Po, called the Marvelous Splendor,
Subdue with my impressive might the myriad lands.
If a crown prince is born in one of the palaces, I will
Slaughter a cow and horse to thank the Three Lights.[8]

Now let me tell you about the empress. The main consort, the empress, was called Precious Virtue (Baode), and she was of the same age as the emperor. Her face was as round as the full moon. Her earlobes hung down to her shoulders,[9] and her eyes were clear and bright. Her entire body was right and proper on all accounts. She was always full of kind goodness, and magnanimous in all affairs. In the eighth year of Marvelous Splendor she suddenly gave birth to a girl. Her father the emperor was pleased and said: "We will use the reign-period as a generational marker, and establish the name according to the situation. Because We were reading a book when this girl was born, her name will be Marvelous Book (Miaoshu)." Later, in the thirteenth year of Marvelous Splendor, the empress again gave birth to a girl. When, as before, this was reported to the emperor, the pleased father said: "As this girl was born while I was playing the zither in the Palace for Communicating with Heaven, so her name will be Marvelous Sound (Miaoyin)." From this time onward the empress time and again prayed to Blue Heaven for the birth of a son. In the eighteenth year of Marvelous Splendor, at night while sleeping in the Palace of Great Harmony, she saw in a dream two heavenly maidens, each thirty feet tall. They wore pearly caps on their heads and were bedecked with jade necklaces: every pore of their bodies emitted a five-colored light. Standing by her bed, they said: "The Jade Emperor of Highest Heaven invites Your Majesty to come to the Heaven of the Thirty-three,[10] so as to meet with the Buddha and hear the Dharma in the Hall of the Good Dharma." The empress agreed to the request, and, once dressed, left the palace. Heaven had sent down a phoenix carriage, which was waiting for her at the gate. In an instant she had arrived at the gate of the Heaven of the Thirty-three. The empress at first saw only a brilliant light that was so blinding that she could not open her eyes. The denizens of heaven said: "Recite thrice the name of the buddha Maitreya, and you will be able to see." She immediately recited the name of that buddha, and indeed could see the extraordinary wonders of this holy domain. The numberless precious halls of the heavenly palace were high and wide, deep and extensive. A heavenly music sounded all by itself, and the colors of flowers were without end. The Great Brahma King and all deities came to the Good Dharma Hall. When they had listened to the sutra, three thousand persons of purple-gold and ten thousand heavenly maidens of impeccable beauty, each seated on a golden lotus throne and majestically floating through the sky, came to the Good Dharma Hall. When the empress saw this, she inquired the reason. Because they had become intimate through their conversation, the heavenly maidens mentioned: "Empress, they are giving you an immortal!" The empress smiled and expressed her thanks to the immortals with a bow. When she had returned to the palace, she awoke with a start. She then composed the following *gātha*:

The holy domain of the empyrean is quite extraordinary,
The precious hall of Daluo Heaven[11] emits a bright light—
Ten thousand immortals all come and congratulate me,
As they give me a girl to take back home to the palace.

When the empress woke up, she pondered the matter in great detail: "What a strange miracle! Even now it is still as if I see that marvelous sight before me! It cannot but be that Heaven will send down disaster and misfortune, or that the earth will awaken clouds of dust. Could it be that foreign countries will create havoc or that the common people will rise in rebellion?" She could not find the peace to sleep, and sat up until dawn, when she went in person to the throne hall to report this matter to her lord and king. She then composed the following *gātha*:

In my dream I went to hear the Dharma in the Hall of Heaven,
The Greatly Enlightened Golden Immortal displayed his light.[12]
As I do not know whether this spells misfortune or happiness,
I've come here with the aim of reporting this to Your Majesty.

The emperor thereupon issued a placard summoning all interpreters of dreams. An elderly man appeared, with white hair and a wrinkled face, wearing a bamboo cap and dressed in a patched cassock, and supporting himself with a staff. Taking the placard down, he entered the palace. Pleased, the Marvelous Splendor emperor asked him: "Where do you live?" "I live in the land of joy (*le*)," the old man replied. Then the emperor asked him: "What is your surname?" "My surname is Mi."[13] The emperor also asked him: "How old are you? And how many years have you been away from your family?" The elderly man replied: "I lost my parents early on, and I do not know my age. At a young age I abandoned the householder's life, and since then have wandered through the countries of the world, everywhere interpreting dreams—I don't know for how long already." The emperor said: "Where is your dream book?" He replied: "I do not rely on a book for interpreting dreams—I have my own considerations." The emperor then told him: "Last night my main consort, the empress, dreamt that she ascended to heaven and in the Good Dharma Hall listened to the Dharma of the Buddha. She then saw three thousand purple-gold beings and ten thousand heavenly maidens, who all seemed familiar to her. They gave the empress an immortal girl to take back to the palace. What does this dream portend?" The elderly man replied: "I will now explain this dream in detail. If the empress ascended to heaven and heard the Dharma, it means she will initiate good deeds, that she will increase the imperial longevity, and that she is bound to become the mother of a buddha. The three thousand purple-gold beings are the three thousand buddhas of the three worlds.[14] The ten thousand immortal maidens are the myriad bodhisattvas. If they gave her an immortal girl to take back with her to the palace, it means she will turn a human imperial family into a Dharma imperial family. Now a bodhisattva of flesh and blood will appear and be born in the palace. By manifesting herself in this world, she will widely display her supernatural powers of omnipresence, and ferry across people without number. This is all it means." He then composed the following *gātha*:

My lord and emperor asks me where I live—
My old home is the land of joy and peace.
Since birth I've been stupid and of no use,
I just pass the time by interpreting dreams.

That elderly man didn't want any official appointment or monetary reward, but just asked a eunuch for a gourdful of water. As soon as he had spit out a single mouthful of water and let out a single shout, his staff rose up from the ground and turned into a golden dragon. Then rain began to pour down, lightning flashed and thunder crashed, shaking with its roar the palace hall. Greatly manifesting his golden body, he disappeared, riding the clouds. When the emperor saw this, he pressed the palms of his hands together, knocking on his teeth.[15] He then composed the following *gātha*:

A single shout, and in an instant the staff became a dragon:
Accompanied by clouds and rain, he returned to the heavens.
Manifesting his golden body, he ascended into the sky—
And the dragon-mien of the emperor showed his pleasure.

The story tells that from this time on the empress was in blessed circumstances. Her eyes constantly saw *ulumbara* flowers swirling about her;[16] her ears constantly heard the playing of a heavenly music; her nose constantly smelled an exquisite perfume wafting about; her body constantly produced a brilliant light; and her throat was constantly moistened by ghee. Accompanied by such auspicious signs, she was pregnant for the full ten months.[17] It was the eighteenth year of Marvelous Splendor, and the nineteenth day of the second month was the birthday of the empress. All the concubines and other palace women celebrated this with three days devoted to enjoying the flowers. In the imperial flower garden there were more than eighty paths for viewing the flowers and willows. These had all been paved with white jade, while the balustrade was fashioned of yellow gold. In addition there were thirty-two pavilions for enjoying the flowers. These were covered with blue and green glazed tiles, with golden beams and jade pillars. The floor was made out of silver bricks interspersed with the seven jewels.[18] Banquets had been set out everywhere, where zithers were played and songs raised in joy. Eventually they arrived behind the Palace of Completed Heaven, where they ascended the Thousand-flower Tower to look and gaze in the four directions. The sun in the cloudless sky was positioned at the hour of *si*.[19] That very moment they saw heavenly flowers scatter their colors, while extraordinary treasure poured out of the earth. The overwhelming perfume of the flowers enveloped and permeated the tower. In that instant she gave birth to the princess. At that time the hundred birds in the sky congratulated her by singing: "A bodhisattva has appeared in this world, / She will ferry across limitless multitudes." Everyone in the palace heard these words. She then composed the following *gātha*:

Enjoying ourselves by viewing the flowers we came to the tower,
Yellow orioles were calling, the hundred flowers were blooming.
How beautiful the spring on the nineteenth of the second month!
This was the day on which the princess was born into this world.

The empress then ordered the concubines and palace maids to wash and bathe the child in a golden basin. All the palace ladies praised the princess, saying: "She is not a mere mortal! Her features are extremely subtle and marvelous, like a pure full moon. Her hands have the sign of the thousand-spoked wheel, her eyes are like *maṇi*-pearls,[20] and her fingernails are like white jade. Gleaming like glass, her face shows the thirty-two marks.[21] Her dark brows and lustrous hair are without compare in the world." The ladies of the Six Palaces agreed: "We should present her to the emperor, so her imperial father may have a look at her." They promptly swaddled her in a brocade coverlet and placed her on a golden tray. The imperial concubines carried her, and the palace maids followed behind. The hundred musicians of the Six Palaces and Three Halls played loudly as they ascended the precious throne hall. Her imperial father was pleased and said: "Since this girl was born after the empress had been affected by a dream, her name shall be Marvelous Goodness (Miaoshan). Tomorrow at the dawn audience We will discuss this with Our ministers, as an edict should be issued throughout the world." He then composed the following *gātha*:

A dragon coverlet woven with gold thread—swaddled in brocade:
On a golden tray she is presented for her lord and emperor to see.
We will share our joy and happiness with the people of the realm,
Even if We would be reduced to poverty, it would be no problem!

But let's not go on about the great joy of the emperor. Let's rather tell about the princess. She grew up inside the palace, where she was treasured by everyone as if she were a jewel or a pearl. When, as she grew up, she had reached the age of ten, the measure of her resolve was large and wide. She was loftily enlightened and profoundly grounded. Without any effort, she fully mastered the zither and calligraphy, colors and paintings, and weaving brocade into patterns. She could prepare all the hundred delicacies and special dishes. Her bodily posture was dignified and serious, [and she exhibited the virtues of] clear purity and appropriate yielding, harmonious modesty and filial obedience. She knew honesty and understood shame and, filled with kind compassion, manifested forbearance. She did not crave anything or cling to anything, and as if by nature kept to a vegetarian diet and maintained the precepts. By day she read the sutras and recited the name of the Buddha, and at night she composed her mind and practiced meditation. Without any slackening she devoted herself to cultivation like this.

She grew up inside the palace and before long had reached the age of nineteen. Time and again the princess prayed to Blue Heaven: "Let me abandon the imperial palace, leave the family and venerate the Buddha, visit an enlightened teacher and follow the instructions of a good friend.[22] I will walk in the right Way without any wavering. Leaving the earth-prison,[23] escaping from this pit of fire, I want to become a buddha and ferry across the multitudes." After she had made this vow, she went in a dream to the top of the Marvelous High Peak,[24] where she received the announcement of her future buddhahood from the buddha Limitless Longevity.[25] When she woke up from her dream, her heart was completely enlightened. She then composed the following *gātha*:

I've grown up inside the palace for a full nineteen years,
But with its myriads of pleasures I've no karmic affinity.
Unshakable and self-realized, my heart does not waver,
From my earliest years I've gone against the grain.[26]

Inside the palace the princess practiced cultivation and studied the Way, but the palace maids and concubines all made fun of her: "Why do you do these things, rather than enjoying all the pleasures [of the palace]?" The princess replied: "Because birth and death are a great matter,[27] I have out of my own nature sworn a vow to ferry all sentient beings across the [sea of suffering], and I have out of my own nature sworn a vow to achieve buddhahood. Alas, sun and moon move like a shuttle, and light and shade [fly by] like an arrow. Constantly I am worried by the thought that as soon as we lose this human body, we will have lost it for over a thousand years.[28] I urge all of you everywhere who understand me: The pleasures of the palace are not necessarily the best, / Much better to become a monk within the Gate of Emptiness."[29] She then composed the following *gātha*:

Wealth and status here in the palace are truly imposing,
The Six Palaces and Three Halls may surpass even heaven.
But do not think you'll live forever without any affliction—
When you die, you'll have to appear before King Yama![30]

Inside the palace the princess practiced cultivation—but how would it end? Let's tell how the Marvelous Splendor emperor ruled the realm with a firm hand: even gods and ghosts were frightened and filled with fear. Those who had merit were rewarded, and those who broke the law were not pardoned. The four chancellors and nine directors served him respectfully, and his millions of troops protected him on all sides. In the rear palace his three thousand seven hundred concubines dined nine times every day, as harmonious music played in accord with Heaven. He lacked neither gold nor silver nor rare treasures. Pondering his position, the only thing he lacked was a crown prince. He then composed the following *gātha*:

Whether an emperor lacks an heir depends on Heaven—
This long tale of cause and conditions is still transmitted.
In a myriad *kalpas*, in a thousand lives, a rare opportunity:[31]
Sit up straight and still your breath, and listen to its telling.

Namo Guanshiyin pusa (*Here one repeats the name of the Buddha and burns and offers [incense]. Whenever one comes across the name of the bodhisattva, the congregation recites the name once. Sound the ruler once.*)

The Marvelous Splendor emperor governed all-under-heaven,
A lord and king in possession of the Way, he ruled the people.
The hundreds of millions of mountains and streams were unified,
The myriads of phenomena praised in concert this Great Peace.
Let's not discuss the emperor's ample possession of the Way,
Let us tell you about his main consort inside the rear palace:
She went by the name of Precious Virtue and was the empress,
A saintly mother of a buddha who had come down to earth.
Her natural beauty from birth was fully perfect in all respects,
Her humane virtue and kind compassion were without compare.
The thirty-six palaces all served her with utmost reverence,
The seventy-two courtyards all venerated her with proper awe.
But even though she was the empress in the rear palace,
She had not given birth to a crown prince, a son and heir.
One after another, she had given birth to three daughters,
And these three daughters I will now introduce to you all.
The eldest sister, Marvelous Book, was the first of them,
The second of them went by the name of Marvelous Sound.

The third of them, Marvelous Goodness, was the youngest,
Her parents loved her best—she was the apple of their eye!

One morning when the emperor ascended the throne hall [for the morning audience], a great rage showed on his dragon-mien, filling his court officials with fear. The emperor did not say a word, but secretly he thought to himself: "The concubines and other women in the rear palace number three thousand seven hundred, but they all are just like bodies modeled from clay or carved from wood. There is not even a single one who is capable of giving me a son and heir! And then to think that the plants and trees of the mountains and rivers each year again in spring open their flowers and form fruit![32] But We lack a descendant, so all Our effort in serving as lord of the country is in vain. If only one of the women in the rear palace would give me a crown prince, who would succeed Our mandate, govern the realm, and glorify his rule, so his fame would spread to other countries—that is Our wish! Today there is none to whom I can complain, so I can only call my ministers to draw near, so they may listen as I tell them in detail my innermost feelings."

If only he had had a son, this affair would have been dropped,
Without a worry in the world, he'd have enjoyed Great Peace.

Namo Guanshiyin pusa

The emperor opened his golden mouth, speaking as follows:
"My dear ministers, come closer and listen to Our concerns.
What is the point in piling up gold and accumulating jade?
In the final reckoning the rarest treasure is not really genuine.
    Light and shade like an arrow hasten the process of aging,
But the state lacks a crown prince, We lack a descendant.
To Our despair today We realize that Our body is aging,
And to govern mountains and rivers We lack a successor.
    If only one palace woman would give birth to a prince,
I would not worry for the peace of this whole wide world.
All you high officials here present in your red and purple,
Who can free me of these feelings of affliction and sorrow?"
    The four chancellors and the nine directors promptly replied,
Following a double genuflection and eight bows they spoke:
"Everyone here at court is a loyal servant and a gentleman,
There is not one person here who disobeys and is not good.

In the palace there are the three princesses, so why not have
Each of them marry a prince consort who will live here at home?
We humbly hope that Your Majesty will regard this proposal,
And with pleased countenance will follow our humble advice."

Each day at the third notch of the fifth watch[33] the emperor would by the light of the moon and the stars be welcomed into the precious hall while the hundred musicians were playing together. The great court bell would be sounded and the great drum would be struck. As a call for silence the whip would be cracked three times with a reverberating roar like thunder. The civil officials and the military officers would be arranged in orderly rows. Following the three prayers and the three praises, they would make twenty-four bows and wish the emperor a myriad of years. One day, when the audience greetings were completed, he asked the regulator of the ranks: "Were all officials this morning present at the morning audience?" The regulator of the ranks reported: "Your Majesty, the chancellor on the left Zhang Gongchen did not take part in the morning audience." So the emperor asked: "And why did he not show up?" The chancellor on the right Xu Zhi stepped forward from the ranks and reported: "Your Majesty, I have learned that he failed to show up for this audience because last night his wife gave birth to a baby boy. I hope that Your Majesty will be so kind as to pardon him for this crime." When the emperor heard this, his brows locked in a frown, and he was very much displeased. "Why did that boy refuse to be born in Our palace? Then he could have succeeded Us as lord once he was grown! Wouldn't that have been wonderful?"

A thousand kinds of rare treasures are not the best,
First one seeks the priceless wish-fulfilling jewel.

Namo Guanshiyin pusa

At the third notch of the fifth watch he enters the throne hall:
Once the large fans are moved aside, one sees the emperor.
Fully armed generals are counted in the myriads of people,
Officials and officers are each positioned according to rank.
In the ritual way they three times wish him a myriad of years,
With twenty-four bows they call themselves his ministers.

The Marvelous Splendor emperor opened his golden mouth,
Asking a question of the assembled officials, right and left.
The court officials, right and left, answered as with one voice
That only Chancellor on the Left Gongchen had not arrived:
"We do not know for what reason this person did not show up,
We don't know why he didn't come to take part in the audience."
But Chancellor Xu Zhi promptly reported to the emperor:
"Your Majesty, please lend your ears to what I have to tell.
It is only because his wife last night gave birth to a baby boy,
That he failed to appear at court. Please be magnanimous."
Upon hearing this, the emperor was afflicted by sorrow:
"Why did this baby boy have to be born in the wrong place?
If he had been born in Our palace, he'd be the crown prince,
Washed and bathed in a golden basin, he'd be Our successor!"
The civil and military court officials stated as with one voice:
"There is no karmic cause why the state lacks a crown prince!
The Three Purities[34] and the High Ruler show no understanding,
Which is why jade leaves and golden branches are not spreading."[35]

At this great audience the emperor's face was distorted by rage. The civil and military court officials all trembled with fear. The entire court knelt down, and urged the emperor: "Your Majesty, please still your rage and be merry! Even though you have not sired a crown prince, we have heard that Her Majesty the empress has three daughters, princesses in the prime of their youth, so you should bring princes consort into your home. Can't they be considered to be directly related vines and tendrils? Later Your Majesty may observe which one of them displays the most virtuous behavior, and raise him. We, your ministers, risk a thousand deaths by offering up our straightforward advice! May Your Majesty decide according to your pleasure whether this can be done." When the emperor heard this advice, he was pleased as was shown by the expression of his dragon-mien, and he said: "Thank you all for your advice. This has eased Our worries." He promptly gave out an order, summoning the three princesses in the rear palace to appear before the throne hall that very evening.

Without the spring wind the flowers will not open,
The flowers need to feel the spring wind's force.

Namo Guanshiyin pusa

Their father's edict summoned them from the rear palace,
It was transmitted to the inner garden as fast as a cloud.
Marvelous Book, Marvelous Sound, and Marvelous Goodness
Made their toilette and then together left the rear palace:
    Their black-silk fine hair done up in coiling-dragon buns,
Eyebrows like green willow leaves in early days of spring;
Their cheeks like peony flowers just at the brink of blooming,
Their three-inch embroidered shoes without a trace of dust.
    Their appearance, their flowerlike faces, like finest jade,
Young in years full of natural charm: in the prime of spring.
They exactly resembled Chang'e leaving the moon-palace,[36]
Were like immortal maidens departing from their paradise.
    "I've no clue why our father the emperor gave this order,
Why this order was issued to summon us to his presence!"
Together they went to the Golden Hall for Completing Heaven,
And with eight deep bows thanked him for the imperial grace.
    In orderly fashion, they approached him, wishing him long life;
With phoenix words and oriole voices they praised their father:
"With your golden wheel you rule the three thousand worlds,
May your lordship be extended for many millions of years!"
    Hearing these words, their father the emperor was pleased:
"My darling daughters, listen now to what I have to say.
Your daddy is getting on in years and has none to rely on,
Because there is no crown prince, no young future lord.
    So I now would like to discuss with you, my children,
How to get a prince consort for you here in the rear palace.
In order of age each of you may tell me whether you want
A civil official or military officer—the choice is up to you!"

The emperor ordered his three daughters to marry a man to wait on them: "What would you like? A literary official or a military officer? Tell me quickly, there're plenty of them." The princess Marvelous Book stepped forward and said: "I, your child, obey my father's command. I would like to have a literary man as husband. First the [possible candidates] have to be investigated to make sure there are none among them who have been punished or committed crimes, or who belong to the lower classes of craftsmen. Outside the gate of the palace a golden placard will be displayed, universally summoning all exceptional men of the whole world for an examination. A flourishing talent who is fully conversant with ten thousand scrolls of books, who only has to lift his brush to complete an essay, who as soon as he speaks completes a poem, who exhibits the virtues of filial piety, righteousness, humaneness, and trust, whose talent and appearance are both perfect, whose figure and energy have the natural charm of youth, who is not too fat and not too thin, not too tall and not too short, whose true talent and substantial learning can be employed according to occasion—only such a man can be considered the greatest treasure of the whole nation, the blazing light of ten thousand states. Only the person who is in the possession of such big capacities for the common good is fit to be my husband!"

The civil arts can bring peace to the nation and joy to the people,
The martial arts can protect the state and bring an end to warfare.

Namo Guanshiyin pusa

The princess Marvelous Book replied in the following manner:
"Your daughter would like to have a literary man for her husband.
First you should investigate to make sure he's not a criminal—
On the golden placard his name should be listed as number one![37]
Knowing the books, understanding principle, handsome to boot,
Proper and imposing—with natural charm, a youthful young man:
Such a prince consort will pacify the wide world with his brush,
The entire nation of Raised Forest will enjoy peace and order.
In the golden palace hall he will be appointed to high office,
In purple gown and jade belt, he'll be known as a loyal servant.
If indeed there is such an intelligent and wise man to be found,
He must be recommended, and I then will marry him promptly."

The emperor said: "Your elder sister obeys her father, and will take a literary man to be her husband. Marvelous Sound, what is your desire? Please tell it to me." Princess Marvelous Sound curtsied, and then said: "As my elder sister has chosen to marry a literary type, I want to marry a military man. But that military man should be perfect in both civil arts and martial skills. He should have the determination to stimulate valor; without wearying the troops he should with folded hands be able to subdue [the enemy]; the neighboring states should maintain the peace, such that warfare be ended forever. With his shout he should be able to still the ranks at court, so that mountains and rivers will be unified. He will dominate the country and manage the army—a formidable fighter without equal! Subject only to the One Man,[38] he will tower above the many. His imposing mien will be awe inspiring, and his personal appearance will be lofty and majestic. I am afraid that when the dust of war rises, he will be needed to protect the state and protect the people. Only someone who has these capacities can be my husband, can be my marriage partner. We really have to be careful."

A thousand soldiers are easily found—that's a common discourse,
But hard it is to find one commander—that is an esoteric tradition.

Namo Guanshiyin pusa

Princess Marvelous Sound hastily replied to her father:
"I would like to have a military man for my husband!
 That military man should be a famous generalissimo,
Leading the troops, protecting the state, terrifying the world!
At his command rivers turn into ice to transport his army,
Like the eight claws of the dragon, he protects the capital.
 He is obeyed by gods and ghosts like a heavenly warrior,
His might is revered over myriads of miles by the masses.
And when the dust of war is raised by the border states,
We need him, I fear, to protect my father's imperial city!"
 Hearing this, her imperial father's face showed his love:
"By nature this girl is filled with a mind of filial piety!"
 He next summoned Marvelous Goodness to step forward:
"My child, please now listen to what I have to say to you.
You are the youngest of our three daughters, and that's why
We cherish you above all—you are the apple of Our eye.
 Your flowerlike face is impeccably lofty and dignified,
Your purple-gold appearance is perfectly proper and correct.
You walk in such measured manner your body doesn't move,
Your voice is distinct and clear but you do not move your lips.

Now We have repeatedly suggested to you that you
Might marry a husband and continue to live in the palace.
If the husband you marry shows himself a loyal servant,
I'll entrust the entire realm of myriad miles to that man!
Your eldest sister marries a scholar as her prince consort,
And your second sister wants an officer as her husband.
My daughter, whatever you want, a scholar or soldier—
Yours the choice, as you wish—tell me and let me know!"

The emperor said: "In Our palace We have only three daughters. As they are now in the prime of their youth it is fitting that they should marry a prince consort to protect the nation and protect the people and to execute transformation on behalf of Heaven. Your eldest sister marries a scholar, and your second sister marries an officer. Firstly they are capable of filial piety, and secondly they are capable of obedience. This shows that determination does not depend on the number of one's years. By nature they understand filial piety, the Great Rite of this world! Marvelous Goodness, what would you like?" The third princess stepped forward and replied: "The body of your child may be the same [as that of her sisters], but her heart is not. Each has her own way of seeing. I implore you, daddy, to look into this as clearly as a bright mirror."

When one expanse of white clouds blocks the valley entrance,
Many homing birds lose their way as they search for their nest.

Namo Guanshiyin pusa

Marvelous Goodness that very moment hastened to reply:
"My father and emperor, please be so kind as to reconsider.
Daddy, you are worried because you lack a crown prince,
But I am sorrowed by birth and death—there's nothing else.
My father, in vain you possess quantities of gold and treasure,
How can you escape from the endless cycle of birth and death?
My fate resembles nothing so much as a candle in the wind,
It's hard to find people of a hundred years here in this world.
Terrifying and ruling the mountains and rivers is a game of Go,
The worldly affairs of a hundred years are all just like a dream.

If one calmly thinks of all the affairs of past and of present,
Even a reputation that rises to heaven turns out to be empty.
Day in, day out their thunderous shouts wish you myriad years—
When King Yama summons you, not one makes himself heard!
A garden hut is a better abode than your palace of yellow gold,
A hempen cassock is a smarter dress than a gown of brocade.
Merit, fame, and power wane: snow melting in boiling water!
Grasp the opportunity to change your ways: practice cultivation.
As long as you still have your breath, you can widely employ it,
But on the day Impermanence arrives, all affairs come to an end.[39]
The civil arts of a literary scholar will all have been in vain,
The martial skills of a military man will have been useless too.
Even though your name was listed on the golden placard,
Your brocade gown and jade belt will have become empty.
I'd rather practice cultivation in the clear breeze by moonlight;
If you study the Way after you get old, it's hard to achieve the fruit.
If I married a prince consort, it would be like being buried alive
In the prison of the earth, with not a single means of escape.
I know that my two sisters are marrying a prince consort,
But my only ambition in this life is to achieve buddhahood.
Whether a civil official or a military officer—I want neither,
Because what I want with all my heart is to become a nun!"

Marvelous Goodness replied to her father: "Even though there may be loyal servants and filial sons, brave volunteers and human men, how can they replace you in the hour of one's death? My heart is pained by the sufferings of hell. Our attachment to life is the cause, and our attachment to desires is the condition. Cause and condition intermingle, and we die ten thousand times to be reborn ten thousand times, changing our head and replacing our face as we wander and roam on the six roads without any hope of deliverance.[40] But as soon as one cuts off attachments and desires, one can achieve buddhahood, and thereby able to vastly manifest [different bodily forms throughout the universe], one can meet [the needs] and bring benefit to all sentient beings so that we all together ascend the shore of Enlightenment!"

A spark from stone, a flash of lightning: it's hard to set a term,
So start cultivating as quick as hell, as early here is still too late.

Namo Guanshiyin pusa

Marvelous Goodness that very moment replied as follows:
"My father and emperor, please listen to what I have to say.
Wealth and status cannot buy you free from birth and death,
Do not cause me to rashly and lightly wreck my prospects.
 It's impossible to fathom when Impermanence will come,
So one should make up one's mind to cultivate the Truth.
Daddy, it would be best to allow me to practice cultivation,
High Heaven will never betray a person whose heart is good.
 So I very much hope, dear daddy, that you will happily
Allow me to study the Way and not repay all your favors.
Riches and poverty and wedded bliss are like a spring dream;
In cloudy forests I will follow the example of the ancients.
 In the domain of the Underworld one has no friends,
In the court of King Yama no mercy is shown, and so,
As the three pathways of earth's prison fill me with fear,[41]
I swear I will never allow my body to be taken by a man."

When the emperor heard this, rage showed on his dragon-mien, and he cursed her, shouting: "You brazen slut! You are a bewitching sprite who has come to haunt Us! We are the ruler of the whole country and the leader of the myriad people. And Our understanding would not be up to that of a mere girl like you? From ancient times till the present age, it has been true that if you have heaven and earth, you have yin and yang, and if you have yin and yang, then you have husband and wife. A man marries, and a woman is wed, such is the normal Great Rite! What kind of nonsense is this?" He ordered his guards to grab her and take her to the execution ground to have her beheaded. The guards to his left and right responded with a thunderous shout, yet still hesitated to lay hands on her.

A blue-green pond of eternity, the moon in the empty sky:
It takes repeated backbreaking effort to know the sound.

Nama Guanshiyin pusa

She had offended her father the emperor, who showed his rage,
In a loud voice he shouted and cursed in a terrible manner:

"Monstrous she-devil, you are quite brazen to talk such nonsense,
How can I listen to the perfidious and evil miasma you spout?
We are the ruler of the mountains and rivers of the whole earth,
Under the canopy of High Heaven I alone am the honored one.
Hundreds of thousands of armored troops submit to my might,
So it's impossible to think that I would be unable to subdue you!
For full thirty-six years I have governed all-under-heaven,
The four seas know my fame, and the myriads of clans all obey.
Throughout the ages the state's orders are spread through the world,
In past and present the king's law brings order to the cosmos.
The executioner's sword will not behead loyal and filial sons,
But when it comes to crimes, blood relationship means nothing:
Mislead your lord and be unfilial, and you will be beheaded!
We'll exterminate this devilish monster, this monstrous vixen!"

When Marvelous Goodness saw how enraged her father was, she stepped forward with folded hands, and said: "If the basin of your belly is like the ocean, it can absorb the hundred rivers. But because of this trifling matter, the breath of your rage resembles a mountain! I implore you, daddy, to show kind grace, and I hope that you will kindly consider [my request]."

A breast like the moon reflected in water: undefiled by dust;
Asceticism like ice and frost: that Way will forever endure.

Namo Guanshiyin pusa

When Marvelous Goodness saw her father's towering rage,
She stepped forward and told him the following, in detail:
"The light and shade of a hundred years are a one-night guest,
Alas, there is no way this floating world can endure forever.
Man and wife by marrying and wedding create suffering,
Widely planting roots for the Underworld, earth's prison.
If you really want to pressure me to marry a prince consort,
My father, you should post a notice and find me a physician.[42]
That physician should really be a renowned physician,
Famous throughout the whole wide world as the very best.

In curing heaven, he should cure it of the hindrance of clouds,
The jade hare and golden crow should not have to move lights.[43]
In curing earth, he should cure it of icy cold and hot heat,
The rivers and mountains of the world should all be equal.
In curing people, he should cure them of high and low status,
Have them enjoy more pleasure than to be found in Heaven's truth.
In the hall of the King of Emptiness I will be the bride,[44]
On the bed of nirvana the wedding will be consummated.
As long as you can find me such a famous physician,
I will not dare make excuses or betray the imperial grace!"

When her father the emperor heard this, he laughed loudly: "You little hussy! You really are a bewitching sprite, a devilish monster! You have lived inside the palace and are only nineteen, and yet you know all these many things! Not studying the virtues of filial piety, brotherly love, loyalty and trust, the Way of human relations, you believe heterodox perverted views and listen to deceiving and misleading words. In past and present people are born and people die, just like there is spring, summer, fall, and winter. When they die, we bury them, and sacrifice to them on the first day of spring and of fall. Such is the Great Rite. And if people during their lifetime have accomplished merit, this will be recorded in the chronicles, so their name will be known to later generations. Filial piety is all there is. What is this nonsense about heaven's hall, earth's prison, and ghosts and gods? What do they look like? The only thing that is true is 'By studying the books one is received at Court.' What's the evidence for 'By reciting the name of the Buddha one ascends to the Western Paradise'? You brazen hussy, you are simply afraid to die and so you cling to life! If you are intelligent, and if you are a smart girl, you will accept your lot, and obey you parents without saying a word. Just marry a prince consort like your two sisters. Then we can wrap everything up all at the same time. It's bound to please you! How could you fall ill at your very young age? Just tell me!" When Marvelous Goodness heard this, she immediately replied.

Even if it is a great master who chops down the parasol tree,
There always will be bystanders who have something to say.

Namo Guanshiyin pusa

Marvelous Goodness stepped forward, curtsied, and said:
"May the jade mirror in your bosom shine on my words.
Firstly I want him to stay forever young without aging,
Secondly I want him to live forever and never to die.
Thirdly I want him to bodily achieve the right fruit,[45]
Fourthly I want him to see his nature, know Heaven's truth.
Fifthly I want his three hindrances to have been annihilated,
Sixthly I want him to have cut off attachments at the root.
Seventhly I want his wisdom to surpass sun and moon,
Eighthly I want him to slake all enmity in the three worlds.
Ninthly I want him to be venerated by all deities and men,
Tenthly I want him to preach the Dharma, saving all beings.
Among the thousands of saints and sages he is the champion,
In heaven and on earth revered and venerated by the masses.
If you find me such a renowned physician, I will promptly
At the Lotus Flower Congregation become his bride!"[46]

The princess replied to her father the emperor: "I want a physician as my husband. But he has to be able to cure all kinds of beings of the phenomena of birth and annihilation, of the emotions of sorrow and desire, of the sufferings of aging and illness, of the restrictions of high and low status, of the humiliations of wealth and poverty, of the worries of liking and hatred, of the feeling of me and you, and of the arrogance of ability and position, thereby transforming the people of the wide world in such a way that they share heart and mind, share form and features, share longevity and life, share name and title, and share peace and joy. The myriad phenomena will all be in order and equally be used. All beings, irrespective of the manner of their birth or their path of rebirth, every wriggling creature imbued with spirit, will achieve universal enlightenment and marvelous enlightenment. They will all obtain the five kinds of vision and the six supernatural powers, the three bodies and the four wisdoms, buddhahood and *bodhi*![47] If you can find me someone who can cure the people of their illness of the heart, I will marry him this very day, and together we will wear the armor of forbearance.[48] We will sleep together on the bed of final nirvana, and sit side by side on the throne of the Emptiness of All Phenomena. This is all I have to say." When her father the emperor heard these words, he gnashed his teeth. His eyes were bloodshot, and his voice roared like the thunder. All those present who saw him were so terrified that their soul left their body and their gall was shattered.

If it wasn't for the freezing cold that pierces the bone,
How could the plum blossom produce such fragrance?

Namo Guanshiyin pusa

When her father the emperor heard this, his heart was vexed,
His face showed the color of ash, his breath was like clouds.
Loudly he ordered his underlings to arrest his third daughter,
And his guardsmen before the hall responded like thunder.
    He ordered the officers in golden armor to his left and right:
"Beat this devilish sprite to death with your heavy cudgels."
The civil and military court officials together addressed him:
"Your Majesty, please pardon her crime, accept our advice!
    The princess is young of years, she lacks proper character.
Display your grace, forgive her crime, and let matters rest!"
The Marvelous Splendor emperor opened his golden mouth:
"You ministers, come forward, and listen to my reasons.
    This wretched brazen hussy's gall is as big as heaven,[49]
Her mouth as sharp as a knife does not accept authority.
Her undivided heart and liver are like bronze and iron,
She refuses to listen to words of virtue and loyal advice.
    Cunning and sneaky, glib and sly, she's not our treasure,
Forgetting favor and betraying duty she is not a jewel.
It's best to eradicate this evil at the earliest opportunity,
Because over the years she will develop into a she-devil."

The Marvelous Splendor emperor beat his table, and cursed her in a loud voice: "You crazy monstrous she-devil! You talk nonsense, your words make no sense!" He ordered her female attendants to strip her of her embroidered brocades and gauze garments, beat her with their staffs, and lock her up in the rear garden. "Once she has died of hunger and cold, We will be freed of a worry!" When Marvelous Goodness heard these words, she secretly smiled to herself. She was only too happy to divest herself of these garments! She kowtowed and left. Once the princess had arrived in the garden, she sighed to herself: "Wealth and status don't depend on garments of gauze and brocade; possession of the Way does not depend on status in the imperial palace." In the garden she quietly practiced silent contemplation. Uncontaminated by even a speck of dust, she deeply entered the trance of meditation. Her thoughts were only on the Way of the Buddha. "To be able to escape from the palace was like getting out of a burning house![50] Thanks to the Three Lights, finally I can practice cultivation to my heart's content and full satisfaction!"

When clouds disperse below the sky, heaven shows its color;
When spring returns to the world, all phenomena are new.

Namo Guanshiyin pusa

The princess straightway left and entered the garden,
Overcome with happiness now she could leave the palace:
"From today I break with wine, sex, wealth, and honor,
Eradicating forever the three pathways and eight dangers.[51]
    Embroideries, gauze garments: a debt of skin and hair,[52]
My entire body now is purified, befitting nonaction.
Once outside the palace gate the universe is wide,
Freely roaming, independent—I thank Heaven's grace.
    The imperial palace is not a place to establish oneself,
My native home originally is located in my own heart.
This garden here is just like the domain of the immortals,
Strange flowers and rare fruits each season are new.
    Because my heart does not cling to birth and death,
I have made up my mind and will cultivate the Way.
I take no joy at all in the thousand kinds of pleasures,
With all my heart I want to achieve the Way's wisdom!"

The princess stayed in the garden, happy in being without worries and cares, and enjoying the companionship of the clear moon and the white clouds. Harboring neither grudge nor resentment, she was always filled with joy. She sighed to herself: "I must have been blessed for a karmic cause, so I am free of all bedevilments and hindrances. Now I have been able to leave the palace, I am like a prisoner freed from her shackles, like a bird escaped from her cage, like a dragon that has found a stream, and like a tiger that has found her mountain. Freely roaming I suffer no worry or obstacle; self-sufficient I am without sorrow." Before long, already a month had passed. Only the empress kept thinking of her and longing for her morning and night. By day she did not eat, at night she did not sleep! She talked with the other women in the Six Palaces about submitting a proposal to the emperor, imploring him to pardon her daughter's crime and assuring him that they would all guarantee her good behavior if she were allowed to return to the palace.

A white cloud may suddenly come to rest on a green cliff,
But nothing will bring the moon down from the dark sky.

Namo Guanshiyin pusa

The imperial concubines of the Six Palaces walked in step,
As they walked to the golden throne hall to plead their case.
A hundred musicians, loudly playing their music, led the way,
While the main consort, the empress, followed behind them.
    Arriving before the hall, she shouted: "A myriad of years!"
Twenty-four times she bowed, her tears overflowing:
"I implore you, Your Majesty, to engender happy joy,
Be so kind as to pardon our daughter and set her free!
    She is our own flesh and blood, the treasure of my heart,
Don't bully and insult her so as to deprive her of her life!
Silly and gullible and very young she lacks proper character,
Unable to distinguish spring from fall, she doesn't follow reason.
    So I implore you, her father and emperor, to still your rage,
And to display your compassion by releasing the criminal!
I myself have given birth to only these three daughters,
Each I've nursed and fed for three years—nine years in total.
    Marvelous Book and Marvelous Sound are doing fine,
But alas, Marvelous Goodness is suffering such misery.
Do you as her father and emperor have a heart of stone,
Forgetting the hardship and pain of your own flesh and blood?"

When the emperor heard this, he laughed heartily, and said: "The understanding of a father and mother is basically the same. Who does not love and cherish his own daughter? But it would be better if she were more filial and obedient. Now We will tell her to correct her mistakes. Tomorrow, following the morning audience, We will go to the garden Ourselves for a visit, and then We will tell that die-hard good-for-nothing girl to return to the palace. All you palace women should come along to talk her around." When the empress had received this order, she promptly accompanied the emperor.

An enlightened person doesn't have to be told many times,
There's no need to beat a resounding drum again and again.

Namo Guanshiyin pusa

The emperor, the empress, and the imperial concubines
Came to the garden, but not in a formal grand procession.
Female servants and female workers led the way in front,
Lower-ranking concubines followed behind in the rear.
    The female officials in charge of flowers welcomed them,
And asked the emperor to rest for a while in a pavilion.
They made twenty-four bows, wished him a myriad of years,
And asked the emperor why he visited the garden in person.
    From the pavilion the emperor addressed them as follows:
"You officials before the pavilion, listen to Our reasons.
Because Marvelous Goodness harbored perverse views,
And silly and foolish did not show a proper determination,
    We confined her here to the garden now over a month ago,
But We do not know her situation since she was brought here.
If you, female officials, know how she has been doing here,
If you know her condition, please let Us know how she is."
    The female officials promptly replied to him as follows:
"Sage and enlightened Son of Heaven, listen to our words.
As we had not received any directive from Your Majesty,
We have not dared visit Her Highness to this very day."
    When the emperor went in person to observe the princess,
She was silently practicing meditation inside a small pavilion.
    He knocked on the door and shouted: "Marvelous Goodness,
You madcap lunatic, you wretched and despicably vile low-caste!
You lack the luck to enjoy all manner of pleasures and good times,
You brought this disaster on yourself, becoming a prisoner.
    But if today you obediently will show a change of heart,
We will pardon you—back in the palace, you'll be a darling.
If you immediately change your mind, it's still not too late,
But if as before you disobey Us, We'll order you extirpated!"

When her father the emperor went to see Marvelous Goodness, he didn't say so out loud, but in his heart he was filled with somber musings, and he could not control the tears that dampened his brocade gown. In person he asked her: "My child, how pitiable you are! You forgot how you sat at the side of your father and mother, inside the Six Palaces, and how you enjoyed the most fragrant foods and drinks, and wore the most brilliantly yellow dragon robes, and inhabited the most colorful towers and terraces! Those who followed you were the prettiest maidens, and those who served you were elegant maids. Every day there were banquets at which the hundred musicians all played. What was ever lacking? If you now obey your father's command and take a husband, when the time comes, I will raise him up so he may glorify the way of the emperor and rule the realm. You will enjoy all the good times of the whole world. Being a Son of Heaven for one day beats being a nobleman for ten thousand generations. What do you think of it? Or would you rather suffer abuse and humiliation?" When Marvelous Goodness heard these words, she promptly replied.

To be hit in the eye by a wedge—who could endure that?
Only someone of the Way will produce water from a fire.

Namo Guanshiyin pusa

The princess immediately replied in the following way:
"My father and emperor, be so good as to return to the palace!
Few understand the sound of the zither without strings,
If you and I would play it, our tunes would not harmonize.
    I do not crave the wealth and status of the imperial palace,
I want to be a 'person of the Way' within the Gate of Emptiness.
I do not want to marry a man who will be Son of Heaven,
I lack the luck to become the empress, his main consort.
    I want to wear the cassock of the Tathāgata Amitābha,[53]
I do not want to wear the brocade gowns of the palace.
Your child regards the three worlds as earth's prison,
So I will never take my body and marry it to some man.
    If I, your daughter, succeed in achieving the right fruit,
I'll repay my parents' favors in the Hall of Universal Light.
Here in the garden I have nothing to repay your favors,
Yet you and mother have been so kind as to visit me.

I only hope that the heart-flower of my nature will open,
When my work is done, my practice complete, I'll return.
Because of birth and death I am willing to brave any danger,
I would not dare carry any grudge toward my sagely ruler."

The emperor said: "All children who do not follow their father's counsel will be executed by Heaven and annihilated by Earth! You oppose me in a thousand ways! Where did you learn all those wild words and weird ideas? In my opinion, all those monks and nuns are nothing but lazy idlers from the common people, or widowers, widows, orphans, and other people without support, who are unable to make a living. So they dress themselves up in an outlandish costume, claiming the Buddha as cause. But they are all, to the very last man, disloyal and unfilial loafers and drifters who merit the death penalty! If you are imitating their kind of behavior, you are definitely damaging the state and disgracing the court! I order you to marry a prince consort who will become emperor. That will mean more wealth and status than if you ascended to heaven! What more could you want?" Marvelous Goodness replied: "When I read the golden writings and jade scrolls, they all state with dazzling clarity that all the buddhas of the three worlds and all the saints and sages of past and present abandoned the five desires and practiced the Way of the Great Vehicle. Once they achieved the universal and correct enlightenment, they universally assisted gods and men. I also read that Brahma and Indra wait on the Buddha to his left and right.[54] Ten kinds of immortals follow the Buddha as he teaches and delivers his sermons. The ninety-six kinds of heretical masters and the fifty kinds of Māra kings follow him and protect him.[55] Then there have been great kings and high ministers, gentlemen, farmers, artisans, and merchants, and old and young men and women who all, because they left the family, achieved the sagely fruit. You are not going to tell me that those were all loafers and drifters who could not make a living?" When her father the emperor heard these words, he indeed uttered not a single word, as he did not know what to answer. He could only suffer his defeat in silence and return to the palace. All the female relatives who had accompanied him followed him back. When the emperor had returned to the palace, he pondered this matter all through the night, but did not know what to do. So he ordered the two princesses Marvelous

Book and Marvelous Sound to go together with the empress and try to talk her around.

As long as the starling remains twittering on its branch,
The phoenix of course will not be willing to alight there.

Namo Guanshiyin pusa

The emperor issued an edict and summoned the empress,
He ordered her to go again and change their daughter's mind.
As soon as the empress had received the emperor's order,
She hastened to go, using fewer than five steps for every ten.
    They had urged her with common sense, fierce like fire!
Who knew that her saintly heart would be cold like ice?
Marvelous Book and Marvelous Sound and their mother
Went straight into the garden, where the empress said:
    "My child, ever since you have been in this place,
Your mother has been awash in tears every night!
I urge you, my child, just marry a prince consort,
And then you can have your wedding with your sisters.
    It's hard to repay your parents' favors in nurturing you,
But by returning to the palace you repay their favors.
If today you still refuse to change your mind, you are
Indeed a person who lacks the heart of filial piety!"

Marvelous Goodness replied to her mother: "I am deeply aware of the extent of my parents' favors, and I will repay them later. Fortunately my two elder sisters will each marry a husband, and they will be able to serve you in your old age. Allow me to leave the family. If I obtain the Way and achieve perfect enlightenment, the first thing I will do will be to ferry across both my parents so they will be reborn together in the Pure Land.[56] I implore you, my mother, to look upon me as someone who was never born, as someone who has already died. The people of this world prize riches and sex, but I want to pacify my heart so it will be still. Riches and sex disturb a person's heart, but once stilled, one sees the Buddha-nature of ultimate truth." When the empress heard these words, she did not know how to reply.

In a quiet night on the cold river the fish refuses to bite,
So one returns in vain, the boat loaded with moonlight.

Namo Guanshiyin pusa

The princess immediately hastened to reply to her mother,
Deeply she bowed down as she laid out her reasons:
"My dear mother, please return now to the inner garden,
Consider me as one who has died, as one never born."
    The empress at that time did not know how to respond,
Utterly disappointed, she did not say a word or a syllable.
When a fierce wind on the Yangzi raises waves and billows,
Of course the helmsman will not try to sail his little craft!
    Her eldest sister Marvelous Book then spoke to her, saying:
"Little sister, you're so smart and intelligent, now listen to me!
Bereft of filial piety and sense of duty, you lack all discernment,
So what is the reason that today you suffer all this hardship?
    Of us three sisters you were by far the youngest, and so
Our father and mother doted on you as the apple of their eye.
We obey our father and marry a prince consort, but you
Are all messed up in your head, you good-for-nothing!
    Now you are subjected by our father to all this misery,
With the result that even we are pained in our hearts.
You ignore all the many pleasures of the palace,
But soon under this heavy burden you will lose heart.
    Be a darling and change your mind, marry a prince consort,
Who'll cherish your flowerlike face and jade-white body.
So we urge you, dear sister, come back to the palace—
Filially obeying your parents beats cultivating the Truth!"

Her eldest sister saw that Marvelous Goodness has lost none of her appearance, but that in fact she had grown even more marvelously beautiful. Truly, a heaven-sent miracle! "You are a girl who is bound to suffer! You don't avail yourself of greening spring to find yourself a husband for life. You'll only understand when you're old, but then despair and despondency will be all in vain! You forget that the wealth and status of our life in the palace of our father, the emperor, is only surpassed by heaven, there is no second family [as rich as we]! We dwell in a myriad-dragon palace, with golden beams and jade columns, silver brackets and golden blocks; we walk on pathways paved with red agate and white jade, interspersed with the seven precious stones, and covered with brocade embroidery; we sit on cushions embroidered with crouching lions, sleeping elephants, and coiling dragons of *maṇi*, sandalwood, and pearls; we sleep on dragon beds of eaglewood and gold foil, inlaid with ivory and rhinoceros horn, inside brocade bed-curtains with paradisiacal flowers made of the eight treasures. The jewelry on our heads consists entirely of curving dragons and flying phoenixes and strings made of a hundred precious stones. The garments we wear are all the most marvelous beautiful gowns covered with the seven jewels, and the mandarin ducks woven into the brocade dazzle the sun as they compete in brilliance. What we eat are the hundred delicacies and the most exquisite dishes, ghee and superior food. We are entertained by a thousand kinds of instrumental music, and when we move about we travel in sedan chairs and are followed by an escort. Every day we are treated to five banquets. We surpass the divine immortals of the eight grottoes. In high heaven, I've heard, the Tuṣita Palace is the best,[57] but here on earth nothing outdoes the dwelling place of our father the emperor. The three of us enjoy such glory and splendor, wealth and status, so what more do you want? If only you hadn't brought this down on you yourself. You had to learn the hard way the hardship you have to suffer today! You crazy hussy, what kind of ghost have you seen? Be a darling and return to the palace, so your father and mother will not be worried any more." When the princess heard these words, she promptly replied.

The bamboo's shade moves across the steps, but the dust is not
moved,
The moon shines down to the well's bottom, but no ripple on the
water.

Namo Guanshiyin pusa

Marvelous Goodness, palms pressed together, replied:
"Deluded, my heart still longs to stay here in the garden.
Joy the cause, hardship the fruit—then all people rejoice,
Hardship the cause, joy the fruit—none wants to hear that.
There's a road that leads to heaven, but none do walk it,
Earth's prison may have no gate, yet people flock there.
If you want to marry a prince consort, do as you please,
And don't worry about me, this totally crazy low-caste!

I, living in pure poverty, want to achieve buddhahood,
Whereas you, craving your pleasures, enter the red dust.
Marrying a prince consort only adds to fetters and shackles,
As you create sinful karma, resulting in the three pathways.
Those who commit sins will suffer the consequences,
Because in the court of King Yama no mercy is shown.
The realm of shade, earth's prison, fills me with fear—
I swear I will never use my body to serve some man."

Marvelous Goodness answered her eldest sister as follows: "Virtue is born from pure simplicity, and luck is born from humble modesty. The wise person believes and enjoys, and clearly understands birth and death. You and I may have the same body, but we do not have the same heart. You marry your husband, clinging to high status. Why are you worried about me? I want to separate myself from favors and cut myself off from attachments, so I may with all my heart practice the right Way!" Her eldest sister then cursed her: "You stupid low-caste! Your intelligence is of no use! You refuse to listen to friendly advice and good counsel. I know that one day you will want to get out, but incapable of doing so, you'll have to suffer!" The second sister then stepped forward to try to talk her around in her turn. How did it go?

If spring returns, it is not because the skill of the painter—
All by themselves the willows turn green, the flowers red.

Namo Guanshiyin pusa

Marvelous Sound addressed Marvelous Goodness as follows:
"My dear little sister, please listen to what I have to say.
Ever since you left the palace, we've had no news from you,
Thinking of you from early till late, I've been awash in tears.
Mother and sister have come on purpose to talk with you,
Follow their advice, do as you're told, return to the palace!
To obey one's parents as if they were Heaven and Earth
Is better than being a monk or a nun, one without a heart.
Be a darling, return to the palace, and marry a husband!
We'll go to the palace together, you'll have a great place!"
When Marvelous Goodness heard this, she was not pleased,
And she told her second sister: "Now you listen to me!

The pleasures of the imperial palace are not permanent,
Like the treasure found in a dream, they're not true.
When one day the notification arrives of Impermanence,
You'll feel remorse for the karma from earlier days.
When once the great limit arrives, no resistance helps,
You'll be arrested by ghosts and meet with King Yama.
If your little sister would marry some prince consort,
I would sink forever, fall forever, and never escape!
You and your sister, marry a husband, do as you please,
I want to avail myself of the spring of youth to become a nun.
There's a road that leads to heaven, and I will walk it,
I've no desire to linger here and go back to the palace."

Marvelous Goodness replied to her second sister: "The pock-marked toad has no light that shines back,[58] the jade hare has no intention of accompanying the moon. Your little sister has searched through the ocean storehouse of the dragon palace,[59] and I am fully conversant with all issues. One road leads to heaven, the other to hell, / It is up to you to choose which one you want to go. / I for sure will walk the road that leads to heaven, / You are tied to the road to the prisons of hell!" When Marvelous Sound heard these words of Marvelous Goodness, her face lost all color: "If you don't want to listen to reason, it's none of my concern! Do whatever you want to do!" Her mother and her two elder sisters could not talk her around, so they could only admit defeat and return to the palace, where they reported to her father the emperor: "The heart of Marvelous Goodness is like iron and stone; it's impossible to make her change her mind! Her discourse does not offer the smallest opening or omission. She is as confident as Mt. Tai, and as determined as the ocean." Her father the emperor said: "She must be a wily she-devil! We have no method to control her." Thereupon he ascended to the throne hall and assembled his high ministers, his civil officials and military officers. "Let's select the best persons! We will first have the two princesses Marvelous Book and Marvelous Sound marry a prince consort." When the court officials had received this order, they immediately set up examinations for literature and martial skills in order to attract the finest men.

Spring moon and autumn flowers—unlimited emotion,
It doesn't hurt to listen for a while to the partridge's call.

Namo Guanshiyin pusa

The emperor then ascended the golden throne hall,
He proclaimed an edict, summoning his ministers.
"Because Marvelous Goodness harbors perverse views,
Refuses to marry a husband and wants to become a nun,
    We have confined her to the rear palace flower garden,
She is imprisoned in a pavilion of the cold palace.[60]
We order the other two girls to marry a prince consort,
To get married now, and not to put off the wedding."
    Once court officials in red and purple received this edict,
The construction of a bunted loft was quickly completed.
The houses along the street burned incense on tables outside,
While all dashing young men milled around on the street.
    The girls could select a man of talent, literary and military:
An embroidered ball was thrown down to settle the match![61]
The princes consort, holding the ball, ascended the palace
To be welcomed by the imperial family and palace women.
    In the high hall the light of the candles dazzled the sun,
As the two princesses emerged through the palace gate.
Organs and fifes, drums and flutes were played together,
Cymbals, clappers, gongs, and bells resounded to heaven!
    The two couples took up position to the left and right,
With eight deep bows they gave thanks for the imperial grace.
After thanking all present they repaired to their rooms,
Inside the chamber flower and candle—the consummation.

One day when the emperor had ascended the throne hall, he summoned the empress, the main consort. "Let's not talk about Marvelous Book and Marvelous Sound. Let's talk about our third daughter, that silly girl. All of sudden half a year has passed by, and we haven't heard anything. How is she doing?" He then ordered the palace maids and elegant maidens: "If you can talk her around so she will change her mind and return to the palace, We will give you a handsome reward." When the palace maids had received this order, they did not dare wait any longer. Hurrying like clouds they went to see the third princess, crying profusely. The princess secretly smiled and asked them: "Elegant maidens, why did you come here, all in tears?" The elegant maidens replied: "In obedience to the emperor's order of this morning we urge Your Highness to quickly return to the palace and marry a prince consort."

When the white dew settles on a field, it is a thousand specks of snow,
When the yellow oriole sits in a tree, the whole branch turns into gold.

Namo Guanshiyin pusa

The palace women, receiving the order, swirled like snow;
As if blown by the wind, they hastened to the rear garden.
Flurried and flustered, as soon as they saw the princess,
They all together bowed down, as tears gushed forth.
"We in the palace are constantly filled with affliction,
As inside the palace we hear no news at all about you.
Princess, your appearance only has grown more marvelous,
Your flower and brocadelike beauty only increases in spirit!
We implore Your Highness to return to the palace, and,
Obeying your father and the empress, to see your relatives.
You should return to the palace and marry a prince consort,
There is no need for you to go so far as to become a nun!"

The princess replied: "I will return to the palace only after I have achieved the unsurpassable right enlightenment, after I have fully achieved the millions of bodily manifestations, after I have manifested the thirty-two marks and the eighty good signs,[62] after in the heavenly palace of the Pure Land my thoughts will follow my body and I will be able to transform all living beings." The elegant maidens said: "If that is the case, then this is not the most suitable place to practice cultivation." The princess then said: "Because you mention it, I'll tell you that I would like to go the White Sparrow Convent of Dragon Tree (Nāgārjuna) county in Ruzhou. There are five hundred nuns there who practice the Way with strictest discipline. I would trouble you to inform my father the emperor and the empress." Having received this order, the palace maids returned and reported to her father the emperor, who said: "If she wants to go herself, that's even better! Truly, when a storm blows on the fire, one doesn't have to make any effort to fan it!" But first he had a secret order transmitted to the abbess that she should persuade his daughter to return to the palace—and that if she failed to change his daughter's mind, her crime would not be pardoned, and troops would reduce the convent to ashes!

All your many affairs with their empty names are snow on waves,
The illusionary image of a hundred years is dew frozen into ice.

Namo Guanshiyin pusa

The emperor's order was conveyed to the flower garden,
But in the garden the princess did not yet know about it.
Then the female officials conveyed the imperial edict:
"The princess is allowed to leave to practice cultivation."
    When the princess heard this, her heart was filled with joy,
With bowed head, palms pressed together, she thanked the gods.
Without choosing a day she immediately wanted to leave;
Immensely relieved and filled with joy she left the garden.
    "The yellow gold of this human world has no value at all,
Most to be prized is one's personal peace and pleasure.
I don't care for embroidered brocade or gauze garments,
In a hempen gown, a white robe,[63] I'll set out on my journey."
    All the women of the palace came to see her off, and
They accompanied her as she exited the main court gate.
Facing the throne hall the princess made eight deep bows,
Wishing the emperor a myriad of years of continued rule.
    With eight bows she wished the empress eternal longevity,
With four bows she asked her sisters to serve their parents.
When she had taken her leave of all her kin in the palace,
She turned around and proceeded to exit the palace gate.

All the civil officials and military officers of the court saw the princess off as she departed through the Meridian Gate; the flower streets had been screened off with silks and fabrics. "We have heard that the ancient books teach: 'Filial behavior is foremost, obedience to one's parents is of utmost importance.' So what kind of principle can it be to betray one's parents and leave the family? What kind of cultivation will you practice? What kind of buddha will you venerate? You only have to filially serve the emperor and obey the empress in the palace, and widely study the *Odes* and *Documents*,[64] and then it will automatically become clear to you that you should marry a prince consort. That is the natural Great Rite! For all human beings, food and clothing are the staples. So what harm is there in enjoying some wine and meat? What sin does one commit by wearing silks and woolens? Among the ancients there were those who never left the gate of their house and yet were able to know the affairs of all-under-heaven; there were those who because of a single recommendation achieved fame and were known throughout the wide world; and there were those who because of their world-famous writings became teachers to emperors. You are not going to tell us that these were all people who left the family to venerate the Buddha? If you establish a reputation for loyalty and filial piety that will be passed on to later generations, what need is there to show and bare your face in public, and thus become a laughing-stock to the people? Guard against rumor and gossip! We, your ministers, commit a crime, as in our ignorance we remonstrate with one so wise, but we implore you, Your Highness, to change your mind and return to the palace. As long as one's words and deeds support each other, all one needs are filial piety, righteousness, loyalty, and trust!"

Once a fine character without learning and without action
Dug a hole in the ground, stupidly wishing to find heaven.

Namo Guanshiyin pusa

Every one of the officials of the court urged the princess
To return to the palace, and to serve and obey her parents.
"Disobeying one's parents means the end of human relations,
For all eternity you'll leave a reputation as an amoral monster!
    If we, your ministers, today are unable to talk you around,
We'll quit our jobs, hand in our seals, and leave the capital!"
The princess immediately answered in the following way:
"Dear officials, please listen for a while to my reasons!
    Thank you very much for your kind words of advice, but
Discussing a dream while dreaming clearly lacks truth.
Your fame may be spread throughout the wide world,
But you'll not escape from the cycle of birth and death.
    Widely learned and erudite, you're intelligent men,
But for all your smarts you've lost both body and mind.
What is the use of your world-famous essays and writings?
They're shackles of fame and fetters of profit, utterly useless!
    Not leaving the gate you know the affairs of all-under-heaven,
But you fail to find the treasure of your own buddha-nature.
The fame achieved by one recommendation is like a flower:
People collapse and flowers fade, all turning to emptiness.

Even though your fame may be transmitted to later ages,
Your soul will not necessarily be reborn in heaven above.
All the phenomena of this world are of a lower order, as
Only the Way studied in the Gate of Meditation is true!"

The princess said: "It is easier to fool a thousand people than to cultivate one's own single body. I am pained by the thought that completion necessarily is followed by destruction, and that birth necessarily is followed by death. Alas, sun and moon move like a shuttle—how much light and shade do we have? Time does not wait on people: the young and the strong will necessarily get older and weaker. All living beings are impermanent, and nothing helps against death. Among the sages of ancient times some had a recipe to transcend life and escape death, and some had a method to see their own nature and achieve buddhahood. All the buddhas of the three worlds[65] were children of their father and mother, and each and every one of them knew his texts and understood principle, but they do not preach that one can achieve buddhahood by staying with the family and being filial and obedient. Each and every one of them abandoned the kindnesses [of his parents] and cut himself off from all attachments, as only in that way could they become a vessel of the Dharma! If this goes even for the ancient sages, how much more so does it hold for me! All those who cultivate their heart should not be dyed by one speck of dust; they should be like the transparent emptiness of the bright moon. As long as one believes that one's own heart is the Buddha, one will eventually achieve buddhahood. But zither and Go, calligraphy and painting, fame and profit, ability and position, purple gowns and jade belts, high halls and large mansions, wives and concubines, elephants and horses and the seven precious stones, lakes of wine and mountains of meat—all these ten thousand kinds of pleasures are nothing but worldly wealth and status. One day your life will end and your eyes will be closed, and your soul will then enter the realm of shade and your spirit will suffer hardship. Your corpse may have been dressed all properly, you may be buried in an inner and outer coffin, you may enjoy sacrifices in spring and fall, it's all an outward show of filial piety and brings no benefit to the deceased. [On the contrary,] it will only add to your sufferings for your sins and greatly create karma for the three pathways.[66] You officials may not believe in retribution, transmigration, and punishment for sins. But you all will have to pass through the hour of your death. Just give it a thought: Where do you come from in birth? Where do you go in death? Do you understand? As long as you do not understand my meaning, you are officials in a dream. When people slander you, you're filled with anger; when people praise you, you're filled with joy. You esteem wealth and status like gold and jade, and you despise poverty and a low-caste like mud and shit. When you see people displaying virtue, you are filled with vexation, but when you see people committing a crime, you're filled with joy. So where is your conscience? Your mouth may be fair, but your heart is not fair; your words may be pure, but your deeds are not pure; you know your books, but you do not know the rites. This is not the way of the princely gentleman."

The meditation gate of great quiescence is unwilling to speak,[67]
Once the sealed lips are opened, the Three Vehicles come out.

Namo Guanshiyin pusa

The princess addressed them in a bitterly biting manner:
"You officials, please listen for a while to my reasons.
Not understanding transmigration through birth and death,
You blabber on in your dream, wasting precious time.
    Today you do not know what tomorrow will bring,
You people all vie to have the upper hand, a vain effort!
Even though you have high status at the imperial court,
You never enjoy the mountain boy's undisturbed sleep."
    All the officials of the court were at loss what to answer,
Dumbstruck and dumbfounded they'd lost their mettle.
In vain they had used their finest words to advise her,
But despite all their earnest talk, she would not go back.
    The court officials thereupon all took their leave,
And returned to court to report to the sagely ruler.
The princess in the end indeed set out on her journey,
And traveled farther and farther from the capital city.
    All her relatives at the capital shed tears for her,
And her close relatives at court were deeply pained.
But the common people of street and ward praised her:
"Rare is a princess with such a heart for the Way!"
    At night when near a mountain she'd rest at the mountain,

And when near a bridge, she would stop by that bridge.
Let's not talk about the daily stages of her journey—
Eventually the princess arrived at the city of Ruzhou.
She had no desire to view flower streets and willow wards—
Her only desire was to continue on in her travels.
The monks and nuns of Ruzhou came to welcome her,
All praising her as a person with a heart for the Way:
"Daughter of the emperor and empress, the third princess
Has taken a vow to practice cultivation here in our city!"
And when she approached the White Sparrow Convent,
She entered the convent's gate while walking on foot.
The bell and drum in the bell and drum towers sounded,
The bell and the drum sounded, reverberating to heaven.
The princess was invited to enter the Hall of the Buddha,
Where she lit incense and paid homage to the Three Jewels.[68]
Firstly she bowed before the purple-gold original image,
Secondly she bowed before all the five hundred nuns.
And all the nuns of the convent praised her by saying
That the princess was not a common mortal like them:
"She understands her own nature and preaches doctrine;
Observe her demeanor: she's one who is born again![69]
She's definitely a buddha who's returned to the world,
She surpasses by far all the nuns in this convent!"

Once the princess had entered the convent, she burned incense before the Buddha. She next greeted the *saṅgha*. Then the director of guests took her to the room of the abbess to pay her respects. After she had had some tea, the abbess started the conversation by saying: "You are a golden branch and jade leaf of the royal house, whereas we in this rustic convent are all daughters of the common people. As nuns we share our cells and live together. You will find this to be very inconvenient." The princess replied: "Studying the Way depends on the heart. How can one make distinctions between high status and low station?" The abbess then asked: "Your Highness, might it not be the case that your stars and planets are mixed up and disordered, that you are not able to follow your heart, that you want to disobey your parents, and that you now use the pretext of leaving the family to come here to find fault with us nuns? Those who defame the Buddha and slander the Dharma are exactly this kind of evil person like you! Why don't you stay in the palace, marry a prince consort, and enjoy to the full all its good times and pleasures? Then you would not waste your greening spring and everything would be fine. Wouldn't that be marvelous? We nuns here wear tattered cassocks and eat thin gruel. It's a lonely and miserable life of grinding poverty. What virtue does it have?" The princess replied: "If one eats gruel, the heart is pure and alert; if one lives in loneliness, one sleeps in peace. I've long heard that your convent houses five hundred nuns, all of whom come from official and noble families, and are intelligent and very smart. Because they understood [the law] of cause and its fruit, they left the family when they were beautiful and charming young girls. If you, my teacher, are able to make them all return to the laity and marry a husband, I too will return to the palace." When the abbess heard this, she did not know what to answer.

To turn iron into gold is an easy transformation,
To suppress her under a mountain was not hard.

Namo Guanshiyin pusa

The princess immediately answered her as follows:
"My dear abbess, please listen to what I have to say.
In entering the convent I hoped to cultivate the Way,
But you do not treat me as a relative in the Dharma.
    While in the palace I had heard such good information,
So how is it you too are all like people in a dream?[70]
May I ask you why you decided to leave the family?
Not everyone who wears a cassock is necessarily a nun.
    I came to this place because of birth and death,
Not loving the imperial palace, I entered the convent."
The nun answered her in the following manner:
"It's not that I was insincere in becoming a nun.
    But I've received a secret edict from the emperor,
Ordering me to persuade you return to the palace.
If Your Highness returns, we are without blame,
If you don't return, he will annihilate this convent!
    Your Highness may be happy to suffer tribulations,
But for what reason should we all be implicated?"
When the princess heard this, she broke into a smile:
"Now I understand why you spoke in such a muddled way!

But if one is a true disciple of the Gate of Emptiness,
One will sacrifice this illusory body for the Dharma.
If the emperor should burn this convent to the ground,
It is its preordained fate, and due to a karmic cause.
Birth is followed by death, completion by destruction,
And rise is followed by fall, whatever you may do.
Let the emperor burn it to the ground if he wants,
Eventually we all must pass through the gate of death."

When the abbess heard this, all the color drained from her face, and she said to the princess: "Your views do not accord with heavenly principle! You are not going to tell me that for Your Highness's sake we all will be implicated and have to share your sufferings? I have served as abbess for over thirty years and never has even the slightest speck of disaster entered the gate of this convent! Your Highness and your father the emperor may be angry with each other, but what does that have to do with our convent?" When the princess heard this, she said with a smile: "The monastic community has six harmonies and five virtues.[71] Such is the behavior according to the Way of monks and nuns. But, my dear nun, your wisdom is narrow and your insight is shallow. Your body may have left the family, but your heart is not dyed in the Way. You do not yet know that among the sages of ancient times there were those who donated their body to feed a tiger, that there were those who cut off a slice of their flesh to feed an eagle, that there were those who set flame to their body like a torch, that there were those who donated their head and eyes, their marrow and brains, their arms and legs and hand and feet, and that there were those who donated their body just to obtain half a *gātha*! All those who donated their body and heart achieved the unsurpassable Way. You cherish your body and nourish your life, so you have not yet done away with your cravings and attachments. If you practice cultivation in this way, it cannot yet be called achieving the Way. It is the original practice of monastics to be able to inflict suffering on oneself in order to benefit others. But to benefit oneself and inflict suffering on others is not the way of the Buddha's disciples. Now you are already quite flurried and flustered even before he has come here to burn down the convent. Come to think of it, you really don't have a heart that penetrates the Way!" When the abbess heard her say these words, she again and again heaved a heavy sigh: "Too bad! Disaster strikes without warning—may Heaven have mercy on us!" She then ascended the Dharma-hall to discuss this matter with all the nuns. So how did it go?

The *ulumbara* flower opens inside the fire, but its golden heart is dew,
The breeze brings you a pure fragrance, which is not of this world.

Namo Guanshiyin pusa

The abbess of the convent ascended her Dharma-throne,
And in the Dharma-hall the gong and drum were sounded.
The assembled nuns of the two sectors attended the meeting,[72]
While on her lion-throne the abbess explained the situation.
"During the over thirty years I have served as your abbess,
All wandering nuns we took in were closer than relatives.
Who could have known that the emperor's third daughter
Would also come here, pretending she wants to be a nun?
This is why I wanted to make this announcement to you all,
What would be the best stratagem to deal with this matter?"
The nuns there present answered her in the following way:
"Dear abbess, it would be best to do the princess a favor.
If kind words failed to persuade her to change her mind,
You should inform the princess of all our bitter hardship."
The nun, adopting their counsel, called Marvelous Goodness:
"Intelligent princess, please listen to what I have to say.
Don't think that leaving the family means endless pleasure,
Only by living here permanently will you know the hardships.
We don't care whether you are a golden branch or jade leaf,
Forget about being an imperial princess or royal consort!
Here you will have to donate your body like a slave, and
With bowed head bow before and serve all the other nuns.
Don't blame me, this old nun, for the orders and demands,
We here don't have the lazy rice to feed any lazybones!
You will start out in the kitchen, doing the heavy work:
Each day you will prepare the rice for five hundred nuns.
From three miles outside the gate you will fetch the water,
You'll carry the firewood ten miles—there is no one else.
You'll rinse the rice, wash the bowls, pick the vegetables,
In doing the kitchen work you will have to be diligent.
In the hulling room and milling place there's no substitute,
When bringing hot and cold water, you'll whirl like a cloud.

When you are lazy or slow, I will hear no idle excuses,
My bamboo rod and meditation staff will show no mercy.
And at the first sign of the slightest disobedience, we'll
Chase you out, and never allow you to enter the convent."

The abbess said: "Don't think that leaving the family means lazy leisure without a worry in the world! In my convent we don't make any distinction between high status and low caste, as everybody has to accept my orders, even if it is all the work in the kitchen. If I tell you to go, you go; if I tell you to stay, you stay. And you have to be careful and diligent! You alone will be responsible for all the tasks of fetching water and hauling firewood, rinsing the rice and picking the vegetables, cleaning the bowls and washing the cups, paying for the vegetables and buying the fruits, burning the incense and changing the water, sweeping the floors and spreading the carpets, refreshing the flowers and hanging up the adornments, sounding the bell and beating the drum, and welcoming and receiving all wandering monastics. The minute you commit even the slightest mistake, it's the meditation staff for major offenses and the bamboo rod for smaller offenses, and you will immediately be expelled from this convent. I inform you of all these matters in advance, so you can make your choice. If you can practice this, then do so." The princess replied: "I happily accept this, and it doesn't matter if I have to do everything." When the nun had explained the situation, she descended from her seat.

The red phoenix faces the sun below the parasol tree,
Never will it share lodging and food with chickens.

Namo Guanshiyin pusa

When the abbess left her seat, she rode her gestatorial chair:
An arhat in the flesh, one who had accumulated great blessing!
All the nuns of the convent escorted the abbess, and after
Accompanying her to her room, they went their own way.
The princess alone went all by herself to the kitchen,
She made no attempt to be excused, did not fear hardship.
The acolyte who served as stoker welcomed her there,
And over a cup of tea they together discussed the work.
All the myriads of tasks she handed over to the princess,

Who modestly and diligently did not shirk the work.
The princess was happily willing and gladly accepted
To serve and wait upon each of the five hundred nuns.
    Whether it was early or late, daytime or evening,
She never complained about midnight's long hours.
She gladly accepted this because of birth and death,
Wanting to escape from this illusory body's suffering.
    During the day she prepared the food and husked the rice,
During the night she pushed the mill and lit the candles.
She received the wandering monastics from all directions
And treated them exactly like the nuns of the convent.
    Because of the many hardships of her heavy labor,
She became so emaciated she was just a bag of bones.
Wanting to achieve buddhahood, to transcend the three worlds,
She would even allow flames to erupt from her mouth![73]
    She did not carry a grudge toward her parents or the nuns,
She only hated herself for her many sins in former lives.
Now that she was here, she felt not the slightest remorse;
Constantly filled with joy, she did not harbor any anger.

When the princess had gone to the kitchen, she managed all by herself both the light and heavy tasks. Because of her heavy labor, her body became exhausted and weary, but even though flames erupted from her mouth, she never felt the slightest grudge or hatred, and was always filled with pleasure and joy. Again and again she prayed to Blue Heaven: "Please assist me by giving me the supernatural strength to donate my body to this work so I can provide for all the nuns. If I indeed succeed in achieving *bodhi*, I will not forget Heaven's grace. Please be so kind as to look down upon me!"

The white cloud atop the mountain: leisure without end,
The brook rushing down the ravine: what haste and hurry!

Namo Guanshiyin pusa

The Jade Emperor up in high heaven observed from afar
How the princess down below suffered such bitter hardship.
Immediately a heavenly command and order was issued,
A heavenly amulet and notification for the Six Nail gods.[74]
    They told the Eastern Ocean's dragon to go to the convent,

And to get into the kitchen by hiding himself in a bucket.
When one drop was spilled, his golden scales appeared,
Whirling, he produced a dragon pond, many yards deep.
The faraway well all of a sudden dried up completely,
As this pure spring was created on the convent grounds.
The spring's water was transparent down to the bottom,
Even if you hauled a thousand buckets, it remained full.
The hundred animals brought firewood, filling the convent,
The thousand birds brought vegetables—flocks like clouds!
The Six Nails and the Six Scales prepared the rice,[75] and
All the other chores were performed by heavenly gods.
Immortals changed the water and spread the mats,
City gods and soil gods lit the candles and the lamps.
Devas and dragons and such divine beings helped out,
Sage monks and bodhisattvas were running to and fro!
There was nothing left for the princess to do, but to
Seat herself in the lotus position there in the kitchen!
The princess was filled with joy about what happened:
"On balance the study of the Way doesn't let one down!"

In the kitchen the princess's dedication to the Way remained firm and unshaken, moving the god of the stove to report her case to the heavenly court. When the High Emperor heard this report, he was greatly pleased, and ordered the Three Officials[76] and the Five Mountains[77] of the Middle World to dispatch the dragons and gods and the six other classes of supernatural beings and to command the Six Nails and the Six Scales to quickly go to the White Sparrow Convent and to do the chores of the princess in her place. He also dispatched the old dragon of the Eastern Ocean to open a well inside the kitchen. He also ordered the running animals of the mountains to bring her firewood, and the flying birds from everywhere to bring her vegetables. All the many chores were performed by heavenly gods and earthly divinities. The princess remained undisturbed and independent. All the nuns of the whole convent were flabbergasted and [the abbess] did not dare to keep this hidden: "Vigilant lips will not mention the faults of someone else; a vigilant person will not hang out with evil companions. If a secret is not well kept, disaster is bound to strike. If one does not make far-reaching plans, one is bound to have immediate worries. I am afraid that we will be implicated in this unpleasantness, so as soon as possible, I will send some people to inform the court."

Leave secretly, come openly, and betray no sign—
Never will they be able to snare you in their traps.

Namo Guanshiyin pusa

Three experienced and capable nuns were dispatched;
With bundles of bedding on their backs, they set out.
They hastened on like a cloud, by day and by night,
And eventually arrived at the capital to see the emperor.
    Let's not talk about their tribulations on the road—
In due time they entered the gate of the great capital.
Their bodies wrapped in cassocks, their heads all bare:
Carrying incense, they submitted a report to the ruler:
    "From the moment the princess arrived at our convent,
She's refused to return to the palace despite our advice.
For this your servants deserve to die a myriad of times—
May Your Majesty in his wisdom pardon his servants!
    When the princess did not listen to our earnest advice,
As punishment we ordered her to the kitchen as a maid.
This punishment was meant to make her change her mind,
But by marvelous magic she managed to move the gods!
    She remains seated in lotus position in the kitchen, while
Devas and dragons and other gods gather like clouds!
The divinities of the three worlds serve as her slaves,
The gods of the five hundred precepts follow her body.[78]
    The Eight Immortals provide her with tea and fruits,
The Lads of Combustion light candles and lamps.
Sweeping floors, spreading mats, and hanging banners,
All this is done by the convent's local protector god.
    At dawn and dusk nobody beats the bell and the drum—
The evening drum and morning bell sound of themselves.
Since ancient times our convent lacked its own well—
A dragon created a dragon pool at the convent's gate!
    The running animals bring firewood, filling the convent,
The flying birds bring vegetables, descending like a cloud!
The husking and milling of rice is all done by ghosts,
Our vegetarian food is all cooked by the Six Nails!
    We nuns would not want to keep anything hidden, so
We have come here solely to report to Your Majesty."
Upon the conclusion of this report by the convent nuns,
Let's attend to the emperor's rage as he heard these facts.

At his morning audience, the emperor saw three nuns who submitted a report to the throne. Following its announcement by the regulator of ranks, the report was opened and declaimed aloud. When the emperor heard its contents, he flew into a rage. He ordered his guards on his left and right to arrest the nuns for interrogation. "I issued an edict some time ago, ordering them to persuade that girl to return to the palace. But now they come here with these devilish words of ghosts and monsters!" Immediately he summoned the two noblemen Zhu and Ye: "Put together our troops as quick as fire and set out! Go to the White Sparrow Meditation Convent in Ruzhou and surround it tightly, layer upon layer. Put the torch to the convent and dig out the foundations, turning them into a lake—no trace is to be left!" When the military commanders had received their orders, they voiced their acceptance like the thunder. After kowtowing, they left the court. Beating the drum and sounding the gong, they collected their troops and officers. Moving and shaking the whole cosmos, they immediately set off for Ruzhou to burn down the convent and annihilate its nuns.

Even though from floating clouds snowflakes drift down,
The full bright moon impresses its seal on a thousand rivers.

Namo Guanshiyin pusa

The officers had received the order to burn down the convent,
Leading their troops they set out, shaking the whole cosmos.[79]
Let's not talk about their daily marches while on the road,
Eventually they arrived at the prefectural city of Ruzhou.
    The common people at Ruzhou were scared and alarmed:
Why was the whole city filled with soldiers and horses?
The White Sparrow Meditation Convent was quite close by,
The troops surrounded it tightly so no breeze could escape!
    The officers opened and declaimed the imperial edict, and
Their fire-spears and fire-arrows flew as thick as clouds!
"All the nuns of the convent, also including the princess,
Are to be burned to ashes and annihilated, sparing none!
    If only one person is allowed to escape with her life,
All your relatives will be killed to the very last man!"
The troops, upon hearing these orders, increased in ardor,
Calling for a storm they started fires, showing no mercy.[80]

In this situation the princess was very much afflicted:
"The whole convent is about to suffer for my sake alone!
It's all because I vowed to become a disciple of the Buddha,
The only reason is I was determined to study the Way!

Now they all suffer the evil ire of my father the emperor,
Who by torching this convent wants to burn it to ashes.
I'm the one who should bear the brunt of his animosity—
But these nuns, my relatives in the Dharma, are innocent!

If our Buddha in his kind compassion deigns to watch us,
He will grant me the Dharma-power to save these nuns.
If the convent is saved from destruction by war and fire,
I later will not dare betray this overwhelming grace!"

As soon as the princess saw flames rising up on all sides and from all directions, smoke filling the whole cosmos, and the nuns of the convent crying and screaming, weeping and wailing, pouring out their grief and bitterly complaining, she immediately and with great devotion prayed to the buddhas of the three worlds and, filled with compassion, addressed the Lord of the Teaching of Spirit Mountain:[81] "Kind father of all manner of sentient beings, World-honored One for a myriad of generations, for many *kalpas* you cultivated your heart, and after six years [of meditation] you achieved the Way. Your marvelous appearance is dignified and impressive, and you have fully mastered all the supernatural powers. The kind grace of our Buddha surpasses that of one's parents, and all the people of the whole wide world are as your single son. I, your disciple, am the daughter of the Marvelous Splendor emperor. Loving and delighting in the Dharma of the Buddha, I entered into this convent to practice the Way together with this community. Because I did not return to the palace despite my father's summons, he has now come to burn down this convent. I hope that you will show your kind compassion by responding to this prayer, as you respond to all requests and fulfill every vow. I am the daughter of the Marvelous Splendor emperor, you were the son of a *cakravartin*.[82] You left the jade halls, I hate the imperial palace. You went to the Snow Mountains to practice the Way, I fled to White Sparrow to leave the family. You are my elder brother, I am your younger sister. You save all living beings from the sufferings of this world, so can't you remove this problem for your little sister?" She pulled a bamboo pin from her hair, and stabbed the inside of her mouth until it filled with blood, which she then spat out into the sky. What was the divine response?

Close-set bamboos don't hinder a stream from passing through,
The highest mountains cannot block a floating cloud on its way.

Namo Guanshiyin pusa

All the nuns of the convent were weeping most piteously,
Pouring out their grudges and complaints again and again.
Looking up to heaven, there was no road leading to heaven,
Turning around, there was no gate to enter into earth either.
  All the nuns collapsed for weeping, bereft of their soul,
There was not even half of a nun who showed any mettle.
The princess prayed piteously to the Buddha in the sky:
"Dear Buddha, you have to respond and save these lives!"
  She spat out one mouthful of blood into the empty sky,
And immediately the entire sky turned a red color.
The blue smoke was transformed into the blackest clouds,
And the blood became a red rain, a torrential downpour!
  The Buddha-hall and bell towers suffered no damage,
They had not been damaged at all, not in the slightest!
The nuns of the convent now were all filled with joy,
They realized that the princess was no common mortal!
  When the troops saw this, they said with one voice:
"The princess is a wily she-devil!" Turning around,
They made their horses head straight for the capital,
Where they reported everything in detail to the court.

When the emperor ascended the throne hall, he saw the troops he earlier had dispatched taking their place in the court ranks, wishing to report. The emperor asked them: "Why is it you officers have returned so quickly?" The commanders then immediately reported: "Your Majesty, the princess is in possession of some kind of magical powers! When we started to torch the convent, smoke covered the wide world, cannon were booming, and the sun was darkened. You only heard the crackling bushes and people weeping and crying. But all of a sudden a heavy red rain came down. The fire was extinguished and the smoke dispersed. When the clouds disappeared and the rain stopped, a white sun appeared in the sky, and the convent had not suffered any damage. We dare not refrain from reporting this!" When the emperor heard these words, his rage rose to heaven. Rising to his feet on the dragon throne, his loud curses reverberated like the thunder: "That must be that wily she-devil! Promptly dispatch more troops to put her in fetters and shackles and take her to the execution ground, where she will be properly dismembered as a warning to the crowd. Only by removing this present danger can We save Ourselves from later consequences!" When the officers had received his order, they traveled the post route like a storm-whipped fire, and they arrested the princess like an eagle grabbing a swallow or sparrow, like fire exploding under water! When the emperor's main consort, the empress, heard about this, her heart and gall dissolved. Hastily she hurried to the throne hall, and weeping and crying she immediately addressed the emperor.

At midnight atop the mountain, breeze and moon so still:
The single sound of the cry of a gibbon from a high tree.

Namo Guanshiyin pusa

The empress was so scared her heart and gall were pulverized,
At a loss what to do, she poured out her grief, weeping sadly.
She straightway walked into the throne hall, and there she said:
"Your Majesty, still your rage, and listen to what I have to say!
    Your servant and maid is aware of the crime she is committing,
For the love between mother and child I don't fear your anger.
Against all convention your maid now ascends the throne hall:
Grant her a pardon, be magnanimous and forgive the criminal!
    For ennobling wife and children one is praised in the chronicles,
Exacting the full measure of the law will ruin your reputation.
Wild tigers may be cruel, but even they still love their cubs—
How can Your Majesty, being a sagely ruler, not show mercy?"

The empress addressed the emperor as follows: "I have enjoyed the imperial grace throughout my life. Because of the degree of affection you have shown me, I now presume on our friendship and have come straightway into the throne hall without any consideration for my own safety, to beg you to pardon her crime. Our little daughter has by her insolence offended Your Majesty. In my ignorance I have thought up a little scheme, which I would like to propose to Your Majesty. If there is a suitable place by the side of the road, we should erect a bunted loft. Together with the palace women and our two daughters, the princes consort and the hundred officials, I will take up position on that loft, where we will wine and dine with a hundred kinds of music and song. Then we will take Marvelous Goodness and have her pass below the decorated loft. Perhaps she will have a change of heart when she sees all this luxury. If so, we may avoid having to witness a separation while alive of flesh-and-blood relatives. What would Your Majesty think of this?" The emperor agreed to her proposal. Immediately an imperial edict was issued, in which the court officials were ordered to quickly erect to the south of the city wall three high decorated lofts and to set out six festive banquets. When the court officials had received this order, they promptly started the construction of these lofts, which were in an instant fully completed.

As soon as you grasp the intention of the crane on its pine tree
branch,
You also understand why the fishes swim close to the river's
bottom.

Namo Guanshiyin pusa

By the light of moon and stars the emperor ascended the hall,
And promulgated an edict to all his court officials, to promptly
Erect three decorated lofts to the south of the city wall, and to
Set out sacrificial libations to be sacrificed to a living soul.
The court officials upon receiving these orders left the hall,
Erected and decorated these lofts—they were done in an hour.
The officers urged on their troops like a storm-whipped fire,
Like dragons and like tigers not to show any sign of mercy!
When they had arrested the princess, they did not say a thing,
But stripped her of shift and skirt, exposing her naked body.
First they took the long stocks and locked them around her neck,
Next they attached the iron chain with its appended bronze bells.
Her arms were tied behind her back, her feet were fettered,
And her body was covered all over with paper-money silver.

On the flag affixed to the stocks large characters spelled out:
"A criminal condemned to die for disobeying her parents."
Her armed escorts pulled her forward, running like a cloud,
They surrounded her on all sides with their spears and swords.
The soldiers shouted again and again: "Hurry up! Make haste!"
Each sounding gong, each roll of the drum was quite frightening.
The soldiers addressed the princess, trying to persuade her
To obey the emperor and marry a husband to avoid disaster.
But the princess immediately replied in the following manner:
"Dear vanguard commander, please listen to what I have to say.
I will rather donate this body and die beneath the sword, but
I will never allow this body to be married off to some husband."
Guarded by her escorts she eventually passed below the lofts—
All palace women saw her and all were overcome by pain.
The good neighbors of street and ward burned paper money,
Thousands of families, myriads of people wept without end.
All the concubines of the palace, all the officials and officers,
All came to offer sacrifice to her and see this darling off.
They offered her soup and gave her food as the zither was played,
They burned incense and bowed down to the saddest of tunes.
After three libations of wine, they would burn the paper money;
Before the pavilion for honoring the soul the prayer was read.

The First Scroll of the Short Version of *Incense Mountain*, the end.

Respectfully carved in the last month of the winter of the seventh year of the Tongzhi reign-period (1868).

The Precious Scroll of Incense Mountain Part 2

The Second Scroll of the Short Version of the *Sutra of the Original Life of the Bodhisattva Guanshiyin*

Now,

(*The members of the congregation, arriving at this point, respectfully stand and remain standing as they listen. The leader leaves his seat and, kneeling, reads out the sacrificial prayer.*)

In the thirty-sixth year, a *jiashen* year, of the reign-period Marvelous Splendor of Raised Forest, on the fifteenth day following the first day of the seventh month, a *yisi* day, we, imperial relatives and officials, respectfully have prepared the ritual pure wine and the appropriate fine foods, and make bold to offer sacrifice to HER HIGHNESS MARVELOUS GOODNESS while she is still alive. As our thoughts go out to Her Highness, tears of pain course down. Because of the measure of her Being she swallows emptiness; on her mind of No-being the moon is imprinted. Her behavior surpasses past and present; her merit transcends the Great Vacuity. As stars move and the Dipper turns, the creatures are exchanged and people fly off. In order to achieve No-birth, she disobeys her father. Right in the middle of her greening spring, the blooming flower encounters a storm. The incense burns but its smoke refuses to rise; the candle is bright but its light is hidden. Forced to depart from the golden palace, she is coerced to go to the Yellow Springs.[1] Her life fades faster than the western sunlight; her body will decompose like the morning dew. We, her servants, have no other means of showing our respect but to give expression to our unworthy feelings. As we send her off on her journey through the clouds, may she deign to partake of these offerings. Alas, alas! Please accept these sacrificial foods!

(*After reading this prayer, one bows down and kowtows. One repeatedly recites "Greatly compassionate bodhisattva Guanshiyin," and regains his seat. Recite the* gātha *and sound the ruler.*)

Now here inside there is no need to hang the silence mirror,
When in the end the heavens dawn, all will be self-so clear.

Namo Guanshiyin pusa

When the sacrifice and libation were done, everyone shed tears,
The whole city was crying and weeping, painfully wounded.
The princess was undisturbed, and, without a worry or care,
Went forward, greatly delighted and filled with a happy joy.
The princess addressed her guards in the following manner:
"What is the reason for this weeping and for this loud music?"
The soldiers immediately answered her in the following way:
"Your Highness, please listen to what we have to say.
The sacrificial offerings set out all along the street over there
Have been all been arranged for by the women of the palace.
With instrumental music and sacrificial gifts they see you off,
Lighting incense, burning paper, and endlessly weeping.
Alas, Your Highness, you are still so young, but beheaded
On the execution ground you'll die and meet with King Yama.
Today one does not know what the next day will bring—
That's why they have arranged these sacrifices for your soul!"

When the princess was captured by the warriors, her fine black-silk hair had been tied to the end of her shackles, and her jade-white face was reflected in the paper coins.[2] Oil and ink smeared her face, and her naked body was stripped of clothing. Her feet were fettered with iron rings, and her hands were tied with a rope of hemp. Soldiers surrounded her—a single mass of swords and spears! To the sound of the gong and the roll of the drum she was led to pass below the lofts. There she saw numberless people clad in mourning garments, who came out to offer sacrifice, light incense, and burn paper money. The princess thereupon asked the soldiers: "What is the reason of that doleful music I hear down the street?" The soldiers replied: "That's because they are offering sacrifice to see Your

Highness off now that you soon will go to the Yellow Springs. That's why they play this music and engage in wailing."

Silently listen to the wind in pines rinsing the rustling green;
Calmly observe the mountain flowers blooming like brocade.

Namo Guanshiyin pusa

When the princess had been told this, she showed a slight smile:
"How laughable that lord and king should play with people for fun!
When the laws accord with Heaven, Heaven and heart are one,
And who would dare harbor a grudge, complain of corruption?
Three thousand legal rules apply throughout all-under-heaven,
And when a crime is committed, family is of no consideration.
This national treasure is transmitted from generation to generation,
From past to present the emperor's law rules the entire cosmos.
An enlightened Son of Heaven governs in accord with Heaven,
And of course the myriad clans will venerate and honor him.
But if the lord ignores the law, his servants too ignore the law,
And his desire to establish a reputation in the world is vain.
From ancient times till the present it has yet to be the case
That people set out sacrificial foods to surprise a living person.
I observe that the people of this world are all moved to tears,
But my heart is still and at peace, like water that is level."

When the empress on her decorated loft saw Marvelous Goodness from afar, she wept and fainted there on the loft. Only after quite a while did she come around. Concubines and palace maids supported her as she descended the loft to talk to her third daughter.

In the hall of yellow gold the pearly screen is rolled up,
Before the green jade steps the mournful cuckoo cries.

Namo Guanshiyin pusa

The empress descended from the bunted loft, awash in tears;
Weeping and wailing most piteously, her tears gushed forth.
All the officials and officers of the court also shed tears,
And all the concubines of the palace wept again and again!

With tears in her eyes the empress addressed her as follows:
"My dear child, why have you become a convicted criminal?
If only today you would be a darling and change your mind,
You'd not have to lose your life to the executioner's sword!
When I raised you, I hoped you'd take care of me in my old age,
Who could have known that now that would turn into emptiness?
My ten months of heavy pregnancy were all a waste of effort,
My three years of nursing and feeding have all come to naught.
When one sees a child grow up, one's heart is filled with joy
At having someone to rely on for old-age care and a burial.
If you discount the kind compassion of raising and nursing you,
You may cultivate all you want, but no Way will be achieved!
By having to endure the many tortures inflicted by your father,
You cause your mother to helplessly suffer in this way!
When I heard that troops had been dispatched to arrest you,
I felt as if heart and liver were being ripped from my belly!
If you still will not obey and marry a prince consort, you'll
Be beheaded by the sharp sword and see the Lord of Shade.
Do as I tell you, accept your lot, and return to the palace, so
You'll save your poor life, and take up your proper duties!"

When the empress had stopped weeping and wailing, she asked Marvelous Goodness: "My intelligent girl, you've forgotten [the poem that reads] 'The love of one's parents is great, / Their care and concern has no end! / Whether rising or sitting—their heart follows close, / Whether far-off or nearby, their thoughts are with you. / Even though a mother turns a hundred, / She still worries about a child of eighty. / Do you want to know when their love expires? / It's only gone when their life is done!' What's so bad about staying in the palace and marrying a man as your father says? Now you are fettered and shackled, your body bared for all to see. The inserted banner proclaims your crime, and soldiers escort and guard you to the sound of the gong and the roll of the drum. You're worse off than a highwayman or a thieving robber. I will be flustered and filled with fear for the rest of my life! How do you dare meet with your relatives in this condition? If having come to this you still won't obey, your life will surely go to the Yellow Springs, and I will try to kill myself! Be a darling and change your mind, and I will report to your father the emperor so he will pardon you and you can return to the palace and marry a prince consort without delay!"

Before the monastery, the horse is tied up at the Hall of Universal
Light,
Outside the gate, the buffalo is tethered at the site of Right
Enlightenment.[3]

Namo Guanshiyin pusa

The princess immediately answered in the following way:
"My dear mother, now please listen to what I have to say.
It's not that your daughter is lacking in loyalty and filiality,
It is because of birth and death that I disobey my parents.
I am happy to sacrifice my life once, dying under the sword,
So I may transcend the myriad *kalpas* and escape *saṁsāra.*
I do not crave the wealth and status of the imperial palace,
My eager vow is that I want to enter the gate of nirvana!
Let them cut this illusory body with knives and swords,
My original nature is perfect and bright, fully indivisible!
Let my father issue thousands of commands and orders,
I refuse, with all my heart, to return to the imperial palace!
Indeed, even if he decided that my life should be spared,
I'd be filled with fear at his sight—I'd never be at peace.
Today the love between mother and daughter is finished,
But we'll meet again in a later life, a coming existence."

The princess answered her mother as follows: "I have heard that the ancient sutras say, 'As long as there is attachment, there is birth. When attachment is exhausted, annihilation follows.' Alas, each and every one in this world craves life, and each and every one fears death. But if one day Impermanence arrives, one's soul departs for the Underworld, the realm of the king of ghosts, without anything to free oneself from karma. Life in this world is empty and insubstantial, like the dew on flowers; a bubble on water, it resembles a particle of dust on a plant. Husband and wife are enemies from a former life, and sons and daughters are like a karmic debt. Mother, please listen to me: the suffering of death is unavoidable. Don't miss this opportunity, and quickly make your provisions for the future. Even if you have filial sons and obedient grandsons, they cannot take your place when Impermanence knocks. But if you are willing to sacrifice this body and practice the Way, you'll achieve the *bodhi* of buddhahood. I refuse to return to the palace today and marry some prince consort!" When Marvelous Book and Marvelous Sound saw that their mother could not talk any sense into her, they both came down the loft to have an earnest word with their younger sister.

The plum blossom in the snow, the moon on a frosty night—
Alas, the color may be the same, but the perspective is not.

Namo Guanshiyin pusa

Her two elder sisters wept most piteously, and weeping said:
"Little sister, you good-for-nothing with no sense of duty!"
Hands clutching gauze skirts, they wiped away their tears,
And begged her: "Dear little sister, please change your mind!
    Be a darling, return to the palace, marry a prince consort,
And avoid having your flesh and body sliced up by a knife!
Once you've died, you will not be able to come back to life,
You crazily seek your own death—nobody knows why!
    Your life hangs in the balance and you're still not afraid,
Just thousands of crafty words—answers like a smoke screen!
Only filial sons and wise wives are found in historical records,
So do not imitate those monks and nuns—low-caste people!
    Cutting off human relations, you lack loyalty and filiality,
The Great Rite of yin and of yang you forever discard.
Take our advice, do your duty, marry a prince consort,
You'll save your life and serve your father and mother!"

The two elder sisters wept most piteously. While tears coursed down their cheeks, sobbing and crying they asked Marvelous Goodness the following question: "Dear little sister, why is it you are so mad and out of your mind that you expose yourself to this humiliation? Even we feel ashamed and afraid because of you! If you still will not obey now, your life is lost!" Hearing this, Marvelous Goodness replied to her elder sisters: "Each should do what she wants! Why should you feel so concerned? The date of birth and death is fixed, so why should I feel any fear? Each and every person in this world craves life, but I alone am willing to die. My sisters, please go back to the palace; there is no need to have an earnest word with me."

One word hits the mark and illuminates myriad phenomena:
The worm bores through the mud, the dragon soars to heaven.

Namo Guanshiyin pusa

When clouds arise under a clear sky, they hide the mountains;
When does a stream, which runs its course, turn and look back?
Her two elder sisters, unable to make her change her mind,
Returned to the court to report to their father the emperor:
  "Marvelous Goodness sacrifices her body and will happily die,
She has no desire to live any longer and return to the palace."
At every place officials and officers offered sacrificial foods,
And this extended delay stretched on until the dusk of day.[4]
  This night the empress was at a loss what to do, and after she
Had returned to the palace she silently pondered her options.
Before the hall an edict was issued, like a storm-whipped fire,
Which once again summoned the princess for an interrogation.[5]
  The soldiers who had received this order then hastened back,
They escorted the princess as she entered the gate of the court.
Carrying shackles and fetters she returned to the inner garden
With the fearful clang and rattle of bronze bells and iron chains.
  Female guards escorted her once she was back in the palace,
They locked her in a cold palace cell with only a single lamp.
The empress and the imperial concubines wept most piteously,
All the women of the Six Palaces were overcome by pain.

That night the empress ordered the imperial concubines of the Six Palaces and the princesses of the Twelve Courts: "If with sweet words and tender phrases you can talk that girl into changing her mind, I will reward you most handsomely!" When they had received this order, they straightway went to the rear palace to talk to the third princess.

Spring flowers and autumn chrysanthemums each have their own fragrance:
Two roads stretch out before you—it's up to you to choose the one to follow.

Namo Guanshiyin pusa

The imperial concubines greeted the third princess with a bow,
Their weeping as with one voice shook the imperial palace.
With tears in their eyes they addressed Marvelous Goodness,
Who was dragging her shackles and supporting her chains.

"One raises a son so as to have someone's care in old age,
To be close to one's own parents beats cultivating the Truth.
We all still remember that day when you took your leave,
Thinking of you both morning and night we're filled with pain.
We all advise you, Your Highness, to marry a prince consort,
And so spare your flesh and body from death by the knife.
The running animals and the flying birds all marry and mate,
So how can one as a human being not be united in wedlock?
Don't follow the example of those losers, those poor nuns,
Who turn into low-caste people and are despised by all!
To practice cultivation in your youth is nothing so special,
One only becomes famous for studying the Way in old age!"

When the palace women went to see the princess, she was bareheaded and her hair was hanging down; her body was hung with paper coins; her neck was locked in a block and her hands were clasped in fetters, and ash and ink smeared her face, as if she were a prisoner from hell. When they all saw her, they could not but burst out in tears. When their weeping was done, filled with compassion they spoke to her: "Your Highness, you have nineteen years of greening spring, you are like the sun rising in the east, like a flower that has just begun to bloom, like a lamp that is burning for the first time, and like a treasure that has just been discovered. So why do you treat your beautiful, flowerlike appearance like shit and mud? Tonight, take our advice, and make use of this opportunity to turn disaster into good fortune, marry a prince consort!"

Following the rain, the flowers on the mountain have increased in color,
Once the wind blows, waves will all by themselves emerge on the water.

Namo Guanshiyin pusa

With kind and friendly words they all urged the princess,
They all urged the third princess to change her mind now:
"The mountains are green, the rivers blue just as before,
So why should you replace your old you with a new you?
If you, Your Highness, refuse to marry a prince consort,
You discard loyalty and filiality, deny human relations.

A hundred years count only thirty-six thousand days,
And how very short are the good times of one's youth?
    Refusing to marry a husband is a crime against nature,
The motivations you have are evil, disturbing the court.
So we urge you, Your Highness, to return to the palace,
And as before, do your duty as someone born in the palace!"

The palace women urged her: "Young women should not practice cultivation! Wait till you're seventy or eighty, when your ears are deaf and your eyes are dim, when your waist is bent and your back is stooped, when you need a staff to support you while walking and people to assist you when sitting down, and when you cannot do any useful work at all, and then venerate the Buddha, keeping to a vegetarian diet—it still wouldn't be too late! So we urge you, Your Highness, to put your sedan chair of earlier days in order once again, to rest on a dragon couch, put on a chaplet and hairpins, and dress yourself in brocade and purple. Pretty maids will swarm around you, and elegant girls will follow behind. That beats being a nun! Moreover, when you stay in the palace, marrying a husband and having fun, you also display complete loyalty and filiality. We wish you a lifetime of harmony, but when you should happen to die, a few extra masses would be read, and a somewhat larger sacrificial meal be set out. A fine grave hill would be constructed, and your own sons and grandsons would of course maintain the sacrifices. On the first days of spring and fall in the family temple and on the taboo days into the far future the rites of sacrificing and sweeping will of course be carried out. But what's the chance that you would achieve some buddhahood? That's all a waste of effort!"

Speaking without illumination all burns down to defamation,
But to remain silent when enlightened is also not acceptable.

Namo Guanshiyin pusa

The princess immediately answered in the following way:
"My bright dear friends, please listen to what I have to say.
You say that one should practice the Way only in old age,
That Impermanence doesn't come and visit younger people.
    But gold and silver, pearls and feathers adorn a skeleton,

Finest garments of gauze and brocade clothe gore and pus.
Once your three inches of breath are cut off, gone like a dream,
Your dead body, bloated and rotten, will be a hill of maggots.
    What is achieved by fame and glory in this human world?
Once you close your eyes, all becomes deepest darkness.
Your beloved wife and children are birds sharing a forest,[6]
On the road to the Yellow Springs you will not meet them.
    If you did not cultivate while alive, your despair is in vain,
Once you're dead, you will not hear of the empty banquets.
A golden casket, a silver chest: buried under green grass,
Sacrifices in spring and autumn: expressing earthly love.
    Each and every one wants to play a tune of a thousand years,
Each and every one craves and schemes to live to a hundred.
Alas, the heart of the people of this world is never satisfied,
But on the day death arrives, all one's affairs come to an end.
    Even a skeleton is still more aware of its true buddha-nature,
For a skeleton will to the end never marry another skeleton.
Today I have seen through the outward casing of the skeleton:
It's dismissed, it's sent away, and I am now my own master!"

The princess said: "The oceans may dry out and Mt. Tai may collapse, but my dedication to the Way will only progress and never waver. Right now the moment has arrived to forget my body for the sake of the Dharma. How could I have any feelings of craving or fear? You are not going to tell me that this body will not die and that we will stay forever in this world? My only wish is to die quickly so I may transcend the three worlds and escape from the six ways. All human beings are from birth the most spiritually gifted [of all sentient creatures]. When people are deluded they are called the profane, but as soon as one is enlightened he becomes a buddha. All who sacrifice body and heart achieve buddhahood. But if I would marry a husband, I would suffer his restrictions and impositions. What would be the sense of that! You all will have to experience the hour of your death. At that time there is no one on whom you can rely, and there is not a place where you can hide. You have to practice cultivation from the earliest moment so as to ferry yourself across [the sea of suffering]. That's the only way to avoid the sufferings of hell!" When the imperial concubines heard her words, they were dumbstruck and didn't know what to say, and feeling downcast they left.

As soon as the metal wind rises, the jade dew turns cool,[7]
And the osmanthus flower fills the sky with its perfume.

Namo Guanshiyin pusa

Marvelous Goodness immediately addressed them as follows:
"Greening spring is exactly the time to settle one's prospects!
All the pleasures in the palace are those of a bird in a cage,
The wealth and high status at court make you a fish in a net.
    The myriad affairs of this human world are all like a dream,
So I want to practice cultivation, study the Truth of the Way!"
The pretty maids and elegant ladies didn't know what to answer,
And without saying another word, they returned to the palace.
    Passing before the throne hall, they reported on their mission:
"Your Majesty, please be so kind as to listen to our report.
The heart of Her Highness is as unshakable as iron or stone,
Kind words of good advice flit past her ears like a breeze."
    Hearing this, her father the emperor was afflicted in his heart:
"I've run out of methods to control her—what can I say?
We will have to go in person Ourselves to the inner garden
And convince Marvelous Goodness to take a husband!"

Her father the emperor said: "As long as one holds the pearl in his mouth without spitting it out, nobody will know it is a treasure, just as the drum and bell in their tower will not resound unless they are beaten. The old books teach, 'When the father is kind, the son is filial. But if the father is not kind, the son will be unfilial.' Thus does the way of father and son have its own principle of reciprocity. We will go to her in person and speak with her face to face." He prayed in the family temple of his own clan, making a wish for the hidden strength of his ancestors, so that this night he might quickly make her change her mind and marry a husband to serve and uphold.

The feral dogs in the wilds may howl like the roaring thunder,
But the noble lion in his den will not be disturbed in his sleep.

Namo Guanshiyin pusa

Dragging up the moon from the water is all wasted effort,
Looking for the sword by the notch on the boat is hopeless.[8]

This night His Imperial Majesty visited the inner garden,
And entered the cell where Marvelous Goodness was kept.
Her father the emperor visited her in person and sighed:
"Alas, my Marvelous Goodness, my very own child! You
Disobeyed your father's orders, so it's fit you are punished,
Now you are a criminal condemned to die for your serious crime."
Her father the emperor was moved to tears big as pearls,
Overcome by grief, his heart was sore, his voice choked:
"If it hadn't been for your sisters' request for your return,
How would you have been allowed to return to the palace?
If you do not marry a prince consort while you're young,
You miss out on greening spring and misapply your mind.
If you haven't known the love between husband and wife,
As a human you have lived your life in this world in vain.
So tonight, dear daughter, be a darling, change your mind,
And avoid having to lose your life and see the Lord of Shade.
But if you still obstinately refuse to have a change of heart,
A single sword will slice you in two, sending you off to darkness!"

Her father the emperor said: "A kind mother's love is like the earth, the stern father is a counterpart of Heaven. How is one different from animals, birds, and beasts, if one does not follow a father's instructions? You should listen to your two elder sisters in the palace! Because they obeyed their father and married a husband, they're now enjoying a hundred kinds of pleasure, and don't lack any of the enjoyments of the divine immortals. But you tonight are fettered and shackled. And why is that? It is because you refuse to enjoy pleasure and are happy to be a criminal. [In this world nothing surpasses the affection between husband and wife who share cushion and coverlet: their love is bigger than mountains and seas!] What kind of notion is that, that you do not obey the instructions of the ancients? [If you would know the pleasures of the forest of hundred flowers, you'd be happy to die for it.]"[9] When Marvelous Goodness heard this, she replied: "My father the emperor, dear daddy, you are misled and deluded and unenlightened, and your perverse heart is all ablaze. This is not the behavior of a lord and emperor in possession of the Way! Daddy, you are the ruler of the myriads of people, the lord of the whole nation. If you cannot control your family, how can you control the nation? If you are a Son of Heaven and an emperor of men, in possession of the Way, how would you, a father, ever think of entering this side palace at midnight, in the third watch,[10] and urge your daughter to marry a husband? How would it look if the world came to know of this?"

A horse—it didn't look like that, a mule it wasn't either,
The very first move you made only brought you disgust.

Namo Guanshiyin pusa

Marvelous Goodness immediately hastened to answer:
"My emperor, please be so kind as to listen to my words.
    A hundred years fly by as quickly as the spark from a stone!
So why are you so narrow-minded, deluded and craving?
You truly are a traveler who has lost his way in daytime,
Call him ten thousand times, and he will not turn his head!
    Even flying birds and running animals all fear their death,
So how can you as a human being not grasp this truth?
Plants and trees have no feelings but understand the seasons;
When we humans grow old and die, there is no substitute.
    Whether we produce good or evil, it's done from the heart,
Becoming a saint or a sage is also achieved from the heart.
We never get fed up watching this show of marionettes,
But alas, at the end comes the moment of the final scene.
    When the nation is settled, Heaven's heart will be in accord,
A truly enlightened Son of Heaven thus has loyal vassals.
But how could it be acceptable for a father to enter this cell,
And at midnight, in the third watch, urge me to marry a man?
    If you have given the order, have the execution performed,
Quickly have me be beheaded and show me no mercy at all.
If I've broken the law, committed a crime, I'm happy to die,
So why is it you have issued an edict to bring me back?
    I now would rather see you, my father, die by the sword
Than that I should ever give up my body to serve a man!"

The princess said: "I would rather see Mt. Sumeru crushed and pulverized, and the thousand times thousand worlds leveled and submerged, than have you raise the issue of my taking a husband!" The enraged emperor said: "You don't know what's good for you! When I tell you to take a husband, he will be emperor and truly rise to the top. That's an exceptionally marvelous good thing. When

I consider what you have been saying, it is all 'Being born from Empty Nothingness,' like the hairs of a tortoise or the horns of a hare, like the moon reflected in water or an image appearing in a mirror—it's all empty deception." The princess replied: "The empty is substantial, and the substantial is empty, but only one who is enlightened will know." The emperor continued: "You are a tender spring flower, so how can you endure heavy snow and icy frost?" The princess replied: "Flowers and leaves may flourish and fade, but their root and source are not darkened." The emperor then said: "But how could your delicate figure bear the tortures of the hundred meltings?"[11] The princess replied: "The illusionary shell is not solid, but the true nature is indestructible." The emperor said: "You girl, even though your body may be like iron, it will not be able to withstand the oven of the execution!" The princess replied: "The true gold that comes from the mine will not be hurt by the fire; when the divine dragon dives into the sea, there's no salt in the water. When the stern orders of my father the emperor are issued, all the officials obey what you say; when the rooster crows in the fifth watch, all the court gentlemen reverentially listen." She also said: "Below the gate of the great sun there are no stars and moons, before the hall of the Son of Heaven there is no poor man. But if you, my father and emperor, cannot control your family, how can you control the nation? You look like a tiger with a paper hat: both ridiculous and terrifying! As to your daughter's body and mind, we each have our own views. So why is it you are so insistent about trying to force me to take a husband?" When her father the emperor heard these words, he gnashed his teeth and rolled his eyes; the breath of his sighs resembled clouds, and his raging voice resembled the thunder. He ran off and went up the throne hall, where he sat and waited for daybreak: "Off with the head of that rebellious child with a heart and liver of iron, that monstrous she-devil, who says she's not afraid to die!"

In the oven with its great bellows her body is purified,
Ghost masks and demon heads can't do a thing to her!

Namo Guanshiyin pusa

When her father the emperor heard this, he exploded in rage,
His face was the color of ashes, his breath resembled a cloud.

Filled with rage and anger he returned to the throne hall:
"That detestable bewitching devil kills me with affliction!"
He waited till the fifth watch, when the audience started,
Then the order for her beheading was issued fast as a cloud:
"If she is not quickly removed, she will be a danger.
If we keep her in prison, it only strengthens her resolve.[12]
If there now still is anyone who will try to dissuade Us,
All his womenfolk will be confiscated, his relatives killed."
As the order was strict, none dared admonish the emperor,
All accepted the fact that the princess would meet her fate.
The Heaven of the Thirty-three was moved and shaken,
The dragon palaces and earth-prisons were all informed.
The eye of the Buddha surveyed and knew all-under-heaven
(His Dharma-body is completely hidden in Great Emptiness).
He stretched out his gold-colored arm that people can't see,
And a dazzling light as of white jade fell on the criminal.
The executioner took his sword and lifted it high, as with
Bulging eyes filled with rage he gnashed his teeth in anger!
With the strength of both his arms: the sword flashed,
And on her neck a dazzling light turned into purple clouds.
You'd have thought that the princess had died by the sword,
Who could know that she would be unperturbed and smile![13]
Both the troops and the people were all filled with joy,
And with one voice they all shouted: "She's no mortal!
Blue Heaven has eyes and protected her from the sky,
Obviously she has not been even the slightest bit hurt!"
The presiding official and the executioner were frightened:
"The princess indeed must be a witchlike she-devil!"
Immediately they returned to the court and reported:
"May Your Majesty pardon our crime and let us speak!"
Hearing this, the emperor's face betrayed his rage;
As he loudly shouted, beating his table, his anger grew:
"If even knife and sword cannot do away with her—
This girl, this monstrous devil, will kill me with affliction!"

When the emperor heard this report, he shook his head and pulled his ears, and his soul and gall both dissolved: "If even sword and knife cannot control her, she indeed is a monstrous sprite! I'll have to discuss some way with the court officials to have her executed so as to avoid later problems." When the princess heard this, she prayed to the empty sky: "Allow me to die, so I will not have to be in conflict with my father, troubling his heart, because it would be my fault if the common people of the whole world would not be at peace." Even before she had finished her vow, the Buddha and Heaven responded and ordained that she would not suffer any pain—like a lamp that's blown out. The executioner then strangled her with the string of a bow, and she immediately stopped breathing and died. That very moment mountains collapsed and trees feel down; birds and beasts madly rushed about, sadly screaming; the sea dried up and the rivers ran dry, leaving the dragons and fishes no place to hide; heaven and earth were darkened; sun and moon lost their light; the whole sky was covered with snow, and every single creature was coated with frost. To the farthest reaches of the earth, to the edges of the sky—both in her own country and in all foreign states everybody knew that the princess had been executed. Each and every one was filled with sadness, each and every one was moved to tears!

Even if they had used iron wheels, they couldn't have hurt her heart,
As in wisdom-*samādhi*, fully enlightened, it enjoyed its own Nature.[14]

Namo Guanshiyin pusa

Marvelous Splendor now had had the third princess strangled,
And this moved to weeping thousands times millions of people.
The empress wept in such a way her liver and gut were rent,
All the imperial concubines of the palace were pained by grief.
Because the pitiable princess had still been so very young,
All the officials and officers at court were awash in tears.
In heaven the heavenly gods all shed tears of compassion,
And on earth the local gods all were wounded in their heart.
The earth moved, the mountains shook, frightening the folk,
None of them was seen walking on the streets or the roads.
The running animals and flying birds were in despair,
Gibbons shrieked and birds cried, weeping again and again.
When the presiding official saw that the princess had died,
He ordered her shot into a pulp with a volley of arrows:
Each and every arrow to be aimed at her heart and liver,
Nothing at all to remain of the skin and flesh of her body!

Before he had finished speaking, the skies all darkened,
A mist arose on all sides, blanketing heaven with clouds.
A black twister arose, shaking the cosmos with its force,
Ghosts wept and gods wailed, frightening the folk, who
Then saw a fierce beast appear, a motley-striped tiger that
Leapt, to everyone's terror, across them in three bounds.
Grabbing the princess in its maw, it took her off to the forest—
The official rushed off to the court to report to the emperor.

The presiding official returned to the court and reported: "Your Majesty, in conformity with your order, we tied the princess up, took her to the execution ground, and had her strangled to death. When we ordered her shot through by arrows and trampled by horses, heaven and earth darkened, and a fierce tiger dragged the mortal remains of Her Highness into the Deceased-Many forest. I don't dare not report this!" When the emperor heard this, his dragon-mien showed his joy: "Our heart accords with Heaven's heart! Those who are disloyal and unfilial should be done away with and annihilated!" The emperor also asked: "What is the Deceased-Many forest?" His ministers replied: "It is a piece of unused public land in the hills. Whenever there are corpses that are left unburied, they are hauled to this place where they are eaten by birds and beasts." The emperor said: "Thank you all for your divine assistance in freeing Us from this worry."

Once one has shed his mortal feelings, the sagely mind is Truth,
Like gold extracted from the ore, the moon emerging from clouds.

Namo Guanshiyin pusa

Let's not speak of the great joy of Marvelous Splendor,
Let's talk about the princess's journey to the Underworld.
The light of her spirit emerged and went to the realm of shade,
Without a care for her illusionary body, which remained behind.
Part shade, part darkness: she went as if in a dream,
Without knowing where she was going, to which village.
"I have no idea which prefecture this is or which county!"
Pondering this, tears dropped from her eyes in profusion.
"If your disciple has been fated to practice cultivation,
May the empty sky respond and show me the way to go!"

Before she had finished her vow, her tears gushed down,
Piteously weeping and wailing she prayed to the gods.
    Suddenly she saw a youth and maiden of spectacular beauty
—Black hair done up in a bun, temple locks trailing—
Who, with banners in their hands, came to guide her.
As soon as the princess saw them, she asked them why.
    The youth and maiden folded their hands and deeply bowed,
And with bowed head and soft words they informed her:
"We are the green boy and girl of the Office of Goodness,
We have been ordered by our king to welcome you here.
    Good people must all be welcomed by us, boy and girl,
But sinners whose sins are many are captured by *yakṣas.*[15]
May we invite Your Highness to visit the realm of shade
And meet with the Lord of Shade in his Yiyang Hall."

When the princess heard this, she could not help being surprised: "You belong to the realm of shade, so what are you doing here, in our world of light?" The youth and maiden replied: "We are here in the realm of shade!" The princess then asked: "But how could I have ended up in the realm of shade?" The youth and maiden replied: "Because you refused to take a husband, you were strangled to death by your father, that's why you've come to the realm of shade! We have long heard of Your Highness's great kindness and great compassion and the lofty transcendence of your style in the Way. The Three Officials reported this matter, and the Ten Kings are delighted to meet you. An edict was issued far and wide to make sure you would be welcomed and invited. There's no need to be frightened; let's set out immediately on our journey." Only then did the princess realize that she had arrived on the road to the Yellow Springs.

Don't think, while alive, that there will be no retribution,
As soon as you have died, it all will be perfectly clear.

Namo Guanshiyin pusa

Once the princess knew she'd arrived in the realm of shade,
She was fearful and flustered, and her tears poured down.
    In this deep and black darkness she had no idea of direction,
At the prospect of the hidden road she was filled with pain.

A youth and a maiden, holding a flag, came forward to guide her,
And following those two she went on with her journey.
First she passed the mighty pass of the Gate of Ghosts,
Even a man made of iron would feel grief at this sight!
The bureaus of the Three Officials allow no corruption,
The heads of the eighteen hells know no mercy at all.
She then saw the iron-bed and bronze-pillar prisons, and
The knife-mountain and sword-tree, both white like silver.
The boiling vats and red-hot ovens would scare anyone,
The freezing cold and the body-saws fill one with fear!
In front of the karma-mirror you see your own sins,
And not the slightest crime of sin here allows for mercy.
A myriad *kalpas* of death and birth—but no one cares!
After your life of a hundred years you alone will grieve.
Male and female ghostly prisoners, millions without number,
Wailed and cried and wept and hollered like cackling geese.
Just think of the thousands of tortures of the earth-prisons:
Who of us will avoid falling down and not visit that place?
She then passed below the Mountain of Wasted Money,[16]
And in the City of Those Who Died Unjustly met with her nuns,
Who complained and cried foul while clutching her gown:
"It's all because of you that we had to die before our time!
If you escape from the three worlds, first ferry us across,
Then we'll be reconciled, and have no cause for complaint!"
The princess immediately addressed these nuns as follows:
"Dear fellow nuns, please listen to what I have to say.
Since ancient times, birth has always been followed by death,
The only difference being whether death comes sooner or later.
If you want to avoid going through the court of King Yama,
You must have completely realized the Truth of Emptiness."

The youth and maiden of the Office of Goodness led the princess by the Mountain of Wasted Money. In the City of Those Who Died Unjustly she ran into some nuns, who grabbed her gown and loudly cried: "We are here because of you! We died unjustly and sank down to this place where we suffer terribly!" The princess said: "You and I had no argument in earlier days, and there is no enmity between us now. The terms of birth and death are fixed, and when that date arrives, your body collapses. Good and evil have their karmic retribution, which you have to suffer yourself. What does it have to do with me?" The nuns said: "Even though that all may be so, we still hope that you in your kind compassion will save us and ferry us across so we may be reborn in heaven."

When you're deluded, you wander in darkness on the six
pathways;[17]
Once you're enlightened, in Emptiness there is no coming or going.

Namo Guanshiyin pusa

"Turn around and you find the road to the Western Paradise!
All that's needed is for a person to be sincere in his vow!"
The princess right then and there pronounced a great vow,
Vowing to ferry across the nuns and free them from suffering:
"If this disciple successfully achieves the right fruit, may
All buddhas of a thousand worlds descend to this darkness!"
As soon as she spoke her vow, she received a response, as
Red and white lotus flowers opened and filled the city walls.
The bodhisattva Kṣitigarbha then addressed her as follows:[18]
"Hail to Your Highness! Tell me, what brings you here?"
The princess greeted him with a bow and promptly replied,
As with lowered head and palms pressed together she said:
"Kind reverend, many thanks for descending in person
And manifesting your golden body in this world of hells.
My only wish is that these nuns may leave this earth-prison,
And ascend to heaven to wander in freedom and joy."

As soon as the princess had pronounced her vow, she saw a bright light, dazzling and blinding. A hundred musicians all played in unison, and the world of the hells was filled with white and red lotus flowers. In the hall of King Yama appeared a five-colored auspicious light. At that time the bodhisattva Kṣitigarbha, seated on his *maṇi* throne, emitted a huge white light, which banished the darkness of the earth-prisons. The *yakṣas* bowed their hands, and the prison guards kowtowed. The princess quickly curtsied, and said: "Great Teacher, when your disciple first left the family, the convent to which she belonged was called White Sparrow. Because I disobeyed my father's command, he tried to burn the convent to the ground, which frightened some nuns to death. This is my fault, and I hope that in your kind compassion you will save them and ferry them across so they may be reborn in your land." When the bodhisattva Kṣitigarbha had heard this, he promptly took these nuns with him and they went to the Pure Land.

Turn around and you promptly ascend the shore of *bodhi*,
No fear there for the iron-faced devils of the Underworld!

Namo Guanshiyin pusa

The bodhisattva Kṣitigarbha rose up into the sky and left,
Followed by the nuns, carried by clouds under their feet.
The princess at this time experienced an increased zeal,
And with the youth and maiden continued traveling on.
The world of the hells had become a realm of free roaming,
And the earth-prisons had become palaces of pleasure.
The heads of the eighteen hells came out to welcome her,
The judicial officers of the Three Offices all received her.
When the princess walked on and came upon a bridge,
Golden bells and jade chimes all resounded together.
There by the bridge, Grannie Meng offered tea and fruits,[19]
And with three cups of tea, her spirits grew even higher.
From the river below the bridge, the sinners cried out—
"From what county and what village do those people come?"
The guardian of the bridge bowed to her and replied:
"These are all people from the world of light who sinned.
Being rich and noble, they thought they would live forever,
And so with fiendish deception, they harmed good people.
During their lifetimes, they did not do anything good,
And now it's too late for remorse as they must suffer.
When they died, they had no meritorious deeds to help them,
And still aren't allowed to come before the Lord of Shade."

When the princess had ascended the bridge and looked all around her, she one moment heard weeping and crying, and the next moment heard sweet music. She then asked the youth and maiden: "What's the cause of this weeping and of this music?" The boy and girl replied: "That music is the music from the halls of the Ten Kings. That weeping is the weeping from below the bridge across the Alas River." When the princess had been told this, she leaned with her jade-white hands on the bridge's balustrade, and with her kind eyes observed the situation below the bridge. She indeed saw a thousand times a thousand, nay, ten thousand times ten thousand, male and female ghostly criminals. She then pronounced the following vow: "I will achieve enlightenment only after I have ferried across these ghostly criminals." As soon as this aspiration was formed in her mind, she saw five-colored lotus flowers bloom below the bridge. When the sinners saw this, they pressed their palms together and were filled with joy. They promptly climbed up to the other shore and departed, after thanking her with a bow.

Transcendence achieved, you straightway enter the Tathāgata's realm,
And you will have nothing more do with high heavens and deep hells.

Namo Guanshiyin pusa

These are the sinners departing to be reborn in heaven,
The Alas River was transformed into a precious lotus pond.
The guardian of the bridge then went, like a shooting star,
To the hall of deepest darkness to report what had happened:
"The daughter of Marvelous Splendor in the world above
Is called Marvelous Goodness—she's no common mortal!
The Office of Goodness dispatched her to tour the hells,
And the limitless power of her vow is incomparable!
When she herself walked over the bridge, she ferried
Across all the evil sinners in the Alas River below!"
When King Yama heard this, his face told his joy,
He issued an edict inviting her to his inner garden.
The compassionate light of the princess overcame the shade,
And the darkness of the iron walls was fully illuminated.
Boiling vats were transformed into streams of merit,
And Sword Mountain became a hundred-flower forest.
Because of the compassionate light of the princess,
All the criminals in these hells were reborn in heaven.
The horse-faced *yakṣas* were all filled with joy,
The ox-headed prison guards all welcomed her!
One moment she heard people singing and chanting,
The next moment she heard the sounds of music.
"I've no clue as to the reason for all of this!"
So she asked the youth and the maiden: "What's going on?"

The youth and the maiden bowed and promptly replied:
"Your Highness, please listen to what we have to say.
The singing and chanting are from ghosts escaping their pain
And going off to heaven, to roam in freedom and in joy.
In front of us you see the throne hall of King Yama,
It's in King Yama's hall that the music is being played."
When the princess heard this, her heart was filled with joy,
And she straightway entered into the Yiyang Hall.

The princess and the consorts of the Ten Kings enjoyed themselves in the hells. That is because all the *yakṣas* had been turned into immortal lads and jade maidens, and all earth-prisons had become the saintly realms of the halls of heaven. The Ten Kings were greatly pleased and invited her to stay so they might venerate her and provide for her. They would properly purify a ritual area, arrange for a Dharma-throne, listen to the sutras and accept the precepts, in order to be freed from the hells. The princess agreed to their request, and ascended the precious throne. She instructed the multitude of ghosts to all approach the Dharma-altar, cleanse and purify themselves of the three karmas, and listen to and accept the five precepts.[20] "Once you have accepted the five precepts, you will forever be disciples of the Buddha. If you are able to keep to the fast for a single day,[21] it is better than accumulating three ounces of yellow gold, as later you will receive one full year of pure blessings. And if you in turn can persuade other people to recite the name of the Buddha, then that is better than building a seven-story precious pagoda. And after your human life has come to an end, Amitābha will personally come to lead you to his land of Ultimate Bliss, where you realize No-being and generate forbearance. This is my advice to you all, rulers of the shade: When will your rule over the Realm of Shade come to an end? When will you be done with your impartial verdicts? From the universal Dharma originates the thought of self and other. When one's enlightenment is fully complete, one achieves the unsurpassable Way." When the kings heard her words on the Dharma, they issued an order to all their offices to release all the ghostly criminals so they might come and listen to the Dharma.

One moment seated in the lotus position in King Yama's hall,
The next moment standing all alone atop Mt. Sumeru's peak.

Namo Guanshiyin pusa

At the moment the princess ascended the Dharma-throne,
Those who accepted the precepts were reborn in heaven.
The princess had not yet finished preaching the Dharma,
When the drum in front of the hall was sounded repeatedly.
The infernal judges in charge of cases all came to report,
After eight bows to the kings they submitted their views:
"Since the moment the princess ascended the Dharma-throne,
She saved each and every sinner in all of our hells.
The new ghosts who are brought in are all released,
Good and evil is discarded, without any distinction!
If you keep the princess here so she will stay forever,
We might as well close the three paths and earth-prisons!"[22]

When the princess had ascended the Dharma-throne and preached the Dharma in the realm of the hells, her audience wanted only to hear more, but suddenly the great ministers of the three pathways and the officials of the eighteen prisons ascended the hall of darkness and reported to the Ten Kings: "Ever since the princess has arrived here, this place is not the Realm of Shade anymore! All our instruments of torture have been turned into lotus flowers, and all the sinful ghosts have been released to be reborn in heaven. Since ancient times it has been the rule that if you have heavenly halls, you also have earth-prisons. The retribution of good and evil brilliantly accords with principle. Who would want to practice goodness if there were no earth-prisons? Your servants dare not refrain from reporting. We implore Your Royal Highnesses to see the princess off so she may quickly return to life." King Yama agreed to their proposal, and promptly issued an edict, in which he notified all of the offices to send the third princess off, so that she might return to the world of men.

King Yama had only to nod and she secretly grasped his intention,
As soon as the *yakṣas* started to speak, she caught their meaning.

Namo Guanshiyin pusa

When King Yama heard this, his face showed his pleasure,
He ordered a notification to be sent out as fast as a cloud:

The infernal judges of all the offices should promptly come
To the Hall of Darkness and listen to what he had to say.
King Yama immediately addressed them as follows:
"Infernal judges and ghostly clerks, please listen to me.
The daughter of Marvelous Splendor in the world of light,
Whose name is Marvelous Goodness, is no mere mortal.
She pronounced a vow to come and visit the Underworld
And save each and every sinner on the three pathways.
But the officials of the eighteen prisons all petitioned
Not to allow the princess to stay here in deep darkness.
The princess has been here for three times seven days,
And I have not the faintest idea where her body may be.
The only reason I have summoned you is to ask you
To help the princess return to the land of the living."

King Yama said: "The only reason I have summoned you is that I want to inspect the ledgers of birth and death." The clerks quickly handed him the documents. The king looked them over one by one, and he indeed found the name and surname of the princess listed in the ledgers, stating that at the age of nineteen she was slated to visit and tour the Underworld. He ordered his ghostly underlings in the front hall to bring in a sedan chair so that the princess could depart. The consorts of the kings saw the princess off as far as the bridge across the Alas River, and when the underlings had taken her to the place where her corpse lay, they all returned to their palaces.

The endless floating clouds are all swept away by the storm,
The one circle of bright moon illuminates the whole cosmos.

Namo Guanshiyin pusa

Now we've recounted the visit by the princess to the Underworld,
We'll expound the circumstances of how she was resurrected.
King Yama's edict ordered that a sedan chair be readied,
And together with an entourage, she set out on her journey.
Banners and flags and precious parasols led the way in front,
And royal consorts and royal concubines all followed behind.
Horse-faced and ox-headed demons together saw her off;
And *yakṣas* and prison guards greeted her in a double file.

When they had accompanied her to the south bank of the Alas,
They took their leave of the princess with a bow and returned.
Because the princess was about to return to the realm of light,
The immortal youth and immortal maiden returned to darkness.

After the princess had crossed the golden bridge [across the Alas River], she traveled on along her way. Suddenly the hundred birds started to sing, and she saw a huge bright red gate, rooted in the earth and rising up to heaven. The locked doors opened all by themselves, booming like the thunder, and that very moment her soul and spirit returned to her body, and she felt as if she were being flung down from heaven! At that very moment, the string around her neck snapped and broke, and she woke up as from a dream. Only then did she realize that she was lying in a wood, but despite much scrutinizing she could not figure out where she was. Her heart was filled with fear, and her mind was flustered. Sad tears choked her voice. Piteously she wept, and her tears were like pearls.

To come back to life from death is something quite extraordinary,
If that secret miracle would bring you back, it would be even better![23]

Namo Guanshiyin pusa

Let's not talk about the Underworld or the Realm of Shade,
Let's rather recount how the princess returned to life again.
The princess found herself lying under the trees of a forest,
Whether turning around or walking about, her bones all hurt.
When she lifted her head and strained her eyes to look around,
She saw from afar the imperial palace and the imperial capital.
"I made a vow that I wanted to escape from the three worlds,
How could I have imagined that today I would return to life?
I broke the law and committed a crime, and was happy to die,
So now, may I ask, where am I supposed to go and settle down?
There's no mountain here where I can live, practicing the Way;
There's no forest here where I can hide away the rest of my days."
The Metal Star of the Great White saw her predicament and,[24]
Flying with the speed of an arrow, came down to the mortal realm.
While in the clouds of the ninth heaven, he transformed his shape,
And so he turned himself into an old man of the human world.

On his head he wore the Daoist headgear of the freely
roaming,
And his body was wrapped in the black gauze gown of a priest.
In his hand he grasped a staff that was taller than his person,
And to his chest he held the *Sutra of Countless Ways*.[25]
With folded hands he stepped forward and addressed her:
"Young lady, what is the cause that brought you here?"
The princess immediately answered him as follows:
"Dear Daoist priest, please listen to what I have to say!"

The princess had come back to life and, breathing heavily with a rasping sound, was looking all around her. When she espied the capital city and the imperial palaces of her father, the emperor, it was like frost had been added to snow, and sufferings doubled by suffering! She deplored that heaven was too distant and earth too narrow, and she thought about the fact she had no place to settle down. Her heart was depressed and filled with despair; she was afflicted and flustered. Her voice was choked, she was overcome by sorrow, her tears streamed down. When she went on ahead, she saw a mountain that was square and broad, level and right. But as she was about to ascend the mountain, she suddenly saw an elderly man standing by the side of a rock who called out to her: "Young lady, why did you come here?" The princess replied: "I want to build a hermitage here in which to cultivate the Way for the rest of my life." The priest said: "Marvelous! Marvelous! If you come to live here on this mountain, you and I will always be together. Whether standing or walking, sitting or resting, we will share our breath and intertwine our limbs. This is a joy that has arrived by itself without being sought! Heaven created in us a fine couple! You and I will become man and wife, a match of yin and yang, and practice cultivation together till we die. Won't that be a joy?!" When the princess heard these words, she promptly replied: "Dear priest, your words do not accord with principle! How can you say such things! Men and women live separate lives; plants and trees don't come in couples. If when cultivating oneself, one does not cut off love and affections, and has not eliminated the lustful heart, then even if you achieve enlightenment it will be a lustful enlightenment, and even after a million *kalpas*, you would still not achieve buddhahood!" The priest then smiled and said: "I am not a mortal, I am Indra from highest heaven. I saw you were coming here to practice cultivation. But this place houses an evil dragon, whose body is huge and whose stench is unbearable: whether coming or going he terrifies people. This is not a place to practice cultivation. But I will direct you to a blessed place. There is a mountain, in this very country, in Pure Heart county of Huizhou prefecture, that is called Incense Mountain. It is a place that has from past to present sheltered immortals. To the left side one hears the roar of the lion, and to the right, one hears the trumpeting of the elephant-king.[26] On Sandalwood Peak all you can see are sandalwood trees, and the Purple Bamboo Grove is filled with purple bamboo. Your Highness couldn't go wrong by settling there to nurture the Way." When the princess heard this, she made a deep bow, and asked him about the details.

Traveling alone and walking alone, without any restrictions—
When you can be relaxed and at ease, you had better be so!

Namo Guanshiyin pusa

"I am grateful to you, Lord Indra, for personally coming down,
And for manifesting yourself in this lower world of mortals.
If truly there is such a place on a famous mountain,
I'd like to hear everything about it, all in great detail!"
    The Daoist priest folded his hands and replied as follows:
"Golden branch and jade leaf, please listen to these facts.
The prefecture is called Huizhou, the county is Pure Heart.
The mountain, called Incense Mountain, is world-renowned!
    Beneath its idle white clouds, it is fit for famous immortals,
In its Hundred Flowers Forest, not a speck of dust is found.
Ordinary folk there are especially capable of goodness,
You won't find even half of a single evil person there!
    No one picks up the gold and jewels lost by others in the street,
Great Peace reigns, gates remain unlocked both day and night.
No freezing cold, no stifling heat: the weather is always the same,
There are flowers, there are fruits: a springtime that lasts forever!
    I implore you, Your Highness, to achieve the right fruit, and
Ferry across the living beings on the roads of the three worlds!"
When the princess heard this, she was filled with joy,
And she set out on her journey, traveling day and night.

When the princess heard this, her heart-ground became clear, so she asked the priest again: "How long is the journey to that place?" The priest replied: "It is not that far, a mere three thousand and some miles." The princess said: "Those three thousand miles are a minor matter, but I can hardly walk for the hunger in my belly. I am afraid that my strength will be insufficient, and that I will not make much progress." The priest replied: "I've got some pills that will enable you to live forever without food; you should take one." The princess said: "I only want to achieve the Way, I do not seek to live forever." From the sleeve of his gown the priest took a peach of immortality, as big as a golden gourd, and he gave this to the princess. "This peach is not a peach from the mortal world, it is a peach from the Garden of Joy in the world above. The one who eats it will not suffer hunger throughout the four seasons and not know thirst for a full year. When traveling, your body will be light, and you also will not feel freezing cold or stifling heat." The princess thanked him with a bow, and each went their own way.

The blue heaven is clear and bright, not obstructed by any clouds,
The pure breeze is limpid and lucid, the light of the moon is new.

Namo Guanshiyin pusa

The priest, returning to the palace, heading for its golden gates,
Took his leave of the princess and went to the courts of heaven.
Slowly he rose into the sky as he was borne aloft by the clouds,
And then eventually the princess also set out on her journey.
    Traveling alone, walking alone, without a human companion,
She covered one stretch of the road to find there was yet another.
She found it very hard to walk on her three-inch arched shoes,[27]
As climbing hills and fording rivers she traveled on alone.
    "During the day the golden crow is my only companion,
And during the night only the jade hare keeps me company.
When I look up and ahead, the road before me is so long,
When I turn around to look back, there's no one behind me."
    As she traveled on, stretch after stretch, she suffered greatly,
Calluses formed on the soles of her feet, her heart was pained.
The Great Lord the Jade Emperor saw her with his own eyes,
And immediately he issued an order that went to the Thunder.
    First he dispatched the inspector-general of the nine heavens,

And next he ordered the god of the earth of Incense Mountain
To transform himself into a brightly hued, motley-striped tiger
And leave the forest, shaking his head and whipping his tail.

The Jade Emperor of highest heaven ordered the god of the earth of Incense Mountain and the inspector-general of the nine heavens to help and assist the princess reach her destination. At this moment the princess was exhausted from the sufferings of the journey. Just as she was about to sit down at the foot of a mountain, she suddenly saw a fierce beast that with its bulging eyes and earth-shaking roar terrified heaven and earth. When she looked more closely, it turned out to be a tiger! So the princess walked up to it and said: "I am an unfilial girl. I went down into the Underworld, but then came back to life again. Now I want to go to Incense Mountain to live in seclusion and cultivate the Way. But alas, my karmic fortune is so shallow and limited that not everything I do turns out as I would wish. Now that I have run into you, I will relieve your hunger with my body, and allow you to eat your fill." When the tiger heard her, it crouched down on its haunches like a gibbon and spoke with a human voice: "I am the god of the earth of Incense Mountain. I have received an order from the High Emperor, dispatching me to guard and protect Your Highness. You don't have to be afraid. I am yours to ride." When the princess heard this, she thanked Heaven with a bow, and mounted the tiger's back. She closed her eyes for a moment, and before she knew it had arrived at Incense Mountain! In a grotto in a steep cliff she saw thousands of tigers gnawing through trees and carrying stones in order to build walls all around. The god of the mountain and the god of the earth protected and guarded her on all sides. Gibbons and monkeys offered her fruits, and the hundred birds brought her flowers. Dragons and elephants served as her entourage, and gods and ghosts served her reverentially. Here there was no division between the human realm and the heavenly realm, and she could meet with denizens of both. From this moment on, the princess was unencumbered and free of delusion. Adapting to her surroundings, her heart was empty, and she achieved the initial stage of enlightenment. Truly, the green pines covered in dew were all Absolute Truth, the moon among the white clouds was nothing but *prajñā*;[28] the persons she was in contact with were all buddhas and bodhisattvas, and the people she sought guidance from were all arhats and holy monks. And in this way, as the crow kept flying and the hare running, before she knew it, nine years had passed.

Freed from the illusory shell she so lived in Absolute Truth,
Only now aware she would not pass through birth and death.

Namo Guanshiyin pusa

The princess lived in lofty seclusion on Incense Mountain,
The spring scene inside her grotto was not of this world.
Everywhere the plants and trees welcomed her with flowers,
All the mountains and rocks greeted her with their fragrance.
The numberless precept-gods guarded her at all times,
Devas, dragons, and other divinities served as her entourage,
Immortals lads and maidens descended from the heavens,
Coming down on clouds they offered flowers and fruits.
The six buddhas of the six directions were her relatives,
And the thousands of saints and sages were her neighbors.
Bodhisattvas and holy monks were her constant companions,
Roaming like a cloud throughout the world they would meet.
Flowers bloomed and willows turned green: nine years passed,
All ten directions heard of the fame of her style in the Way.
"I've had no news at all from White Sparrow Convent—
I've no idea whether I will ever meet with them again!"

When the princess first ascended Incense Mountain, she practiced quiet-sitting in her rock chamber. Undefiled by a single speck of dust, she entered deeply into the trance of meditation. She did not rely on the sages and she did not betray her sunlike spirit. She did not make any discrimination on the basis of saintly and mortal passion-realms, and she did not feel any love or hatred on the basis of the defined domains of good and evil. She simply discarded all emotions and silently probed and searched. She silently attained and abided in her original nature as the source. In this way her whole body became light and at ease, and the demon of sleep could not possess her. She happened to hear the cry of the gibbon resound through the valley, and her divine understanding was cleansed of delusion, and suddenly she was completely liberated, as if she had forgotten both heart and phenomena. Her name became Contemplating the Cries of the World. Only then did she understand that there is a nonphenomenal body in the phenomenal body: when the turning light shines on itself, one achieves full enlightenment. The princess said: "How could I have achieved the right fruit today if it had not been for the White Sparrow Convent?" As soon as this thought formed in her mind, Heaven and Earth were informed.

If I had not then visited that place in person,
This *ulumbara* flower would still be buried.

Namo Guanshiyin pusa

As soon as this thought formed in the princess's mind,
The god of the earth of White Sparrow was also informed:
"Marvelous Splendor harbored most evil intentions,
Committing arson, he burned this convent to the ground."
The protective deity rose on a cloud to the upper world,
Before the third heaven's gate he submitted his brief:
"I come to report about the doings of Marvelous Splendor,
So I prostrate myself and kowtow in order to report."
As the High Emperor listened to the official's report,
Adjusting his crown and grasping his belt, he laughed.[29]
He then dispatched the heavenly agents on duty that day
To transmit his order throughout the whole wide world.
The High Lord the Jade Emperor addressed his court:
"All you True Rulers, who fill the heavens, please listen.
In the mortal world lives a certain king of Raised Forest,
Who, inexplicably raving mad and completely insane,
Defames the Buddha, destroys the Dharma, kills nuns:
As an inquiry is called for, I have summoned the gods."
The thirty-three heavenly gods all exploded with rage, and
Not a single one of them was willing to show any mercy!

The Jade Emperor summoned by his command all the gods of the nine heavens to deliberate: "The Marvelous Splendor emperor, bereft of the Way, eliminates the Three Jewels! This crime cannot lightly be pardoned. So I dispatch the disease-spreading agents of the Ministry of Epidemics to give a disease to the Marvelous Splendor emperor. He will suffer from the *kāmalā*-illness.[30] Interrupting his blessings, he will suffer retribution in this very life!" When the

Ministry of Epidemics had received this order, it didn't dare tarry or linger. On horses of storm and in carriages of clouds [its agents] straightway went to the world of men. Truly, good fortune follows from the blessings of goodness; disaster strikes because of accumulated evil. The net of heaven is wide, so wide: retribution and response are extremely quick.

Good and evil eventually are all repaid in the end,
The only issue is whether it happens sooner or later.

Namo Guanshiyin pusa

The High Lord of bright heaven listened to the report he gave,
Then together the six heavenly ministries deliberated over it:
"This detestable Marvelous Splendor is bereft of all reason,
He burns a convent to ashes, annihilates the Three Jewels!
　　During his life he will be punished by the *kāmalā*-disease,
Upon his death he'll fall forever into the iron-wall prison.
Grab that Marvelous Splendor, give him three hundred lashes,
Beat him all over his body, and show him no mercy at all!
　　First inflict him with racking pain and burning fevers,
And then swathe his entire body with this evil illness."
They quickly dispatched the Five Epidemics to go down,
As soon as they got the order, they hastened like clouds.
　　Riding on clouds they came down to bring this disease
To the still unsuspecting emperor of Raised Forest.
Right this moment the emperor ascended the throne hall,
When the epidemic-gods saw him, they said to each other:
　　"This Marvelous Splendor cuts quite an exceptional figure,
Awe inspiring, imposing and tall, as mighty as a dragon!"
But before the fading moon and stars had hid their light,
All of this suddenly changed as disease racked his body.
　　Despite his illness, every day he ascended the throne hall,
Terrifying all his civil and military officials and officers:
The skin and flesh all over his body rotted and fell off,
And an unbearable stench spread through the palace!
　　From ancient times such a disease had never been seen,
With every remedy applied, the illness only worsened.
It was then that the epidemic-gods returned to heaven, as
The emperor's body was forever swathed in suffering.

When the Marvelous Splendor emperor first became ill, his body suffered from cold shivering and hot fever, and his head and eyes felt drowsy and heavy, while all his bones were racked by pain. Later his skin began to burn and itch, and then it cracked and broke open all over his body. Pus and blood oozed out, and the stench penetrated far and wide, filling the whole palace with fear and causing everyone to puke and vomit. The imperial concubines and pretty maids all excused themselves and refused to wait on [the emperor], and the princesses and the princes consort covered their nose and kept their distance, afraid to either look at him or approach him. Truly, you consult the oracles and pray to the gods, but the gods don't respond; you offer sacrifice and take medicine, but the medicine doesn't work. The empress was the only one who did not budge from his bedside, but all her efforts were useless.

Despite his illness the emperor each day ascended the throne hall. Soon his whole body was rotten through and through. Within one month his hands were balled up in fists, his feet were curled back, and his entire head was covered with sores. The hair on his brows and at his temples had all fallen out, while maggots crawled in his skin and flesh. Cramps and pains racked his body. His ears were blocked, his nose had collapsed, his eyes bulged out, and his teeth had rotted away. His gums were exposed and his tongue was swollen, and his fingers had dropped off at the joints. His Great Peace crown was covered with green flies, and his dragon robe was streaked with gore. His precious tablet and jade belt were dyed with pus, and his cloud-topped boots were smeared with blood. The imperial body was visibly wasting away, and his disease was becoming ever more serious. When he itched, he itched to the marrow of his bones, and when he felt pain, the pain wrenched his liver and gut. From this moment on he did not take pleasure in anything. His gold and silver and precious stones were now as disgusting to him as [the walls of a] a prison, and tender lamb and fine wine were now as disgusting to him as mud and shit. The dragon robes of embroidered brocade were now as disgusting to him as fetters and chains, and all the various sorts of instrumental music were as disgusting to him as crying and weeping. His ivory-inlaid dragon couch was as disgusting to him as knives and swords, and the concubines and pretty maids were as disgusting to him as vipers and tigers. Each day and each night lasted longer than a thousand years. Frantic and frenzied, he wept and wailed, disturbing heaven and earth. Pus and blood streamed from his eyes, ears, nose, and mouth. Moving or turning around was nearly impossible, and the pain was unbearable. Only then was he no longer able to ascend the throne hall. "I've no idea what karmic cause from a former life has made me suffer this discomfort, but when I observe the symptoms, there is truly cause for worry and fear."

The emperor then ordered that a placard be posted, calling on all the famous physicians of the whole world, and stating that whoever could cure him of this disease would be allowed to choose his own promotion or reward. When, with her Buddha-eye, the princess on Incense Mountain saw this, she discarded her illusory shell and, manifesting her true Dharma-body, emerged riding on a cloud from her heavenly grotto. Contemplating the cries of the world, she has only to hear a word to save those who suffer!

It was by his own actions that he caused this affliction—
But few repay a favor shown, more will betray a favor.

Namo Guanshiyin pusa

The emperor had a placard posted by the side of the gate,
And at Incense Mountain the princess learned about it.
She discarded her illusory body and then transformed
Herself into an old beggar-monk from the world of men.
On his head this monk wore an old torn monk's hat,
And his body was wrapped in a threadbare cassock.
His face was covered by sores—a scary sight!
With bundle and staff he emerged from the forest.
In the wink of an eye he arrived in the capital city,
Tore off the golden placard, and then explained why:
"This old monk can cure the Son of Heaven's disease,
Without any medicine the disease will be eradicated!"
The soldiers guarding the gate collapsed in laughter:
"What a laugh, you crazy monk! You're afflicted yourself!
Your face is covered with sores you cannot control,
Why don't you cure yourself if you have the herbs?
Of the millions of well-known physicians of the world
We've already done away with countless famous names!
By your looks you are not some wonder-working wizard,
And yet you have the incredible gall to enter this gate!

Now be so kind as to hang up that placard nicely again,
Unless you want to lose your life and visit the Lord of Shade.
Our firm orders, the law of the land, make no distinction:
We don't care whether you are a layperson or a monk!"
The monk approached them and spoke as follows:
"Dear gentlemen, please be so kind as to hear me out.
Humans suffer from four hundred and four diseases,
And each and every one of these diseases has its root.
With a prescription but lacking the herbs there's no cure,
Without a prescription but having the herbs there's hope.
If I, this poor monk, really did not possess the herbs,
How would I dare enter the great gate of the court?
A precious pearl in a linen sack is often ignored,
A brocade bag stuffed with chaff fools the crowd.
Let's stick to the present, and forget about the past—
Please announce this old monk to your saintly ruler!"

The soldiers guarding the gate had a good laugh and said: "This crazy monk has no idea what he is crashing into! You're a guy who has no idea of life and death! The court and the state are not to be trifled with by the likes of you!" Before they had finished saying this, someone shouted: "Reverend, come here! The ancients said: 'A monk should respect the Buddha.' Let me explain things to you. God knows how many learned scholars of the Imperial Secretariat and renowned physicians have been unable to cure the emperor. It's just too laughable! How could you save someone else when you cannot even control the rotten sores on your face? You must be some rascal monk! It's obvious that you come here to seek your death. Now hang that golden placard up again, and then quickly make yourself scarce. If you tarry and the officers arrest you, your life will not be spared!" The monk said with a smile: "My dear gentlemen, why do you try to bully me? I left the householder's life at an early age, and I have traveled though seventy-two countries. Whether it is evil diseases that affect the body, or corpses and skeletons—without using even a single dose of a miracle cure, I remove the root of the disease and bring the skeleton back to life. Irrespective of how many diseases our father the emperor is afflicted by, they all have their causes. Don't ridicule me for the sores on my face; I know the prescription but lack the herbs. As for the disease of our lord and emperor, I have the herbs but need no prescription." The officer on duty that day said: "This monk speaks quite convincingly." As quickly as a shooting star, he announced the monk's arrival and presented him to the emperor.

Flowing over rocks, the river cools down the atmosphere,
Passing through flowers, the breeze brings their fragrance.

Namo Guanshiyin pusa

The officer on duty that day went inside the palace,
And reported to His Majesty in the Golden Bells Hall.
With eight bows he kowtowed, wished him a myriad of years,
Then in plain language said: "I report to Your Majesty
    That some meditation master has arrived from abroad,
At a full sixteen feet tall, he is not your ordinary guy.
On his shoulder he carries a gold and tin staff with six rings,
And his body is wrapped in the robe of a Buddhist monk.
    His mouth mumbles Sanskrit sounds no one understands,
And his hands finger a hundred kinds of *maṇi*-pearls.
From his staff hang a bundle of herbs and a calabash,
Their fragrance bombards your nose, fills the whole town!
    His head and face are covered with sores of some kind,
But his friendly words and good talk make perfect sense.
He says he can cure every manner and kind of disease,
For he's roamed the rivers and lakes and met with experts.
    In foreign countries too, he's sought the advice of sages.
And now he's removed the placard and entered the court.
As he doesn't dare ascend the hall without authorization,
I have first reported this so that Your Majesty is informed."
    Hearing this, the emperor showed his joy on his face,
Lifting his fists,[31] he bowed slightly to thank his officials:
"This is most likely some saintly monk come to save Us!
With some appointment or a reward—I won't forget his favor!"

The commander on duty then asked the emperor for his decision, and brought the monk into the court. As soon as the emperor saw him, he was filled with joy, and he asked the monk: "Where did you receive your training?" The monk replied: "I received my training in the country of Joy."[32] "How many years have you practiced the Way?" "It has been only nine years since I entered the monastic order." "Who is your teacher?" "My teacher is Siddhartha."[33] "And what is your name?' "My name is Potalaka." "From whom have you learned your medical skills?" "I have met with the Medicine King and the Medicine Chief."[34] The emperor also asked: "Can the disease with which We are afflicted be cured?" "I can cure it, but I will have to feel your pulse in order to diagnose the disease and effect the cure." The emperor promptly presented him with a decorated stool, and the monk took a seat. After some time, he said: "Now that I have felt the pulse I can assure you that there is no need for any worry."

When the four diseases leave the flesh, the three bodies become manifest,
Once the heart-flower opens and expands, the myriad dharmas are clear.

Namo Guanshiyin pusa

Please realize that joy and suffering share the same body,
Good luck and disaster always depend on the person himself.
When the emperor heard the report, his face showed his joy,
And he had a lavish banquet laid out to regale the monk.
"If you can cure Our body, so We will be healthy and hale,
A gold and silver jade begging-bowl will express Our thanks."
The monk made a slight bow and then promptly replied:
"First I will have to feel the pulse so as to know the cause."
The emperor stretched out his arm for the monk to feel:
And the latter saw that the symptoms were truly quite serious.
"If Your Majesty wants his dragon-body to recover its health,
Three marvelous medicines can fully eliminate the disease."
When the emperor heard this, his heart was filled with joy:
"Dear eminent monk, please tell me quickly so I may know!"
The monk immediately replied in the following manner:
"Your Majesty, please be so kind as to listen to my words.
Since ancient times, medicines have cured nonfatal diseases,
From the start, the Buddha has delivered those with the karma.
This medicine cannot be bought on any street or market,
And no pharmacy in the world has ever heard about it.

All you need is the arm and eye of one without anger:[35]
Mix them into a magic pill, and the disease will be gone!"
When the emperor heard this, his face exploded in rage,
And his shouted curses roared like thunder for all to hear.
"Even if I would offer a million pounds of yellow gold,
Who'd be willing to slice off a part of their body with a knife?
However much that body part might hurt, they'd still cherish it—
And trees and rocks are the only ones that do not feel anger!"
He ordered his guards to grab the monk and, once beheaded,
To pulverize his body out on the street as a warning to others!
"With his witchlike words he stirs up delusion. Unpardonable!
Deceiving the ruler he betrays the state—a most serious crime!"

When the emperor heard this, his face turned the color of iron, his eyes were like arrows of fire, his breath resembled a misty cloud, and his shouted curses were like thunder. "Take that crazy monk and the officer who introduced him and have them both sliced according to the rule. From ancient times till the present, even the most afflicted person, whose body is blanketed with a hundred diseases, who lacks the clothes to cover his body and the food to fill his belly, and who collapses on the street, a low-caste beggar, even such a person still loves and cherishes his body and his life. If you would ask him whether he would be willing to donate his arms and eyes, wouldn't he be filled with anger and hatred?" The monk smiled and replied: "May Your Majesty calm down a little—in all affairs practice patience! I, this monk, have received the full set of precepts, and imitating the ancient Buddha, I engage in preaching. Every single word and every half sentence has its source and origin. How would I dare announce this at court if such a person did not exist!" The emperor asked: "In which prefecture and county is this person to be found? What is his name and surname? We will personally summon him and ask him right here in this hall whether he would be willing to donate his arms and eyes. But what will We do if that person is not willing?" The monk smiled and said: "Don't think it will be a person without arms and eyes that will appear before the Son of Heaven!"

As soon as you have the power to turn yourself around,
Each and every issue and problem will then solve itself.

Namo Guanshiyin pusa

The rustic monk bowed slightly and promptly replied:
"Your Majesty, calm your rage and listen to my reasons.
At present such a person without anger may be found—
Living in seclusion on Incense Mountain now for some years,
    This person practices forbearance, without anger or hatred
And is always filled with joy, never showing any anger."
When the emperor heard this, his face showed his joy,
And lifting his fists, he bowed slightly to thank the monk.
    "As long as Our body becomes hale and healthy again,
We will repay you for your favor in this golden hall.
What is the distance from here to Incense Mountain?
And what kind of treasure should I give to this person?"
    The monk bowed slightly, and then promptly replied:
"This person cares only for cultivation, and not for gold.
All you have to bring is a single box made of sandalwood,
And pray to the immortal there in front of the hermitage."

The emperor said: "I still can't completely believe that there is such a person to be found." And he ordered officers of his bodyguard to bring that person to the palace. When the members of the guards heard the emperor's decision, they asked the monk: "How far is this Incense Mountain from here?" The monk replied: "From here to Incense Mountain is about three thousand miles. But you don't need any post-horses: you'll arrive there as soon as you set out on the journey. The place is called Transparent Heart county in Huizhou, and the mountain is called Incense Mountain. There's an immortal who lives on that mountain, whose heart is as unshakable as iron or rock, and who has no desire for the gold and silver of this world. With no craving for fame or profit, this person has forever broken with the world of dust, and can donate his illusory body as easily as taking off some dirty clothes. I implore Your Majesty to dispatch an official, who should take with him a single imperial edict and a single box of fine incense. If he goes there and prays to him, that immortal will be only too happy to make the donation." When the emperor heard this, he was filled with joy, and immediately dispatched Liu Qin to go there as quickly as a shooting star!

Be willing to believe a grafted tree can produce flowers!
Too many smart and intelligent people never reach home.

Namo Guanshiyin pusa

The emperor dispatched Liu Qin with these instructions:
"We are afflicted by a disease of the most serious nature.
Fortunately a monk has arrived who promises to save Us
With a rare and marvelous medicine that can be found.
    All he needs are the arms and eyes of one without anger
That will be mixed into a magic pill that will save Our life.
So you have to go on Our behalf to Incense Mountain,
And simply ask for the arms and eyes of that immortal."
    When Liu Qin received this order, he was all hurry,
He didn't dare excuse himself for reason of hardship.
Kowtowing, he left the court as fast as a shooting star,
Raised his whip, mounted his horse, set out on the trek.
    Let's not say more of all his adventures while on the road,
Let's talk about Incense Mountain's Purple Bamboo Grove.
    On the mountain, flowers were blooming like brocade,
While *kalaviṅkas* and parrots vied in beautiful songs.[36]
Here thousands of saints and sages often came together
For the sole purpose of discussing the mystic teachings.
    Liu Qin straightway entered the hermitage, where the
Immortal was seated motionless in the lotus position.
When Liu Qin saw the person there, he was filled with joy,
And dressed in his court robes, he burned his incense.
    Kneeling down on one knee, he loudly proclaimed the edict:
"Great Immortal, please be so kind as to lend Us your ear.

"The emperor's edict: 'We have learned, Great Immortal, that you have long lived in seclusion in this hidden valley. Your style in the Way is lofty and transcendent, and your fame has spread throughout the entire cosmos. *Devas* and humans reverentially look up to you, and mortals and sages all seek your advice. With kind compassion you care for all kinds of living beings, loving them as if they were newborn infants. It has been forty-five years since We, this diseased lord, established the great state of Raised Forest. All-under-heaven has been at peace, and We have shared our joys with the people. But for some unknown karmic cause, We were suddenly afflicted by a disease. All the prescriptions that have been tried out have proved to be ineffective. Now We have encountered a monk who can concoct a medicine in which he needs to mix the arms and eyes of a person without anger in order to render it effective.

We implore you, Great Immortal, to kindly make this donation. If We recover from this illness, We will not forget to repay your favor.' Such is the edict."

To gouge out, to cut off—just like the autumn wind does when it arrives:
It doesn't intend to make people shiver, people shiver of their own accord.

Namo Guanshiyin pusa

Liu Qin opened and proclaimed the imperial edict,
Raising it with both hands up to the crown of his head:
"We implore you, Immortal, to show your compassion,
And give Our servant the magic pill to bring back."
Hearing this, the face of the Immortal showed joy:
"The emperor should not worry about the disease, as
For five hundred generations, I've practiced forbearance,
Not feeling any hatred or grudge, and not feeling anger.
Please feel free, dear general, to cut off what you need,
As my only wish is that our lord and emperor be cured."
Liu Qin kowtowed, and then promptly proceeded to act,
Drawing from his scabbard a shining, silver-white blade.

Hearing these words, the immortal promptly agreed: "I offer my left eye and arm to our lord and emperor." Now that Liu Qin had received permission, he could not but apply the knife. At first, fresh blood spurted in all directions, but then it was just like paring off a piece of sandalwood, each and every inch fragrant. He placed the arm and the eye in a golden box and, after thanking the immortal with a bow, straightway returned to the capital.

The fame and value of this feat is not at all small,
Who is there to compare in all of the golden halls?

Namo Guanshiyin pusa

Once Liu Qin had obtained the immortal's medicine,
He promptly returned to the capital in just a few days.
After arriving, he went straight to the imperial palace,
When the emperor saw him, he asked how things went.

Liu Qin made a slight bow and then promptly reported:
"Your Majesty, please be so kind as to listen to my words.
Your servant obtained the medicine from the immortal,
Who indeed was filled with joy and did not feel anger."
The monk was immediately asked to mix the medicine,
Which was promptly prepared and presented to the king.
The emperor used the medicine and after a single night,
One half of his body was cured, the other still afflicted.
His left side was completely healed, as in days before,
But his right side still suffered—not even one whit less!
The emperor asked the eminent monk the question:
"Why is my affliction not yet fully done away with?"
The rustic monk immediately replied as follows:
"This is not at all due to lack of sincerity on my part!
The arm and eye of a single side cure only one side,
The arms and eyes of both sides cure the whole body.
If Your Majesty wants his whole body to be cured,
The only thing to do is go and ask the immortal again!"
When the emperor heard this, his face showed his joy,
And he promptly issued an order summoning Liu Qin.
When Liu Qin again had received the imperial order,
He took his leave with a bow and went out the gate.
His fast steed seemed to fly as he set out on his journey,
Not shirking the hardship of high hills and long roads.
Eventually he arrived once again at Incense Mountain,
That holy realm of divine immortals and eternal spring.
When he approached it and spied it through the forest,
Liu Qin was overcome by divine joy at first sight.
He dismounted from his horse, entered the hermitage,
And brightly burned incense sticks to express devotion.
Bowing eight times, he kowtowed and, unrolling the edict,
In a loud voice proclaimed it to the immortal:

"An imperial edict: 'Great Immortal, You have been so kind to Us as to cheerfully donate the arm and eye of your left side, and Our disease has also been cured on the left side. But the disease on the right side has not diminished a whit. At this time, well aware of Our crime, We cannot but implore you to again to show your great kindness and great compassion. If We are cured from this disease, We will everywhere establish monasteries, and every family will set up an image that is faithful [to your appearance]. We will venerate none but the Great Dharma so that it will spread throughout the world. This country as well as other states will make annual offerings of incense and candles, and each year will present flowers and fruits. We implore you, Great Immortal, to cheerfully make this great donation!' Such is the edict."

If there is a river, it can reflect the moon on an autumn night;
If there is no mountain, it can't be wrapped in evening clouds.

Namo Guanshiyin pusa

As soon as Liu Qin had finished proclaiming the edict,
He made eight bows before the immortal and prayed:
"May you in your kind compassion take pity on him,
Our emperor will not forget the favors you show him!"
Hearing this, the immortal only smiled and said:
"Dear general, there is no need for your mumblings,
I would not object to donating my entire body and life:
My only wish is that our emperor be cured of his illness."

The immortal said: "I will offer the arm and eye of my right side to our lord and king, so the evil disease that afflicts his body may quickly disappear. I pray that the emperor's body may become like the medicine tree that cannot be invaded by any disease, and that he may rule the mountains and rivers eternally, and that he may live forever and never grow old!" Now that Liu Qin had received permission, he could not but apply the knife. After wrapping up the arm and eye and storing them away in a brocade bundle, he returned with the momentum of a cloud.

Forgetting both quiescence and illumination, observing the undeluded mind;
Returning to the root and going back to the source, one achieves realization.

Namo Guanshiyin pusa

As soon as Liu Qin had obtained the immortal's medicine,
He kowtowed, bowed a hundred times, and left the convent.
Cracking his whip he got on his horse—like a flying arrow,
Up the mountains, down the ridges—like a speeding dragon!

We will not talk of the wind and frost while on the road—
From afar he observed the capital city as he drew closer.
His horse was exhausted, he was tired out, and it was late,
So for the time being he took his rest at the post station.
Sitting up, he waited for the fifth watch, went to the palace,
And entered the gate of the court in his court robes and belt.
He promptly presented in person the arm and the eye;
Lifting them up with both hands, he told what had happened:
"The immortal cheerfully donated them and made a prayer,
Made a wish that the emperor's disease be done away with,
And that he might rule the entire cosmos and never grow old,
Enthroned like the heavenly Indra up in his Dragon Court."

When the emperor heard the report of his minister, he laughed heartily and said: "That Heaven should produce such a good person!" When he also saw the arm and the eye, he lifted his fists and pressed them together, expressing his thanks to Heaven. He ordered the Court of Imperial Banquets to take good care of Liu Qin, and summoned the monk to mix the medicine. The monk placed the arm and the eye into a box, which he then carried into the inner palace to show them to the empress and the concubines. Let's see what happened!

This unhitches the heavenly moon and stars from their orbits,
The lotus-breeze shakes the brocade of rivers and mountains!

Namo Guanshiyin pusa

He carried them into the palace to the Brilliant Yang Hall,
Where kowtowing, he presented them to the main consort.
The empress scrutinized them in person, with her own eyes,
And saw the immortal's arm and eye very clearly indeed!
The immortal's hand showed the thousand-spoke wheel—
That's one of the thirty-two marks that's rarely heard of.
Before she had seen the hand and the eye, things were fine,
But now that she had seen this sign, she was filled with pain.
"The hand of my child showed the thousand-spoke wheel,
And now both that hand and that eye look exactly like hers.
I have no idea what became of Marvelous Goodness,
As the only way for me to meet her is in my dreams."
The empress wept in the most gut-wrenching way,

And as she wept in the palace, she choked and fainted.
All the women of the inner palace were moved to tears,
And the immortal's arm and eye were then taken away.
    Let's not talk of the empress, who fainted from weeping,
But listen to me as I return to the subject of the king.
The monk mixed the medicine and presented it, and
Wherever the medicine was applied, it brought relief.
    The emperor used the medicine, and after one night
The disease had been eradicated from all of his body!
The emperor's dragon-body was hale and healthy again,
And a Great Peace golden placard was posted at the gate.
    From the vermilion steps an edict was proclaimed:
"We have regained Our life, and Our soul is restored.
Heaven bestowed on Us a saintly monk who saved Us,
He must have been Our parent in an earlier existence!
    We hereby proclaim that Liu Qin is promoted in rank,
He will be named a marquis and appointed as general.
We reward him with gold and silver and precious stones,
Brocade gown and jade belt, and the title 'Loyal Vassal.'
    The rank and salary of all court officials will be raised;
By an act of Grand Pardon, We will release all criminals.
All the prefectures throughout the land will be ordered to
Sponsor a vegetarian feast for the recitation of sutras."
    With a bow he asked his physician to ascend the hall,
And had him sit down on the nine-dragon throne, saying:
"Dear Master, allow me to thank you for your visit, please,
Allow Us today to give expression to Our heartfelt feelings."

The emperor consulted with his court officials and said: "It is out of the ordinary that today We should have regained Our life! This is like coming back to life from death, like flames leaping up from cold ashes, like a withered tree sprouting flowers! Heaven dispatched this heavenly physician, and Our gratitude is immense—he is Our parent from a former life! We should inform all-under-heaven by a proclamation, and pardon criminals on a large scale. We will for a while turn the main hall into a preaching hall, and use the dragon-throne for the time being as a Dharma-throne, and in so doing prepare a ritual space. By decree We will confer on this monk the title of Greatly Precious Dharma King and Meditation Master Commanding the State. He will be subject only to

High Heaven, and be superior even to Us, the One Man!" The civil officials and military officers wanted to honor the monk as the emperor's teacher, but he said: "That's not what I wished for! You should think of the immortal of Incense Mountain who donated his hands and eyes. If you have the intention of repaying favors, you should go in person to Incense Mountain and present your thanks face to face." As soon as the monk had said this, he rose into the sky and was gone.

The oriole sings, the crane cries, the phoenixes dance:
How many people know the hidden meaning of this?

Namo Guanshiyin pusa

The monk, flying on his tin staff, soared up into the sky,
And from the sky he left the following message to the king:
"Don't forget your suffering once you're freed of suffering,
Remember a favor well whenever you've enjoyed a favor.
    I am the Bodhisattva Who Contemplates the Cries of the World,
I came for the purpose of saving you from your disease.
From now on practice the saintly Way with a true heart,
Make sure that the numinous Truth is not defiled by dust.
    The cosmos is bound to go through many more changes,
A floating bubble, this world of dust won't last forever.
Asuras are caught up in anger, *devas* take their pleasure,
Ghosts and gods suffer sorrow, birds sing their sadness—
    It is only humans who are capable of becoming buddhas,
So I urge you, my lord and king, to practice cultivation.
Transcending enlightened and vulgar: the right fruit achieved;
A clear breeze, a full moon—you will realize no-delusion!"

When the Marvelous Splendor emperor himself heard these words, he bowed a hundred times toward the sky and kowtowed. He then returned, and as soon as he had ascended the throne hall, he issued an edict, directed to all the high ministers and the women of the palace, in which he ordered them to keep to a vegetarian diet and to cleanse and purify themselves, body and heart. Then both those in the inner palace and those in the outer would take up flowers and incense and, astride their elephants, immediately set out for

Incense Mountain to thank the great immortal face to face and repay his virtue!

Once your heart is fixed, you personally ascend to the Flower Store Realm,[37]
Once you've escaped from Māra's net and snares, you'll never sink down.

Namo Guanshiyin pusa

The emperor ordered the imperial cortege to be called out,
The dragon pavilion, the elephant boxes without number,
For the empress, the princesses, and the princes consort,
The women of each of the palaces, and the many relatives.
The four chancellors and nine directors, all in attendance,
Set out at the same moment as they started their journey.
They had barely left the imperial city and its golden hall,
When the text of the edict already had arrived in Huizhou.
Huizhou's officials and officers welcomed the emperor,
In their court robes and belt they came out to greet him.
From afar, Marvelous Splendor saw Incense Mountain,
Its slopes all covered with dark pines and green bamboo.
He had no desire to view the beauties of rivers and hills.
When the cortege halted, he emerged from the dragon pavilion.
Proceeding on foot unattended, he ascended Incense Mountain,
With lowered head he entered the straw-thatched hermitage.
Bearing precious incense in both hands, he offered it up,
And he performed a hundred bows as he recited his prayer:
"Kowtowing We prostrate Ourselves, knowing We've sinned.
If We have recovered our life, it is only due to your grace!
The merit of this feat, Immortal, is far from insignificant:
We may be compared to a withered tree springing again to life!
Because of this, the entire court has come to express thanks,
And we hope you will be so kind as to accept Our sentiments."

The Marvelous Splendor emperor personally visited Transparent Heart county in Huizhou. When he saw Incense Mountain, it was still twenty miles away. From afar he saw how purple clouds encircled its emerald peaks, and how a rain of flowers fell from the clear sky. Its hundreds of peaks rose out of ancient mountains, and its thousands of cliffs knew no autumn. The emperor then announced that he was going to dismount from his carriage, and together with the women of the palace, he ascended the mountain on foot. On the top of Sandalwood Peak, in Purple Bamboo Grove, he indeed found a straw-thatched hermitage. He promptly ordered all the musicians to play their instruments, and dishes of fruit and delicacies were all carried to the mountain. They approached the dwelling of the immortal, each bearing incense and flowers and bowing all the way. The emperor, wearing his golden crown, holding his royal tablet, and dressed in his dragon robes, stepped up to the burner and thrice offered incense. Touching the ground with his head, he made a hundred bows, and prostrating himself, he said: "We now first burn precious incense and next offer vegetarian food as a small expression of Our simple sincerity, and We hope that in your kind compassion you will deign to look down upon Us!" At that moment the immortal was seated in lotus position on a rock and, absorbed in silent meditation, did not reply.

Thousands of mountains cannot block the view of the moon
As her undiluted clear light is exceptionally brilliant tonight!

Namo Guanshiyin pusa

The emperor looked up and observed the immortal's face—
She was seated in lotus position and did not rise to her feet.
Without her arms and eyes her appearance was quite different,
And so the emperor failed to recognize his own flesh and blood.
    Face covered with blood and grime, she had no arms or eyes,
She did not utter a single word or syllable—it truly was hard to
        tell.
The emperor immediately addressed her in the following way:
"Immortal maiden, please be so kind as to listen to Us.
    Because Our body was suffering from a fearsome disease,
You, immortal maiden, were willing to mutilate your body.
Even if We pulverized Our bones, that favor can't be repaid,
Because you saved our miserable life from the brink of death.
    As an offering We've prepared incense and vegetarian foods,
And the entire court thanks you in person for your signal favor!
As We have nothing else by which We can repay you for your grace,
From the heart, We express Our mortal feelings with this incense!"

The emperor said: "We are the ruler of the mountains and rivers, of the wide world, and the emperor of the entire nation and its ten thousand clans. Grateful for your favor, great Immortal, We have come from afar to thank you face to face. So why don't you say even a single word and insist on keeping silent?" The emperor retired shamefacedly, and then told the empress and the concubines to bow before the immortal and ask her how she was doing. So let's see what happened!

Awe inspiring the blaze of her might consubstantial with Great
 Emptiness:
Whether in the heavens above or in the world of men, she is
 without equal.

Namo Guanshiyin pusa

The empress then promptly went inside the hermitage,
With the imperial concubines all following behind her.
They lit a candle: its blaze illuminated mountain valleys,
They burned incense: the smoke rose up in huge clouds.
 When she had made her bows, she stepped forward to look,
But the immortal's face was covered with blood and grime.
The black balls of her two eyes had both been gouged out,
She was missing both her arms, the knife marks still visible.
 The empress immediately called for scented bathing water,
And washed her with scented water, so as to know the truth.
Time and again she pondered all the details of the matter:
"She looks exactly like Marvelous Goodness, my child."
 The empress wept in a most gut-wrenching way,
Each time she wept, she would faint, then come around:
"My child, we have been apart now for a full nine years,
And all those years your mother never stopped crying.
 How many times did I search for you in my dreams?
My weeping would wake all the women of the palace.
During the day I did not eat, nor sleep during the night,
Sorrow and worry became a disease, I lacked all spirit.
 In the palace I never dared raise my voice in weeping,
Afraid your father would hear and be filled with anger.
I took no joy at all in the thousand kinds of pleasure,
All the thoughts of my heart were with you, my child!

If you are my child, please don't try to conceal it,
But tell me the truth so your mother may know!"
This time around the immortal spoke and replied:
"Dear mother, please listen, and I will tell you.
Considering that the favor of nurture is hard to repay,
I left the family to study the Way for my parents' sake!
If I had not been the daughter that you gave birth to,
How would I have been willing to cut off my limbs?
I did not care about the pain and hardship I'd suffer,
With all my heart I wanted to save my father's body.
You, the empress, are the mother who gave me life,
Now Heaven has allowed us to finally meet again!"
She wanted to embrace her mother but had no arms,
She raised her eyes to look up, but now had no pupils.
When the empress heard this, she wept most piteously,
And because of her weeping, she fainted then and there!
The entire palace and the entire court all shed tears,
Their piteous wailing even shook the heavens up above.
When the emperor was told this, his heart was shattered,
He shook his head and pulled his ears, driven to distraction!
Knocking his knuckles, he now was filled with remorse:
"This frightening development really fills me with shame!
I hate myself for lacking all foresight in the beginning,
I have eyes, but still failed to recognize a good person.
In vain I ruled mountains and rivers as king and emperor,
To no use I served as lord and king, was called a sage!
If I only had earlier known that a candle is still a fire,
I'd long ago have escaped from bitter transmigration."[38]

The emperor said: "How beautiful the scene of Incense Mountain! / Blooming flowers cover the earth with brocade. / The trees on the mountain add to the green, / The ancient grotto by white clouds is hidden. We could never really believe there were mountain landscapes as beautiful as this!" Next he said to his court ministers: "When Marvelous Goodness was strangled to death with a bowstring, she was hauled away by a tiger and her body was never recovered. How could she still be alive?" The court ministers reported: "If good and evil would not have their retribution, the cosmos would be guilty of partiality. This immortal truly is the princess." The emperor said: "If it is established that she is Marvelous

Goodness, may High Heaven be moved to restore her arms and eyes, so that she may be as beautiful as before!"

We can't continue to be vainly filled with desperation,
Enough said about clouds, as the ocean becomes clear!

Namo Guanshiyin pusa

The Marvelous Splendor emperor personally bowed down,
He kowtowed, and with folded hands pronounced a prayer:
"If indeed she is Our own daughter, may High Heaven
Not betray a person who has shown so much filial piety!
    Restore her hands and eyes as they were in earlier days, and
We will abandon Our name and fame and become a monk!"
He made a hundred bows, and had not yet finished speaking,
When suddenly and without any warning, dark clouds appeared.
    Then, a moment later, the clouds cleared and the sun came out.
In the clear light, sunny and bright, the scene looked like spring.
The immortal was as beautiful as a flower beginning to bloom,
Her brand new face surpassed even her earlier beauty at eighteen.
    Meeting again with close relatives, she wept most piteously,
And poured out her deepest feelings to her father and mother:
    "All the stars in the sky surround and bow before the polar star,
In the world below, there's no river that does not run to the east.
For all eternity, the heaven will be able to cover the earth,
So of course a filial child will always serve both his parents.
    Because of the importance of the matter of birth and death,
I abandoned my parents in order to go and cultivate the Truth.
If I had not cut off the affections and abandoned my parents,
For thousands of *kalpas* I would not have achieved the Way,
    That unencumbered and unhindered perfect Universal Principle—
Forgetting the world and forgetting the Dharma, fully free!"

At this moment the body of the immortal was like pure glass, showing her true golden form inside. When the clouds cleared away and the storm died down, there appeared a blinding blaze of light, and suddenly the appearance of the immortal was even more beautiful than earlier at the age of eighteen. Of such a situation it is said: "Bright oh so bright shines the sun up in heaven, / Huge oh so huge the numinous might of the Buddha!" Those who believe in the teachings cannot but be filled with fear!

She who achieved Non-action, Guanshiyin,
Releases or holds at will, all spontaneously.

Namo Guanshiyin pusa

The immortal indeed had achieved the Way of No-birth,
The entire cosmos, even plants and trees, basked in her grace.
Indra and Brahma and all the *devas* were filled with joy,
The thousands of saints and sages offered congratulations.
 The bodhisattva, opening the storehouse of the dragon palace,
Expounded the Marvelous Dharma and manifested the Truth.
"You, my stern father Po Qie, are now sixty-eight years old,
Born in a *mao*-year, in a *mao*-month, in the hour of *mao*.
 Your name, my kind mother the empress, is Precious Virtue,
And your age is, I find, exactly the same as that of my father.
I, your daughter Marvelous Goodness, am now twenty-eight,
Born on the nineteenth of the second month, at the hour of *si*.
 Because a crown prince had not been born to the palace,
I wanted to repay the favors shown by my father and mother,
I wanted everyone to change their mind and practice the Way,
Because Impermanence fears neither the emperor nor his kin.
 It has not been easy to obtain this human body in this life,
Once one has lost this human body, it is hard to obtain it again.
In myriads of lives, of *kalpas*, it is rare to have this chance:
Your imperial visit to my hermitage must have a karmic cause.
 The great matter of birth and death is not a trifling matter—
How much time do you have? Don't be muddleheaded now!
When you come to a mountain of treasure, grab the treasure!
Don't go away empty-handed, for there'll be no second time!"

The empress asked her daughter: "You went to the Underworld, and then came back to life again. Please explain in detail the affairs of the Underworld. We notice only that people die in the thousands and ten thousands, but where is there anyone who comes back to life?" When the immortal heard her question, she immediately replied.

If the Buddha's Dharma could not provide this kind of proof,
How could the ancestral teaching continue to the present day?

Namo Guanshiyin pusa

"When I entered the Underworld it was as if I was dreaming,
On the roads of the Yellow Springs deepest darkness reigns.
A youth and maiden carrying banners went ahead and led the way,
I followed that youth and maiden, and went onward and onward.
    Then later I saw prison wardens bringing a sedan chair,
Ox-headed and horse-faced demons greeted me in two rows.
As I straightway entered into the Yiyang Hall of King Yama,
The Ten Kings and their consorts all came out to greet me.
    The three pathways were transformed into realms of roaming,
Five-colored auspicious clouds filled the deepest darkness.
Sinner ghosts who had long been imprisoned were all set free,
And new souls who had just arrived all received a full pardon.
    But the infernal judges in charge of cases came to complain,
And so I was promptly escorted back to the world of the living.
I found, when I'd come to below the trees of Deceased-Many,
That local gods of mountain and earth had protected my corpse.
    My body of flesh had not decomposed and was still firm,
So my spirit entered once again into that old physical body.
When I came back to life it was like waking up from a dream,
The string of the bow had snapped, all my bones were hurting."
    Remembering their earlier conversations, she asked her sisters:
"My dear elder sisters, please listen to what I have to say.
Boasting of your filial piety, you married a prince consort,
So why did the two of you not donate your arms and eyes?
    The one who can't repay a favor in a time of need is not filial,
He shows ingratitude for all his parents' feeding and nurturance.
In this world of men your title may be that of princess or more,
But in the Underworld they have never heard such distinctions.
    The king of ghosts and his ghostly agents recognize no status,
The infernal judges and the infernal clerks show no mercy at all.
They don't ask whether you were a queen or perhaps a princess,
They don't care about 'emperor's kin' or 'kin of the empress.'
    If you do not enter the Lotus Congregation while you are alive,
You will not avoid sinking down into the hells upon your death.

If human beings wish to avoid the sufferings of transmigration,
They should with all their heart recite the name of the Buddha."

The immortal said: "Since ancient times, the Dharma of the Buddha instructs the emperor and his ministers to help all sentient beings, generation after generation, to understand the teachings of the Buddha. But if I look into the ancient chronicles and inquire into them deeply, there never has been anyone like you, my father, whose wisdom so lacked perspicacious illumination, and whose behavior so lacked proper measure. You sought to exterminate the Dharma with cruel punishments, persecuting and harming it without end. You were concerned with only your own pleasures, and didn't consider the sufferings of others at all. Now, ordinary people may be be cheated and abused, but High Heaven cannot be deceived. So when that fearsome disease visited your body, your remorse was of no use." When her father the emperor heard these words, his tears streamed down like pearls, and the ranting rage he would have once indulged in was stopped by this one speech.

Who recognizes the jade that's hidden in the rock of Chu?
One only sees the treasure once the stone has been broken.[39]

Namo Guanshiyin pusa

The immortal then addressed this question to her father:
"My father and emperor, please listen to what I will say.
You thought your dragon-body would always be healthy,
But in fact you too were visited by a fearsome disease.
When you saw that I cultivated my heart, you objected,
Repeatedly giving stern orders that I should be beheaded.
When I think back on that time, where would I be now?
Dear father, how would I have been able to see you again?
Officials and officers may be famed as loyal and filial,
But if an evil disease visits your body, kin doesn't count.
If a prince consort would be able to die in your place,
Your Majesty could live forever, never having to die!
No one can escape or flee from the hour of one's death,
Rich or poor, high or low, all go to the deepest darkness.
Each makes that journey alone, no substitute is allowed,
So what merit have you amassed to avoid punishment?

Others may fear your evil, but Heaven knows no fear,
Others may cheat the good, but Heaven always is fair!"
Her father the emperor, when he heard this question,
Cast down his eyes, his pearly tears flowing copiously.
"My darling daughter, please don't bring up the past,
For now We will join you here and cultivate the Truth!
I hate myself for my lack of foresight in the beginning,
Only today I've been enlightened—too late for remorse!"

The Marvelous Splendor emperor implored the immortal: "When We think about those days, We are overcome by shame and remorse, and We are fully aware of the punishment We deserve. To Our regret, We lacked a lofty and brilliant farsighted clarity. We were muddled and deluded for a while, just like the sun when it is obscured by clouds. Now We see that you truly do not harbor a grudge from before, but even have the grace to repay past favors. Please forgive Our crime, and allow your father to leave the family, so We may on this mountain devote Our thoughts to the Way of the Buddha and fully manifest the Gate of the Dharma that in its unlimited capacity ferries across all sentient beings."

If this body is not ferried across in this very life,
When and where will it ever be ferried across?

Namo Guanshiyin pusa

The Marvelous Splendor emperor only now was enlightened,
He abandoned the throne as he wanted to practice cultivation.
He divested himself of the myriad glories of the palace halls,
He forever discarded the thousand kinds of wealth and status.
The concubines and palace women all were converted, and,
Maintaining the pure precepts, they abandoned the red dust.
Golden crowns and jade belts were all consigned to flames,
Dragon robes and precious tables all reduced to white ash.
Ascending the altar, he received the precepts as a disciple,
And by study became an old monk on Incense Mountain.
When Heaven disperses the clouds, the Three Lights shine:
He experienced that the mortal heart is the Buddha-heart!
The court officials of the entire country practiced the Way,
Completely enlightened, they understood mortal feelings.

When the three roots are grasped,[40] one goes to the Pure Land,
Just like all the myriad streams pay homage to the patriarch.

At that moment, the buddhas of the ten directions manifested a flowery throne of precious jade and in the most subtle and marvelous tones they praised him: "How good! How good is this great emperor! His karmic good fortune is deep and wide. He donated one daughter so she could leave the family, and as a result all the different branches of his family can now ascend to heaven. He was also able to abandon the throne and cede the country, and come and visit this straw-thatched hermitage. In this life he was an emperor; in a future life he will become a buddha." When the Marvelous Splendor emperor received the announcement of his future buddhahood from the buddhas, his heart was filled with joy, and he composed the following *gātha*:

(*The recitation of the name of the bodhisattva and its repetition by the congregation here come to an end. Sound the ruler. The* gātha *reads:*)

The bodhisattva, kind and compassionate, came down to the world,
And she grew up to adulthood inside the walls of the royal palace.
I urge all disciples of the Buddha to follow the example she provides,
For, in truth, no one has ever been betrayed by the study of the Way.

After the Marvelous Splendor emperor had spoken this *gātha*, he lived in seclusion on the mountain and cultivated the Way. More than twenty years later, when he had reached the age of eighty-nine, and knowing in advance that his time had come, he announced to the congregation that he was to depart from this world. He then composed the following *gātha*:

Abandoning the imperial throne, I entered True Emptiness,
And thoroughly probed into pure vacuity and silent nirvana.
All that remains of me now is this unenlightened outer shell,
And that I entrust for its final performance to Old Uncle Fire.[41]

Let's not recount how the Marvelous Splendor emperor went to the Pure Land. Let's recount how the one who was now the Bodhisattva

Who Contemplates of the Cries of the World, when her work was done and her merit complete, received the announcement of her future buddahood from the Buddha. This moved the thousand times thousand worlds to shake in six different ways. A precious parasol came down from the sky, and a golden lotus emerged from the earth. The buddhas of the ten directions, the bodhisattvas and holy monks, Indra, Brahma and all the *devas*, and the dragons, the gods, and the six other classes of supernatural beings all came to Incense Mountain, and together they composed the following *gātha*:

Cheerfully she made the great offering with kindness and compassion,
Though in the imperial palace, there was not a single person who knew.
If in a single moment a mortal is converted, the heart becomes buddha,
And all the many myriads of phenomena will give off a radiant light.

Among the congregation on Incense Mountain, there was a certain Sir Moon Parasol.[42] Leading a contingent of five hundred, he came before her throne, knelt down and asked: "What is it that is called the outer way, and what is it that is called the right Way? May you in your kind compassion illuminate our blind delusion." After he had expressed this wish, he remained on one knee with palms pressed together. His eyes remained constantly fixed, and with all his heart he gazed eagerly upward. It was then that the immortal taught the monks and nuns, laymen and laywomen: "How can I not explain it to you, since you have asked so sincerely for an explanation. Those who practice what we call the outer way look for the Buddha outside of the heart. They visualize the crown of the head and become entangled in phenomena. They see a light between the brows and the nose, and knowing Emptiness they cling to Being. But is there really any extraordinary excellence to be found in a phenomenal body?[43] They practice semen retention, and terminate the red and the white. They collect yin to supplement yang. They practice the work of the ten stages. They know the divine affairs of luck and misfortune. They secretly transmit marvelous methods, and establish and revere oaths and vows. They sit like a block and guard emptiness. They themselves know the roads and routes, and the seals and names of their birth and death, and with their colleagues they ascend to the highest ranks, roaming through fine realms where they can observe all phenomena, but they do not allow other people to know them. They claim to be in possession of the Way and establish sects and schools. They practice magic and abstain from grain, and by manifesting miracles they delude the masses, deceiving and denying the sages and saints![44] All these are false ways. Those who practice them may be compared to gibbons and monkeys who, arm in arm, dangle from a tree on a steep cliff in the attempt to reach the river below and grab the moon—it is all wasted effort that will turn to nothing. People with the right cause and the right view are never like this." He then replied with the following *gātha*:

Those wishing to penetrate the true pure realm of the Tathāgata,
Should purify their body and heart until they are perfectly empty.
Don't study spirit-journeys, don't follow alchemical methods—
Only now we see that our earlier efforts were wrongly applied!

At this time the immortal told the disciples: "Once in the past, numberless *kalpas* ago, during the time of the buddha Ratnagarbha,[45] I was the first crown prince in the Palace of Pure Sounds. I left the family and practiced the Way, and to this very day my body and mind have not wearied. Each and every one I save and assist, transforming my body according to need. The current emperor was a patron of mine in that earlier existence, and Marvelous Book and Marvelous Sound were good friends in that earlier life. All the other palace women and ministers were faithful donors who aided my cause, and in that earlier life we established a good bond. As a result we have followed each other from age to age." She then composed the following *gātha*:

In immeasurable light, I purely contemplate the cries of the world,
As I have come to this land to ferry across all sentient beings.
For a long time I lived secluded on Potalaka, rarely known to men,
It was in Manifest Dew of the Tang dynasty I first became known.[46]

From this time onward, the immortal was known as the Bodhisattva Who Contemplates the Cries of the World. Her Self-so body is enveloped in strings of jewels, and on her head she wears a pearl crown. In her hands she holds her pure vase and a willow wand, and her feet rest on a thousand-petal lotus flower. Streaming from the crown of her head, a white ray of light universally illuminates the innumerable worlds. All the people then asked the Buddha: "World-honored One, as to the original life and the causal ground of the immortal of Incense Mountain, please allow the faithful to joyfully proclaim what it is they receive and uphold." He replied with the following *gātha*:

This tale of cause and circumstances is not something rare,
As it is received and upheld by all of the saints and sages.
Pull the nail from your eye and remove the barrier of clouds:
The one nature is perfectly bright, equal to Great Emptiness.

At that time the World-honored One said to the monks and nuns, laymen and laywomen: "Listen attentively, and I will explain everything to you. This is the brightest *tathāgata* of the Right Dharma among the ancient buddhas. Of all the buddhas, her kindness and compassion are the greatest. Out of pity for all living beings, she manifested herself in the mortal world. She appeared to enter into the stream of transmigration, and her transformation allowed her to share the experience [of sentient beings]. She was able to donate her body and heart in order to save those who are deluded so they might go to the Pure Land. She donated both her eyes, and now she has received a thousand eyes in return. She donated both her arms, and now she has received a thousand arms in return. That is why she is called the one with a thousand arms and a thousand eyes, the greatly kind and greatly compassionate one, the one who saves from suffering and from hardships, the one of wide and great numinous might, the *tathāgata* who responds to prayers, the one of right and universal wisdom, the one whose illuminated behavior is perfect, the unsurpassed mahāsattva who knows how to go into the world of men to save them,[47] the hero who regulates and rules, the teacher of *devas* and humans, the Buddha, and the World-honored One. These are the ten titles of the Bodhisattva Who Contemplates the Cries of the World." And then he recited the following *gātha*:

The compassionate teacher Guanyin suffered Māra's enmity,
She left this great teaching that is transmitted to the world.

Never again say that a woman can have no accomplishments:
Her work done, her merit complete, she became a buddha.

Namo Guanshiyin pusa
(*The following* gātha *has eight lines. The recitation of the name of the bodhisattva and its repetition by the congregation concludes this [ritual of] merit.*)

This tale of cause and circumstances has been told to the end,
The old mirror, now bright again, illuminates the many worlds.
Those whose faith is up to it achieve the right enlightenment—
If one does not achieve buddhahood, one becomes an immortal.
This sutra of the first life of the One Who Contemplates the Cries
Is of universal benefit to all sentient beings in the entire world.
May you read or hear it, understand it, and grasp it completely—
Now that this work is fully concluded, I wish you Great Peace.

The end of the scroll.

(*Recite the* Great Compassion Dhāraṇī *once. Then strike the chimes and recite the last four lines loudly.*)

The Second Scroll of the Short Version of *The Sutra on the Original Life of the Bodhisattva Guanshiyin*

The merit of expounding this scroll is quite superior,
May the limitless superior blessing all be transferred.
My universal wish is that all who have sunk and drowned,
May quickly go to the realm of the Buddha of Limitless Light.

The leader, who is now back in the midst of the congregation, kneels down and reads out the Buddha's various texts of repentance. He then leads the congregation in reciting the name of the Buddha.

(The End)

Composed by the meditation master Puming of the Tianzhu Monastery of the Song dynasty.
Edited by the later student Jinghong of the Clear Plum Court.

The Precious Scroll of Good-in-Talent and Dragon Girl

Edited by the Angler of the Misty Waves

We unroll and open this precious scroll, proclaim the true traces,
The golden burner's incense smoke spreads an auspicious aroma.
Listen with pious reverence, you good men and faithful women:
It dispels disaster, lengthens your life, and brings endless fortune.

The story of this precious scroll took place during the Qianfu reign-period (874–879) of the Tang dynasty (618–906). In the Immortal Peach village of Hanyang prefecture of the Huguang area lived a certain grand historian named Chen Debao. His office was of the highest rank, his position exceeded that of all other officials, and he was in charge of the great affair of court protocol. He was able to influence the ruler above and to benefit the people below. Each and every civil official and military officer at court respected him. He was as pure as water and as bright as a mirror, and his fame reverberated through all the four directions. But at the age of fifty, he still had no heir to play at his feet. His wife, Lady Han, was already forty years of age. Wise and virtuous, proper and upright, she often urged the grand historian to take a concubine, but he adhered to the proper, and never wavered in his devotion. As his wife saw no other way out, she urged the grand historian to join her in making a pious pilgrimage to the Mahāsattva of the Southern Sea and pray in front of her lotus throne for a son to continue the ancestral sacrifices of the Chen family. What did the grand historian think of that?

When Lady Han alerted him to this possibility by her words,
The grand historian, hearing this, secretly sighed to himself:
"Day and night I keep wondering why I as yet have no son,
It must be because I made mistakes in discharging my duties.

But I find myself free from shame before the window's light,[1]
My unalloyed natural goodness is a match for Blue Heaven,
Is a match, above, to my lord and ruler, to Heaven and Earth,
So why am I punished by being denied a son to play in my lap?"
Lady Han urged the grand historian again, speaking as follows:
"Fate is what determines whether a son comes to you early or late.
The one who responds to all requests is the bodhisattva Guanyin,
Ask her a thousand times, and she will help you a thousand times.
If you, Grand Historian, are willing to pray with a devout heart,
You'll acquire a son to continue the sacrifices to the ancestors."
The grand historian acted according to the lady's advice, and
Filled with pious sincerity he made a pilgrimage to the mountain.[2]
"If we have come to Mt. Putuo, it is for no other reason
Than to ask for a son, a new sprout. And if you, our Buddha,
Are able to give us a child who'll continue the ancestral line,
We will offer incense and repair the monastery's main hall."

The Mahāsattva of the Southern Sea was aware of the pure and pious sincerity of Grand Historian Chen in coming to her mountain and asking for a son, but alas, fate had determined that he should remain childless. This was a karmic fruit from a former life. But in this life he was pure and upright as an official. In all his actions he displayed expedient means,[3] and everywhere he accumulated hidden merit. His virtue matched Heaven and Earth and, truly, his name was worthy of being listed among the immortals. If she would bestow on him a son who would realize the Way, then his entire family would all ascend to heaven! How could any worldly good fortune compare with this? Yesterday, Jinzha had stopped by,[4] and from him she had heard about a good friend of Jinzha's named Summoning Riches Lad below the throne of the Heavenly Official for Bestowing Riches in the Communing-with-Heaven Office, whose mind was set on the Way. Even though he had set his mind on goodness, out of his unalloyed compassion he had, by distributing too much wealth to people, disrupted the Heavenly Emperor's system of rewards and fines, and in so doing ruined the fruit of his karma. Because of this, the HEAVENLY EMPEROR had been filled with rage, and he had been demoted and sent as punishment to be reborn in the realm of dust. The mahāsattva thought it would be a good idea if she ordered Jinzha to go and fetch this lad and give him to Grand Historian Chen as his son. As his energy and nature were not of the mortal world, she could later ferry him across so that he would be able to cultivate and achieve the right fruit. In this way he could not only repay the grand historian's favor of raising and nurturing him, but also help the seven generations of the ancestors of the Chen family to ascend to heaven. In this way he would adhere to the HEAVENLY EMPEROR'S system of rewards and fines, and still bring about the retribution of good and evil. After Jinzha had accepted the mahāsattva's holy command, he thanked her with a kowtow for her Buddha-grace. Immediately all the divine generals appeared below her lotus throne, along with the crowds of arhats and the Jiedi-gods,[5] the merit-officers of the day, the monastery gods and the gods of the earth, all those gods who protect the Dharma and sing her praises without end. Three times they walked around the bodhisattva,[6] and with the palms of their hands pressed together they recited a thousand times HAIL THOU BODHISATTVA GUANSHIYIN WHO ART GREATLY COMPASSIONATE AND GREATLY MERCIFUL, WHO SAVES US FROM SUFFERING AND WHO SAVES US FROM DANGER, WHO GRANDLY EXTENDS HER NUMINOUS RESPONSIVENESS, AND WHO FOLLOWS THE SOUNDS TO SAVE FROM SUFFERING! When the bodhisattva had descended from her Dharma-throne, the crowd bowed and retired—but enough about that.

Let's tell again of the grand historian, who returned home
To find that the lady was pregnant and expecting a child.
 Before they knew it, days and nights had quickly passed by:
After ten months the baby was ready to come into the world.
When she gave birth to a boy, the whole household rejoiced,
The family, old and young, were happy and filled with joy.
 "The year of his birth was that of *yiyou*, the month, *jimao*—
The crow flies, the hare runs: he'll enter Penglai and Yingzhou;[7]
Jiachen is the number of the day, and *bingyin* that of the hour—
Dragons whistle, tigers roar: he will return to heaven's palace.
 This boy has never been of the common mortal kind, and
As soon as he grasps wind and cloud, he'll become a dragon."
At the birth of his son, the grand historian was filled with joy,
Cradling him in his arms, he observed his physical features:
 "The crown is flat, the forehead broad: this is proper and right,

His Star of the Ground rises straight up to Dipper and Cowherd.[8]
And the Five Mounts and Four Conduits are very clearly visible,[9]
The three sections of head and body are equal, the earlobes rich.[10]
His mouth is square, edges and corners are carefully crafted,
His one pair of phoenix eyes rests on the tallest of parasol trees.[11]
But I also see that
He closes his mouth, guarding his spirit—breathing like a turtle:[12]
His single breath is not dispersed among the five element-phases.
Walking like a crane, breathing like a turtle is what immortals do—
How will he be able to continue a family line in the mortal realm?
I am afraid that
He is not a man to stand below the gate with its vermilion steps,[13]
He is bound to follow in lofty traces on the three immortal isles.
I, this old man,
Cannot help but fear that the Chen family will remain without heir,
I asked for just a single vein to continue the root and ancestor.
Not for nothing have I followed the proper way all of my life—
Let's keep this little one born of our flesh to extend the family!"
When the lady heard the grand historian speak in this manner,
She continued to comfort the grand historian's heart without end:
"With pious sincerity we asked for a son, and moved the Buddha:
The mahāsattva then sent us a son to continue the Chen family line.
What we should do now is offer incense, go and repay the vow,
So he may lead a long life, without disaster, and without danger."
The name chosen for the child was Chen Lian ("Continuation"),
A prayer for the unending proliferation of the Chen family root.
Before they knew it, days and nights had quickly passed by:
Sun and moon moved like a shuttle, even faster than the wind.
With every day Chen Lian grew smarter and more intelligent,
At the age of three, the little boy could already recite his texts.
When he opened his mouth, every word accorded with Truth,
Whatever he uttered, whatever he said, was out of the ordinary.
But when they wanted to send him to school to study the Books,
He said to them:

"I don't want to study the Books, I'm too lazy to make the effort.
It's not my wish to become an official or to become an officer,
But to search for my roots by studying the Way of the immortals!"

When his parents heard him talk like this, they were both pleased and startled. They were pleased that a little boy of three could be so supernaturally intelligent, but they were startled because they feared that he might not grow up to be the son and heir of the Chen family. But after all, since he was only a toddler whose understanding had not yet developed, for now they could leisurely teach and guide him, and later decide what to do.

Alas, when Chen Lian was five years old, Lady Han fell ill, and he felt completely disconsolate. When her disease had progressed beyond cure and she suddenly died, the sweet five-year-old child tossed and turned without relief, and filled with grief, he cried out piteously: "Oh, my dear mother!

Since my birth I have never left mother for even half an instant,
Whenever my mother went here or there, I would rush forward.
My mother loved me like a treasured jewel, and I followed her,
Holding her hand or clutching her gown, wherever she went.
Not for even an hour or a minute did I leave my mother's side,
But today you abandon your son to sleep all alone by himself.
I keep on asking: My mother, where you are going?
It is only right that your child should accompany you.
I am happy to follow you whether in life or in death,
But it is too pitiable to brusquely abandon your child.
The weeping cuckoo spits out blood as it cries, and
Each and every branch is dyed red by its tears of blood.
My mother, you should have taken me along with you,
Why am I left to imitate the cuckoo with every cry?"
Chen Lian continued weeping in this most heartrending way,
Each and every word so mournful it shook and moved Heaven.
The grand historian could not stop himself from crying,
Hastily he cradled his sweet son in his arms, called him darling.
Moved to grief because the lady had abandoned the boy,
He was even more saddened seeing the boy weeping so piteously.
His grieving heart was confronted with more to add to his grief.
As he grieved and watched his sweet son, his grief grew greater.

The entire household, old and young, they all shed sad tears. The servants came forward and together urged the grand historian to take good care of himself as his health was of greatest importance. He should consider the well-being of the young master, who was completely dependent on him for all matters. They then dressed the lady and placed her in her coffin, and when the funeral had been completed, he took care of his orphaned son—like a jewel, like a treasure!

Chen Lian soon reached the age of seven, and the grand historian summoned him and said: "My son, come here! You are still young and your understanding is limited, so I will engage a tutor to teach you the Books—scholarship is inexhaustible! In the future you may plan for a career, so as to bring glory to your ancestors and renown to your family, in this way fulfilling the great obligation of a lifetime." Chen Lian promptly knelt down before his father and spoke as follows:

"My father, I do not belong to the mortal kind of men,
I want to ferry my parents back to the land of immortals.
    The Spirit Peak is the original home from which I hail,
One wayward thought and I was sent down from heaven.
I constantly long for the pleasures of the Peach Banquet,[14]
I have no desire for the red dust and its long entanglements.
    I love neither merit and fame nor riches and status—
The splendor of glory is just a midnight dream.
A hundred years add up to thirty-six thousand days—
How many days in a human life are nice to look at?
    Love and attachment of wife and children: a candle in the wind,
And beautiful houses and good fields are only frost on the tiles.
Much better thus to engage in fasting and to cultivate oneself,
So as to escape from earth's prison and ascend to heaven's hall!"

When the grand historian heard the little boy speak in this way, he shed sad tears: "My boy, you are still so young in years. You know nothing of the affairs of this world, so how could you know about heaven's halls and earth's prisons? Don't talk such nonsense! If you do not listen to your father's instruction, you are committing an act of unfiliality. As a human being in this world, you must obey Heaven, Earth, your ruler, your parents, and your teacher—that is the great beginning of being human." Chen Lian kowtowed and begged forgiveness: "I will never again fail to obey your fatherly instructions!" The grand historian's anger then turned into joy: "My son, only by being willing to do this can you be said to be acting according to the Way and principle.

My son, if you are willing to follow my instructions,
You will not betray your mother's grace in raising you.
My son, if you are able to walk the way of filial piety,
You will not betray your father's unalloyed concern.
Your father will soon reach the age of sixty years,
I'll make arrangements for you so I don't have to worry:
There is a Master of the Way at Hemp Maiden's Grotto,
Of great integrity, he knows both civil and military arts.
My son, if you become his pupil and receive his teaching,
We may plan for a career that'll bring glory to the family.
In computation and interpretation he's deeply abstruse,
With administration and strategy he's fully conversant.
My son, if you are willing to study with all your heart,
You will have a great career, quite out of the ordinary!
My son, you must make every possible effort, so
Devote yourself to your study, do not shame the Chens!
In that place there are no pungent foods and spices,
So that will fit with your refusal to eat pungent foods."[15]

When Chen Lian heard this, he was greatly pleased. He promptly asked his father: "How far is that Hemp Maiden's Grotto from here?" The grand historian said: "It is located on Iron Mountain, which is not far from here. Ever since the Master of the Way arrived here, he called it Hemp Maiden's Grotto of Two Immortals Mountain." The little boy then asked: "When can we go there?" The grand historian said: "We can go as soon as tomorrow! The eighth month is *dingyou*, a month that indicates the noble man. The first of the month is *bingchen*, a day that is situated in the Great Yang—a lucky star shines high above. You, my son, were born in the year of the rooster, and *chen* harmonizes with *you*, which means that you are suited to entering school, and that effort will bring great profit." He right away informed the Master of the Way that on the next day at the hour of *si* they would arrive in the proper way so his son could then become his pupil. The grand historian meticulously made all the necessary arrangements, and the next day he accompanied his son to Two Immortals Mountain so he might bow before the Master of the Way and become his pupil—but no more about this.

Let's talk about the mahāsattva Guanyin. "Seven years have passed since I sent that lad down to the mortal world. He was given the name of Chen Lian and was born into the realm of dust. He does not eat any pungent food: his root in the Way has not yet been obscured, and his single-minded heart is still undivided. If I do not provide him guidance along with the Way and its Virtue, I fear he will end up taking the wrong road. 'By practice people grow distant.' Availing myself of the opportunity that 'his hole of passion has not yet been opened,' I will lead him into the Way, so he will avoid stumbling into the domain of misty flowers.[16] I will entrust him to my old friend, the Perfected Man Yellow Dragon. He and I are inseparable friends in the Way from an earlier existence. He has now built his hut in Immortal Peach village in Hanyang prefecture, so as to ferry people across. I will have to entrust it to him to guide and ferry across Chen Lian. Then later, Chen Lian can enter my service at Mt. Putuo." She immediately dispatched Jinzha to Two Immortals Mountain. The Perfected Man Yellow Dragon, who already knew about everything, agreed to all her requests—but enough about that.

Let's not talk about the mahāsattva and the Perfected Man,
Let's tell of the grand historian, who accompanied his son.
One of heart they arrived at Two Immortals Mountain, and
In Hemp Maiden's Grotto the father explained his purpose:
"Greet the teacher with four genuflections and eight kowtows—
I completely rely on you, dear sir, to instruct my ignorant son.
Young of years, his understanding is not yet very perceptive,
I pray you, dear teacher, to treat the boy with some leniency.
On the first and fifteenth he should practice his essay writing,
On the second and sixteenth he should train in the martial arts.
The civil arts on the odd days, the martial arts on the even—
Let him give all his efforts to civil affairs and martial skills."
After the grand historian had entrusted him so to his teacher,
He also impressed on Chen Lian not to slacken his effort, and,
Having said what he had to say to Chen Lian, he returned home,
And when he got home, he felt lonely and sad, awash in tears.

After Chen Lian had seen his father off back to his home,
He was called in by his teacher, who asked about his likings:
"You are still only so young, and your knowledge is small—
What kind of skill would you in your heart most like to learn?
Whether the civil arts or martial arts—the choice is up to you,
Seeking riches and high status will all be easy to accomplish."
Chen Lian without hesitating addressed his teacher as follows:
"I, your student,
Do not want to seek riches and status, do not want to seek glory.
I want to seek the divine immortals' ways of leaving the world,
I want to learn how to achieve a diamantine indestructible body.
I want to achieve the not-being-born and not-being-extinguished,
I want a life eternal without aging, lasting a myriad of springs.
This is your student's heartfelt wish, which is why I beg you,
My teacher, to please enlighten the ignorance that beclouds me."

The Perfected Man laughed heartily and said: "Your age may be small, but your delusion is big! You have not yet put in any hard work, you have not yet accumulated any merit, and you don't have even a clue, but yet you want to to live a life eternal and never grow old!" Chen Lian replied: "My dear teacher, a terrace of eight feet high rises from a foundation in the ground. If I do not establish my purpose from earliest youth, I will die in old age without having accomplished anything. Having a purpose in life does not depend on one's age, but, lacking wisdom, one will become a centenarian who has lived in vain." The Perfected Man continued: "You are the son of a prime minister. Your father sent you here because he wants you to devote yourself to the study of books and to practice and study the civil and military arts, so you may become an official or an officer and bring glory to your ancestors. He definitely did not tell you to cultivate the Way. So how would you be able to face your father? Even I as your teacher would be unable to face your father." Chen Lian said: "Teacher, don't worry. I will make sure that you do not suffer the blame. It is I, your student, who refuses to study the civil and martial arts, and insists on cultivating the Way. My father definitely will not blame you, my teacher. It is all my own responsibility." "If you truly want to cultivate the Way, you have to be able to abide by the rules of the mountain before you can cultivate the Way. You'll have to be able to do all kinds of heavy work, such as brewing tea, cooking rice, hauling water, and chopping firewood. You'll have to be able to eat yellowed leeks and bland rice, and to be able to wear a raggedy cassock and hempen clothes. Only if you are able to abide by all of these many rules will you be able to cultivate the Way!" Chen Lian replied: "How can one obtain the sweetest of the sweet without experiencing the most bitter of the bitter?" He then composed the following *gātha*:

Only because of birth and death, endless *saṁsāra*, does your pupil
Want with all his heart to escape from that cycle of suffering.
I implore you, my teacher, to show me some kind compassion,
I will be happy to be ordered about and serve as your servant.
My single-minded heart is undivided: I will not waver or regret,
I am eager to practice meditation, seated in the lotus position.
I'll take refuge in the Three Jewels, uphold the five precepts,
Unshakable in my determination to escape from the Red Dust.

Testing him, the Perfected Man found that he did not waver, and realized that his determination was that of the brave man who does not fear and of the wise man who is not deluded. But then he tested him once again to see how he would react. The Perfected Man spoke once more, saying: "So you really want to cultivate the Way. But what will you say if your father comes and orders you to return home?" He replied: "He who has left the family does not return to the family." The Perfected Man was pleased and said: "Yes, yes, yes! You truly have the talent in your breast!" And he gave him a religious name, calling him Good-in-Talent (Shancai).[17] From this moment on, he called him by the name of Good-in-Talent. Even though he was still young in years, he really was quite determined. From that day onward he took all the heavy work upon himself, and he was willing to carry out all the tasks of hauling water and carrying firewood. Despite all these hardships, he never showed any resentment that the true summation was so hard to achieve. His father also understood that his son was unwilling to devote himself to the study of the Books, and often sighed over his bad luck. He would often invite him to come back home, but his son always refused. Now he had practiced austerities for three years and had just turned ten. This was the year that the grand historian was celebrating his sixtieth birthday, in grand style. So let's see whether Good-in-Talent returned home.

The Perfected Man thought to himself: "I have to test him once again to see how he holds up." He then instructed Good-in-Talent: "I want to descend the mountain to visit a friend. I may be away for eight or ten days, I don't know exactly. You take care of everything in the grotto. I'm leaving now."

Good-in-Talent immediately wanted to ask some questions,
But the Perfected Man had gone, as if borne by the wind.
He rushed after his teacher because he wanted to see him off—
How could he know his teacher had departed as if on wings!
"I don't have the faintest idea where my teacher has gone,
He has left me behind, his orphaned disciple, without support.
With my teacher here on the mountain, I had a companion,
But now my teacher has gone, I don't know how to survive.
All alone and by myself, I have no clue what I have to do,
He has not even left me with a stratagem that I might use."
Considering all possibilities, he had no stratagem, no clue,
And as his tears streamed down, he was truly pained at heart.
He walked to the front, then to the back, at a loss what to do,
He went inside, then went outside again, still awash in tears.
He looked up and then looked down: without any companion—
The more he thought and pondered, the more he was afflicted.
"How would he want me, his pupil, to behave should I
Find myself attacked by highwaymen, bandits, or robbers?
How would I, all alone and by myself, be able to flee,
Should I find myself surrounded by wolves, tigers, or panthers?"
As he pondered these matters, he lacked the nerve to stay,
All of a sudden he found himself overcome by worries:
"Considering all the possibilities, there is no other way out,
But to go back home for the moment, stay there for a while.
Pondering all the solutions, that is now the only thing to do.
It doesn't mean that I am wavering in my holy commitment.
My father served at the imperial court as prime minister,
Dependents and servants crowd the house with their number.
Once home, I'll be respectfully called 'the young master,'
There's nobody there who would not respect me greatly.
I used to dine on special foods and fine dishes in season,

My body was always clothed in exquisite silks and gauze—
But because of birth and death I came to cultivate the Way,
And was willing to wear a raggedy cassock full of patches.
    If my feet are shod in straw sandals, that is my own wish,
Hauling water and carrying firewood—no problem at all!
It is not that I want to belong to the low and despised classes,
It's that I want to avoid the three paths, stop birth and death![18]
    So if I descend the mountain today it is for no other reason,
Than to go only for a while, waiting for my teacher's return.
        Moreover, my
Father is celebrating the great event of his sixtieth birthday,
And for a long time has been inviting me to come home.
    In front of my teacher I once declared I'd never go back,
That's why I've repeatedly disobeyed my father's command.
But if I descend the mountain today for just a short while,
It's to wish my father longevity, in accordance with the rites.
        The only thing is that
    It is hard to go home to see my father in this torn cassock:
As soon as he sees me, my father will be pained in his heart.
The affection between father and son is forged by Heaven—
        I only fear
The gossip of all the relatives—where can I flee for shame?
    The neighbors on all sides will all say I am lacking in luck;
Not made to enjoy my good fortune, I've turned into a slave.
But today I cannot take that dire disgrace into consideration,
Facing insult and humiliation I will return and go back home."
    It is difficult to explain this hardship and suffering fully,
All day long his tears streamed down in an unending flood.
The best thing would be to descend the mountain right away,
And once he got there, he could then decide what to do.

Our story tells how Good-in-Talent, having concluded that there was no road for him to ascend to heaven and no gate through which to enter earth, made up his mind to descend the mountain. "I'll have to lock the gate of the grotto, and then I will straightway descend the mountain. Then, when my teacher returns to the grotto, I will come back to serve him."

He hastily walked as fast as he could down the road,
And suddenly found himself midway down the mountain.

He then heard someone calling from the woods for help,
Piteously imploring him to be so kind as to save her life.
    When Good-in-Talent heard this, he looked all around,
But there was not a trace of the one who was calling out.
He could only hear her calling, but he could not see her.
When he listened, the voice came from among the pines.
    "Who are you who time and again begs me to save her?
Are you some monster? Or are you an immortal maiden?
Please tell me where you are hiding yourself,
And also tell me in what way I can save you!"

Good-in-Talent thought to himself: "She begs me to save her life! People who cultivate their behavior should employ expedient means wherever possible. If I did not try to save her, it would not be right." And so, even though he was frightened, he forced himself to ask: "You who want me to save your life—I ask you, who are you? Tell me your name and surname, because only then I can save you. If not, I will continue on my way down the mountain." That bewitching sprite replied:

"I implore you, dear monk, please listen to me,
I am a little snake-sprite from these mountains.
Because I offended an immortal, I'm confined,
So I implore you be so kind as to set me free.
    For a full eighteen years I've lived in this jar,
I am now so starved that it's truly pitiable!
If you, dear monk, are willing to save me, I will
Express my thanks with a thousand-storied pagoda!"

Good-in-Talent replied: "How do you want me to save you?" The snake-sprite said: "By the side of the pine tree is a huge rock. Below it you'll find a tiny jar. You only have to remove the sealing skin, and I will be able to come out." Good-in-Talent did exactly as he had been told. When he lifted up the rock, he indeed found a small jar. When he had removed the sealing skin, there was a flash of light from the bottle, and a little snake wriggled out onto the ground. Then she immediately transformed into a terrifying creature more than twenty yards long with eyes as big as copper bells! When he saw this, Good-in-Talent was so frightened that his soul left his body. The snake-sprite addressed him as follows:

"Many thanks, my dear monk, for having saved me,
Having saved me, this snake-sprite, from suffering!
I am starved and the pangs of hunger are unbearable,
So I'd like, my dear monk, to eat you as a little snack."

Good-in-Talent cursed her: "You evil beast! How can you be so devoid of decency? Now that I have saved you and set you free, you should repay the favor I've shown you. But you want to eat me! You repay a favor with a feud—how could there be such a principle in the world?" The snake-sprite replied: "In this world it is common practice to repay a favor with a feud." Good-in-Talent said: "Now that we find ourselves in this situation, let's travel onward. Once we have asked three people, and they all say that it is common practice in the world to repay a favor with a feud, then I'll allow myself to be eaten by you, and I will die without any regret. But if a favor has to be repaid with a favor, you cannot even touch me!" The snake-sprite said: "I have also cultivated the Way, for a few hundred years, and I have only heard that a favor is repaid with a feud. I've never heard that a favor is repaid by a favor. I've now spent a full eighteen years in this jar, and I haven't eaten a thing. I'm really starving, so please, allow yourself to be eaten!"

Good-in-Talent said to the snake-sprite: "Now listen!
You and me, the two of us, cannot reach an agreement,
So we will put the question to anyone we come across:
If it's 'a favor is repaid by a feud,' I will accept defeat.
 After we've asked three people, you may then eat me,
But first we'll have to see what these three have to say.
If each of these three says a favor is repaid by a feud,
I will die without regret, and I will be happy to do so."
 From a distance they saw a man who came their way,
It happened to be the Golden Buffalo Star from heaven.
Good-in-Talent stepped forward, greeted him with a bow,
And then asked him: "Dear sir, can I ask you a question?
 Is it the way of the world to repay a favor with a feud,
Or is it the case that a favor should be repaid by a favor?"

The old man said: "It is always the way of the world to repay a favor with a feud. It is never the case that a favor is repaid by a favor." That snake-sprite started to jump up and down for joy: "Little monk,[19] you're bound to die. Quickly allow me to eat you!" Good-in-Talent replied: "We have asked only one person; that's not enough testimony. We still have to ask two more people. If they all say that a favor is repaid by a feud, it's still not too late to eat me. Don't be so eager! I cannot escape from you anyway. You, old man, you say that a favor is repaid by a feud. I really don't understand why that is the case. Please explain it to me, so I may die in peace." The old man said: "I will explain it to you. I happen to be the Golden Buffalo Astral Official, the Great Strength King. Originally I was not willing to descend to the mortal world, because I knew that the ten sins of the living beings of this world are unpardonable. It was all because of the boundless vow of Lord Kṣitigarbha to ferry the people across.[20] He saw that the living beings of the eastern world bloodied their hands in digging the soil and planting the fields. In tears he urged me to descend to the mortal world and assist the living beings. When we arrived at the southern gate of heaven, I saw how the evil miasma of the living beings rose up to heaven. They definitely repay favors with feuds! But the boundless vow of Lord Kṣitigarbha was deep, and he said: 'They surely repay a favor with a favor. It is not possible that they repay a favor with a feud. If I am unable to see such living beings, may my two eyes fall down upon the ground!' He strongly encouraged me to go down to the mortal world, and when I was not paying attention, he pushed me out the gate of heaven! When I crashed to the ground, I lost all teeth in my upper jaw. When the living beings saw how great my strength was, they pulled a rope through my nose to lead me hither and thither to pull the plow and drag the harrow. Whenever I walked just a little bit slow, they would whip me with a green bough and curse me, calling me a 'rotten cow.' Whenever I stopped for even a moment, they would curse me, calling me a 'lazy cow.' Whenever I felt hungry and ate a mouthful of grass, they would curse me, calling me a 'thievish cow.' And then when I grew old and could no longer do any work, they wanted to kill me and flay my skin, pull out my tendons, and eat my flesh. That's the extent to which they are devoid of a conscience! Now that I have told you this, is it the rule that a favor is repaid by a favor, or that a favor is repaid by a feud? Because Lord Kṣitigarbha could not see the evil of the living beings of the eastern word, and had earlier made a vow, both his eyes fell down to the earth. There they turned into snails, which are trampled by buffaloes. It's all too pitiable, too saddening, too bad!

"It's too saddening: these evil men are without foundation,
They don't want to repay a favor, they repay it with a feud.
I pulled the plow and dragged the harrow, heavy as rocks,
But the eight-foot-long hempen whip whipped my back.
    If the soil was too heavy or the water too deep to plow,
And my tears would stream down because of my hunger,
They would constantly curse me in language most foul,
With every word they would curse me: 'You rotten cow!'
    My only wish was to rest for a while in the early morning:
'You don't do a thing from midnight till the hour of noon!'
When I was hungry and ate of the grass that grows by the field,
All the laborers, old and young, cursed me: 'You thievish cow!'
    All I got to eat throughout the year was only straw, whereas
The rice and grain I helped plant was all harvested by others.
The white rice they harvested was cooked as food and eaten,
The glutinous rice was made into wine to entertain friends.
    Millet and rice and cotton flowers—all was provided for,
Beans and wheat and sesame seeds—all were harvested.
But when bringing home a bride or marrying off a daughter,
The first thought if money was short was to sell off the buffalo.
    When they saw that I had grown old and lacked strength,
They sold me to the butcher so he could turn me into beef.
I was tightly bound with a hempen rope and hit with an axe,
My skin was flayed, my flesh was cut—what feud did we have?
    My tears gushed down as I was totally overcome by pain,
My four legs all facing up to the sky and my life now gone.
When my skin was flayed, it was made into a booming drum,
Which scares Heaven and Earth, distressing ghosts and gods.
    I will take revenge on the people who killed me, and I
Refuse to forgive and forget the people who dined on me.
This is how evil the heart is of the people in this world:
You do them a favor and they will repay you with a feud."

When the snake-sprite heard this story, she wiggled her head and whipped her tail and said: "Fine! Fine! Fine! I'm really starving. Little monk, quickly relieve a little of the hunger in my belly!" Good-in-Talent said to her: "I've told you this before. We will ask three people, and you can eat me only if they all say that a favor is repaid by a feud. Now we have asked only one person, so how can you want to eat me right away? After we have asked three people, then you may eat me and I will die without regret." The snake-sprite said: "Little monk, there's no need for me to fear that you will escape to heaven. We'll do as you say. After we have asked two more people, I will eat you anyhow." As Good-in-Talent was walking on, he was weeping—

Our little Good-in-Talent was frightened in his heart,
While the snake-sprite followed him, whipping her tail.
He had only thought to go home and have some fun,
Never thinking that midway he'd be eaten by a snake.
From a distance they saw a man coming their way;
When he got closer, he turned out to be a Daoist priest.
"Such a Daoist priest must of course know principle,
And clearly understand the causes of favor and feud."
Awash in tears he addressed him and asked the question:
"Is it a common habit that a favor is repaid by a favor?

"My dear priest, please allow this monk to ask you a question. Is it the way of the world to repay a favor with a favor, or to repay a favor with a feud?" The Daoist priest replied: "It is the way of the world to repay a favor with a feud; there is nobody who repays a favor with a favor." When the snake-sprite heard this, her joy was beyond words: "My dear priest, you are so right! You little monk, quickly let me eat you!" "We have asked only two people, so how is it you again want to eat me?" The snake-sprite said: "Four does not block Six. You have no idea how unbearable my hunger is! You are someone who has left the family; you should show a little more compassion! You must have heard that in ancient times the Buddha Śākyamuni sacrificed his body to feed a tiger and that he cut off his flesh to feed an eagle!" Good-in-Talent said: "Well, I am not the old Buddha who sacrificed his body to feed a tiger and cut off his flesh to feed an eagle. As long as we have not asked three people, I am not giving up hope. That Great Strength King, the Golden Buffalo Astral Official, also provided me with an explanation, so, Daoist priest, you should also provide me with an explanation of why you say that a favor is repaid by a feud, so that I may die in peace."

Good-in-Talent asked the Daoist priest the question:
"What is the reason that a favor is not repaid by a favor?

To repay a favor by a favor is the correct moral principle,
To repay a favor by a feud is not the way it should be."

The priest addressed him with the following clarification:
"You are young, your understanding is not yet developed.
I am no one else but Master Zhuang, and I am
A renowned philosopher of the Western Zhou.[21]

Studying with Grand Superior I learned the Great Way,[22]
He taught me amulets and mantras to save the people.
I am even capable of bringing the dead back to life,
But who in this world ever repaid me for my favors?

Today I came here by way of Mount Southern Flower,
And in a pavilion there I saw a pile of white bones.
My heart was filled with a most compassionate wish
To bring the man back to life so he could return home.

But alas, it turned out the corpse was no longer whole:
It had been partly eaten by wolves and dogs.
Reciting true words, I summoned the god of the earth
To investigate that dog and wolf, and borrow a heart.

The god of the soil, thus instructed, without any delay
Arrested a dog and a wolf, and took their lungs and heart.

"That god of the soil brought the wolf and the dog before me. I promptly took out the wolf's heart and the dog's lungs, replacing them with lumps of clay. After I had sprinkled them with talisman-water, the wolf and dog returned to the mountain as if nothing had happened. The fellow was still was missing a thigh, so I used a mulberry branch for the bone and clay for the flesh. As soon as I had sprinkled him with a mouthful of holy water, he returned to life. He promptly got back on his feet, rubbed his eyes, and stretched himself. Then he addressed me, saying: 'I've slept for quite a long time!' He then looked all around him. 'Aiyo! Where have my luggage, bedding, and umbrella gone? You priest, don't laugh at me. Quickly give me back my bedding, luggage, and umbrella! There is no one in front of us, and there is no one behind us, so who but you could have taken my stuff? If you don't return my stuff to me, I will take you to see the magistrate at his office!' Pulling and dragging me, we arrived at the office, and he immediately started to beat the drum.[23] The district magistrate promptly opened up the court for the interrogation. I told him what had happened. 'Magistrate, if you do not believe me, I'll use my holy water to perform a test.'

The man turned back into a pile of white bones: the mulberry branch and the clay were clearly visible, and the wolf's heart and dog's lungs had not changed. He was a skeleton! Only then did the magistrate believe my story to be true. Only in this way was I able to escape with my life and arrive here! Now this is called 'repaying a favor with a feud'!

"How sad it is to see such a skeleton bereft of feeling!
You bring him back to life, but he becomes an enemy.
My compassion was aroused—he could not be saved,
In this world of ours, everybody is an evil skeleton.
    Dragged by pigs, nibbled on by dogs, picked at by crows,
Beaten and blown by rain and wind—truly lamentable!
As the moon at night as before shines on the dry bones,
The white clouds are the coffin lid, a cool spring flows.
    I know not the surname or the name of that skeleton,
But my unalloyed compassion was repaid by a feud.
In this world of ours, everything always goes this way:
Wolf's heart and dog's lungs everywhere stay in place."

When she heard these words, the snake-sprite's joy was beyond words. Wagging her head and whipping her tail, she took on a threatening posture, and again she wanted to eat Good-in-Talent. A weeping Good-in-Talent begged her: "We still have to put our question to one more person! Until we have arrived at the Yellow River, I will not lose heart. If we put the question to one more person and that person also says that a favor should be repaid with a feud, you may eat me, and I will die without regret."

Good-in-Talent was so scared he was shaking all over,
The snake-sprite followed behind him, showing her might.
Good-in-Talent was so scared he didn't know where to go,
His life at this moment resembled a candle in the wind.
    As he walked along the road, he was weeping,
Crying and weeping in a most heartrending way.
As he wept for a stretch, he walked one stretch:
Then he saw a young girl coming toward him.

When Good-in-Talent saw this girl, he walked up to her. "My dear girl, could I ask you a question? Is it the way of the world to repay a favor with a favor, or to repay a favor with a feud?" The girl said: "The rule is that a favor is repaid by a favor. How could one repay a favor with a feud?" The snake-sprite was enraged and said: "Aiyo! You little girl, you really do not understand the affairs of this world. The two people we met earlier said that a favor is repaid by a feud. How dare you now say that a favor is repaid by a favor! Those two elderly gentlemen a moment ago were well experienced in worldly affairs, and they supported their argument with watertight evidence. And you want to tell me that they are no match for you, a little hussy without any proof or evidence?

"This is the day I am definitely going to eat you!
You little hussy are devoid of any intelligence!
The earlier statements were supported by proof,
Your words are devoid of any supporting facts.
    I first intend to eat the monk as my main dish,
And then later I will have you as a little snack!"
Slithering closer she was truly about to eat them:
Her heart was suddenly filled with blackest evil!

The snake-sprite said: "This little monk is just a starving bag of bones. Even if I ate him, it still would not be enough. So I will eat him together with you, little girl!" Wagging her head and whipping her tail she made ready to eat them. The bodhisattva touched her just once with her immortal fly whisk, and the snake-sprite immediately collapsed on the ground. The snake-sprite remained stunned for a moment, and the girl said: "Evil beast, how do you dare act in such an impudent manner, unaware that Heaven's chastisement is inescapable. The crimes you've committed are as big as a mountain, and your accumulated sins are as deep as an ocean! Because of this, the Ancestral Teacher of Pure Yang,[24] afraid in his compassion that you might be executed by the Thunder, confined you in this jar, hoping that you would abandon the crooked and return to the straight, reform your evil ways and follow goodness. But even after eighteen years in this jar, your evil heart is still not reformed, and your old desires are still the same as before. Now you had been set free by the monk Good-in-Talent, you should have repaid his favor. But you want to devour him and repay a favor with a feud, without considering that the Five Thunders are inescapable, and that Heaven's Principle cannot condone this!" The snake-sprite replied:

"You have eaten your fill and cannot feel the pangs of hunger in my belly. What is this nonsense about the Five Thunders and Heaven's chastisement? I've never believed in any of that crap! I'm definitely going to eat the two of you as little snacks!" The girl then said: "You evil beast, what cheek! If you really want to eat the two of us, there is no problem at all. I have here this little jar. If you can wriggle into the jar and then wriggle out again, you may eat the two of us. But if you cannot wriggle into the jar and then wriggle out again, forget about it!"

That snake-sprite thought to herself: "I spent eighteen years in that jar! Why would I not be able to wriggle into the jar and then wriggle out again? You, little girl, this will be your death! Give me that jar and I'll give it a try! I'm really going to eat you." The girl took out a tiny earthen jar. As soon as the snake-sprite saw it, she shook herself a few times and transformed herself into a tiny snake. After she had wriggled into the earthen jar, she shook her head and then turned around, saying: "Fine! Make the opening a little bit bigger, so it is easier for me to get out." The bodhisattva replied: "You evil beast, do you still think you can get out? If you do, it will only be one hundred eight thousand years from now!" "Aiyo! Who will you be then?"

The bodhisattva then answered her in the following way:
"I am the bodhisattva Guanshiyin of the Southern Sea.

You, you animal, are totally bereft of moral principle,
Without any conscience you repaid a favor with a feud.
Today you may still think that you will get out again,
But you'll not be set free for a thousand, a myriad of years!

You may have cultivated yourself for three hundred years,
But acting against the Dharma, you're a witchlike sprite.
If the heavenly immortal had not confined you in his jar,
You would have been killed by the roar of the Thunder!

Convinced of the extent of your own Dharma-power,
You did not realize there'd be no escape from the jar.
Your whole body is racked by pain as if cut by swords,
Your belly now feels as if it were pierced by arrows."

"This kind of pain and suffering is truly unbearable!

I now realize that

The string of my evils is complete, my life is in danger.
Dear bodhisattva, I beg you to show me forgiveness,

I am fully willing to
Leave the crooked, return to the straight, and cultivate myself."
With each and every word she begged bodhisattva Guanyin:
"I'll never again waver and act like a witchlike sprite!
If you, Bodhisattva, are willing to show me compassion,
I will protect Buddhism for a thousand, a myriad of years!"
"Sinful beast, your heart is far too evil, and so I fear
That later you will once again harm people and kill them.
When your poor life was saved, the favor was not repaid,
Instead, overcome with black desire, you wanted to eat him.
If such a witchlike sprite like you is not done away with,
I fear you'll bring harm to later generations without end.
If you indeed still hope to get out of this jar one day,
It can only happen once your
Poisonous heart has been completely turned into cinnabar.[25]
Your entire body will have to be turned into a tree of *bodhi*,
Shedding your snake body, you must convert to Buddhism.
And if just once again you turn from the straight and narrow,
A hundred days, I promise, and you will turn into bloody pus."
"The pain and suffering in this jar are truly unbearable!
I beg you, Bodhisattva, to show me your kind compassion!
If I do not abandon the crooked, and return to the straight,
Arrest and confine me for the rest of my poor little life.
From now on I will never falter in my desire for the Way,
With all my heart and without doubt, I'll cultivate the Way,"
The bodhisattva was bound to display her compassion,
And with her willow branch
She sprinkled a single drop of sweet dew into the jar.
The snake-sprite immediately felt
Clear and cool throughout her body, relaxed in spirit,
And the craving hunger in her belly was also relieved.
The bodhisattva took the jar with her to the Southern Sea
So she could cultivate perfection in the Roaring Tides Cave.
The bodhisattva then turned around to ask Good-in-Talent,
To ask Good-in-Talent in turn what it was he truly desired:
"Do you want to go back home and see your father, or
Do you want to come with me and cultivate yourself?"
The virginal lad Good-in-Talent bowed with sincere piety
To express his thanks to the bodhisattva for saving his life:

"I was on my way back home, but that was not my intention,
Who'd have known that I'd run into a snake-sprite midway!
If you, Bodhisattva, had not come and saved my life,
I would not have been able to survive this ordeal.
From now on I only want to follow you, Bodhisattva,
And if that means walking on fire, I'll gladly do so!"

The bodhisattva said: "If you are happy and willing to cultivate the Way, I will take you with me to Mt. Putuo. It will take you several years of bitter cultivation to complete your training, after which I will transmit to you the method of seated meditation. Only then will you be able to fully accomplish the Great Way. Please memorize carefully:

"Your behavior in cultivating the Way should be clear,
Make not one mistake on the road of birth and death.
If you persist in the forgetting of your body and limbs,
The Self-so True Buddha will display his full body.
When the moon is completely round at midautumn,
The flood has not yet come, the water's not yet tranquil.
Then your mental ground is calm and without any care,
Your body will rise freely and enjoy mystic pleasures.
When first you meditate / and become aware of causes,
You must fully understand 'thus-come and thus-gone.'[26]
This waxing and waning—/ who ever understands?
Freedom from delusion depends on the central mind.
Harmonize inhaling and exhaling, / separate upper and lower,
So one yin and one yang will be stewing in the tripod.
In the crescent-shaped burner / creation is born:
Travel down the twelve stories of the layered tower.[27]
When water and fire cooperate, / Qian and Kun move,[28]
Yin and yang unite their virtue and also their brilliance.
The spirit-light shines, / and the jade hare rises:
The golden crow wakes with a cry the midnight moon.
On the year's shortest day / a new yang emerges:
Red lotuses manifest numerous new flowers.
In utter bewilderment, / in deepest darkness:
Nothing generates Being—enjoy Ascending Peace.

Miraculous mysticism / and numinous miracle!
The myriad phenomena all return to the root.
The Three Teachings / all share the same root:[29]
Sages, immortals, buddhas are one and the same.
The fire of *samādhi* / is called 'noncompeting'
And brings about a sixteen-foot purple-gold body.[30]
They may burn incense, / they may recite the sutras,
But how can any of them ever know this one Truth?
But now on this day / I transmit this teaching to you:
Cultivate it piously from dawn to dusk—don't slacken!"

The bodhisattva said: "Good-in-Talent, memorize this well, and on no account slacken in your practice. I will now take you with me to Mt. Putuo. After you have practiced for three years, I will come again to see how you are doing. That little snake-sprite I will take to the Roaring Tides Cave. Once she has there completely transformed her poisonous heart, I will transmit to her the method to refine her nature, so she can join the ranks of the immortals. The poison of her heart will turn into vipers and scorpions. When her heart is good, it will instantly be transformed into *bodhi*. We'll see how she behaves, and then make our decision accordingly." After the bodhisattva had given her instructions, Good-in-Talent kowtowed repeatedly to express his thanks.

The mahāsattva Guanyin set out for the ninth heaven, and slowly she rose up into the sky. From the edge of a cloud, the bodhisattva observed the billowing ocean of suffering, the inexhaustible domain of dust, and sighed:

"White clouds and flowing streams—what does one see?
One who coolly observes the dusty world finds it empty.
On a crane-bench alone, he sings of the miraculous cinnabar,
Not submitting writings for fame and profit at Phoenix Pond.[31]
Muddleheaded, they will miss out on the Buddha-mind—
The multitudes on earth are deluded, so few are enlightened!
If they are not persons so predestined by the nines and sixes,[32]
Will they ever recognize the obvious ladder leading to heaven?"

As the mahāsattva was observing the world from the edge of her cloud, she noticed an auspicious aura rising up into the sky from far away in the western lands, and she knew this meant that there was a good and virtuous disciple to be found in the western regions. "I'll have to go there to have a look!" When she arrived there and pushed aside the clouds to have a look, it turned out that a white parrot had been able to practice filial piety, which explained the appearance of this auspicious aura:

"So it happened that this divine bird from the western regions
Was born in these eastern lands with a heart of filial piety.
As its true nature was displayed, a bright light shone forth,
And its filial heart moved me to come and visit this spot."

The bodhisattva noticed that the gods of the earth were keeping watch over this parrot, so she immediately asked them: "What happened to this bird?" The gods of the soil then provided a full account to the bodhisattva:

"This bird's been as white as silver from the day of its birth,
Although a parrot, it was capable of filiality toward its parents.
    When its mother fell ill, she longed to eat some red cherries,
So it flew to the east of the city to pluck some red cherries.
Who could have known it would be captured by hunters,
Who would lock it up in a cage for longer than a year.
    By then all hunters had been converted,[33] so they changed
Their means of livelihood and became virtuous people.
Each day it urged people to practice expedient means,
And many great sinners were awakened by its preaching.
    East of the city lived a certain millionaire named Ren,
The violence and evil he committed were beyond words.
But even he was persuaded by this parrot to convert,
And his wife and concubine began self-cultivation.
    This moved Bodhidharma from the western regions[34]
To teach it a trick by which to escape from its cage:
By pretending to be dead even though it had not died,
It managed to escape from the cage and go back home.
    It found the cherries it wanted to take to his mother—
How could it know its mother had gone to the shades?
Heartbroken, overcome by grief, it died from weeping—
Now we stand guard over the corpse of this filial bird.
    As we did not know, Bodhisattva, you were arriving,
Please forgive us for being so slow to welcome you."

As soon as the bodhisattva had heard from the gods of the earth this story of maternal love and filial piety, she immediately poured a single drop of sweet-dew water into the mouth of the parrot, which in an instant returned to life. She quickly ordered the gods of the earth to find the souls of the parrot's parents, which after a short while, they were able to do. The bodhisattva in her kind compassion immediately sprinkled the souls of the two birds with the sweet dew of her willow wand, and cleansing them from all the dust and pollution of former lives, she ordered them to be reborn in the world of men. She then took the parrot with her to the Southern Sea, and sighed:

"I had ferried across Good-in-Talent and the snake-sprite,
Now this bird's filial heart invoked the Buddha's presence.
If an oh so tiny parrot is capable of practicing filial piety,
How can a human being not understand the filial impulse?
    Today I take you with me to my Southern Sea, where you
Forever will be the Dharma-protecting bird before my throne.
With me you will meditate there on the Way of the Buddha:
No birth and also no annihilation—eternal spring forever!"

The bodhisattva instructed the gods of the earth: "Thank you very much for standing guard over this filial bird. Now, you may all leave." The gods of the soil kowtowed to thank her for her grace and left.

Riding her cloud, the bodhisattva returned to her mountain,
And before realizing it, three years had gone by in a flash.
The virginal lad Good-in-Talent's work was completed,
The bodhisattva guided him in shedding his mortal body.
    One grain of golden cinnabar is heavier than a pound—
Those who can fathom this truth will live a life eternal.
Build a base and sweep it clean of all your dusty cares,
Refine yourself till the six roots are all refined and pure.[35]
    Increase the fire of *samādhi* below the earthen pot,
And in the Yellow Court refine your original nature.[36]
Empty your myriad cares, cut off both color and form,
Do not cling to ways of the world, achieve the cinnabar!
    Separated from color and form, forget them completely—
A spark of one's nature's light: empty and numinous![37]

I tell this to all you gentlemen who study the Way,
This is the one and only standard for all eternity.
  When after three or nine years your work is done,
You will live forever and enjoy everlasting spring!

One day the bodhisattva arrived at Mt. Putuo and said to the virginal lad Good-in-Talent: "Please tell me how your work has been going." Good-in-Talent replied: "Mahāsattva, please let me explain. I hope that you, my buddha, will show me your compassion, as I don't know whether I am doing well.

"The numinous terrace swept clean, there's no thought,
In emptiness and nothingness the mystic work is done.
The hundred veins have all returned to the point *wuji*,
I've gathered the single true breath preceding creation.
  The nine-cycle divine cinnabar enters the golden tripod,
The four seasons proceed smoothly, creation is numinous.
The Dharma-wheel constantly turns in the No-birth land,
A sagely sun, a sagely moon illuminate the golden court.
  As fire and water cooperate, the true mercury appears,
And turns into one clump of gold made of purest yang."

The bodhisattva said with a smile: "Even though your work has reached this stage, you still have some more work to do in order to progress. But today I have come for the purpose of taking you to a place where we may have some fun." Riding a cloud, the mahāsattva took Good-in-Talent with her to a tiny island, which was nothing more than a single white rock surrounded on all sides by water. As soon as the bodhisattva with her willow wand sprinkled [some sweet dew] on the sea, myriads of lotus flowers appeared. As soon as Good-in-Talent saw these lotus flowers, his heart was filled with joy. But all of a sudden he saw a golden whale emerge from the sea, stormy waves rise up mightily, and white billows surge up to heaven, all of which frightened Good-in-Talent. While the bodhisattva stood on the head of the whale, Good-in-Talent walked on the lotus flowers, and in this way they leisurely arrived at the Purple Bamboo Forest. There he watched as the white parrot came flying toward them, carrying a rosary in its beak. The bodhisattva has preserved this picture in the world.[38] It was at this moment that the virginal lad Good-in-Talent escaped from the mortal world and achieved perfect truth. It happened on Good-in-Talent Rock, which to this day is to be found in the Southern Sea.

The bodhisattva said: "If one son achieves buddhahood, all nine classes of relatives will ascend to heaven." Because at this time Good-in-Talent's mother, Lady Han, was still being kept in the world of darkness,[39] she promptly ordered a Jiedi-god: "Go to the palace of Kṣitigarbha and ask the Teaching Lord of the Dark World to look into the case of Lady Han. Enlighten her as to the Great Way, and take her to the Heavenly Palace of Ignorance, so that she may practice cultivation in the Hall of Taking Pleasure in Goodness. When her work has been completed, she will once again be promoted and rewarded. Because his father, Grand Historian Chen, has not received any news from his son since the boy descended the mountain, he is day and night overcome by sad thoughts, and has no desire at all to serve as an official at court. He wishes to send up a request to be allowed to take his leave from the court and return to his village, but alas, the current emperor will not grant his request because he so appreciates his undivided loyalty. Moreover, all his life he has been able to influence the ruler above and to benefit the people below, his merit covers the world and his virtue moves the god. The SUPREME DEITY has registered his name in the jade tablets, so he may, once he has died and returned to heaven, be able to practice cultivation. His case has been settled by an edict of the BUDDHA." As soon as the Jiedi-god had received the bodhisattva's holy order, he went to the palace of Kṣitigarbha—but enough of that.

Let's tell again of the snake-sprite. After having cultivated herself for seven years in the Roaring Tides Cave, she had completely transformed her poisonous heart, obtained the Way, and realized perfect truth. Her practice of refinement had resulted in the creation of a night-shining pearl, and she herself had been transformed into Dragon Girl. That's why it is said "Dragon Girl at seven years offered a shining pearl." The mahāsattva in her kind compassion took her into her service. She brought her to the northern rock, where she escaped from the mortal world and achieved perfect truth. This took place at Dragon Girl Rock, which is still to be found at Mt. Putuo.

The Precious Scroll of Good-in-Talent has come to its end,
May all you who are present develop a heart for the Way.

Cultivating yourself with purpose, you can become a buddha,
These true and substantial words are no unfounded fiction.
As a human being we should never waver for an instant,
But should turn ourselves around and begin self-cultivation.
Congratulations, good men and faithful women, because
Together at Numinous Mountain, we will see the Buddha!

The faithful believer Zhou Hongyuan has respectfully seen to the cutting of the printing blocks.

Notes

Introduction

1. For a comprehensive study of the cult of Avalokiteśvara/Guanyin in China, see Chün-fang Yü, *Kuan-yin: The Chinese Transformation of Avalokiteśvara* (New York: Columbia University Press, 2001). This work contains an extensive bibliography of primary and secondary materials on Guanyin. Patricia Eichenbaum Karetzky, *Guanyin* (Hong Kong: Oxford University Press, 2004), provides a very brief outline of the development of the cult of Guanyin, focusing on the bodhisattva's representation in art. Recent years have witnessed an outpouring of comparable Chinese studies on Guanyin.

2. For a detailed study of this sex change, see Rolf A. Stein, "Avalokiteśvara/Kouan-yin, un exemple de transformation d'un dieu en déesse," *Cahiers d'Extrême Asie* 1986:17–80.

3. The origin and development of the legend of Princess Miaoshan has been studied in great detail by Glen Dudbridge, *The Legend of Miaoshan* (Oxford: Oxford University Press, 2004). This is a revised version of the author's *The Legend of Miaoshan* (Oxford: Ithaca Press, 1978). The revised version incorporates the findings of his article "Miaoshan on Stone: Two Early Inscriptions," *Harvard Journal of Asiatic Studies* 42.2 (1982): 589–614.

4. Dudbridge 2004, pp. 47–56.

5. A rare example of a *nianhua* (new year's print) showing four scenes from the legend of Miaoshan from Linfen in Shanxi is reproduced in Po Sung-nien and David Johnson, *Domestic Deities and Auspicious Emblems: The Iconography of Everyday Life in Village China. Popular Prints and Papercuts from the Collection of Po Sung-nien* (Berkeley: Chinese Popular Culture Project, 1992), pp. 168–169.

6. The same design is still found in the frontispiece of a woodblock edition of 1931, kept in the Harvard-Yenching Library (Patrick Hanan Collection). Popular woodblock prints of the nineteenth and early twentieth century often add Weituo in the upper right-hand corner. See, for instance, the examples reproduced in Wang Shucun, comp., *Guanyin baitu* (Guangzhou: Lingnan yishu chubanshe, 1995), which focuses on the popular iconography of Guanyin. Weituo is the guardian god facing the main hall of a monastery. One legend about his

association with Guanyin tells that when Guanyin manifested herself as a beautiful young girl in a boat on the Jialing River, offering herself in marriage to anyone who could hit her with a piece of silver (in this way collecting donations for building a bridge), the only piece of silver to hit her was the one thrown by Weituo, who had the assistance of the immortal Lü Dongbin. Guanyin thereupon manifested her true nature to Weituo, who became her disciple. See Yan Suhui, *Guanyin xiaobaike* (Taibei: Yushushe, 2001), p. 107. Other versions of the legend are linked to the completion of the famous Luoyang Bridge near Quanzhou in Fujian. See Li Miao, comp., *Guanyin pusa baojuan* (Jilin renmin chubanshe, 2001), pp. 134–142. Because of these stories Weituo and Guanyin are often refereed to as "face-to-face husband and wife" (*duimian fuqi*), a couple who live in close proximity but who are not allowed to consummate their marriage.

7. See Kenneth Ch'en, *Buddhism in China: A Historical Survey* (Princeton: Princeton University Press, 1964), pp. 340–341.

8. The information on the cult of Avalokiteśvara in India is summarized by Yü 2001, pp. 7–14. On the cult of the horse-headed Guanyin, see Robert van Gulik, *Hayagriva: The Mantrayanic Aspect of Horse-Cult in China and Japan* (Leiden: E. J. Brill, 1955).

9. Mahayana means Great Vehicle. In contrast, the earlier teachings of Buddhism came to be designated as Hinayana or Lesser Vehicle. This earlier tradition of Buddhism, which spread to Sri Lanka, Burma, and Thailand, often was referred to as Theravada or School of the Elders in English scholarship, but nowadays is more commonly referred to as "mainstream" or "Nikaya" Buddhism. The classic study on the early dissemination of Buddhism in China is still Erik Zürcher, *The Buddhist Conquest of China: The Spread and Adaptation of Buddhism in Early Medieval China*, 2 vols. (Leiden: E. J. Brill, 1959).

10. Rebirth was unknown as a concept in China before it was introduced by Buddhism. Although early Buddhism taught that what was reborn was a constantly changing continuum, Chinese Buddhism came to teach that every person had an individual soul (*shen*) that passed through an endless chain of lives. By the tenth century, it was commonly held that every soul following death had to subsequently appear before the Ten Courts of the Underworld, to be judged for its sins and virtues while alive. The leader of these Ten Judges was King Yama. Each of the Ten Judges might condemn a sinner to long and gruesome sufferings in one of the many hells; the final judge determined the nature of one's eventual rebirth. See Stephen F. Teiser, *The Scripture on the Ten Kings and the Making of Purgatory in Medieval Chinese Buddhism* (Honolulu: University of Hawai'i Press, 1994). Buddhist popular preaching vividly contrasted the joys of heaven to the tortures of hell.

11. Many *jātaka* (tales of earlier lives of the Buddha) tell stories of the future Buddha donating his body to animals in need of food, or willing to suffer great tortures in order to hear the Truth. See Reiko Ohnuma, *Head, Eyes, Flesh, and Blood: Giving Away the Body in Indian Buddhist Literature* (New York: Columbia University Press, 2007).

12. See Richard Payne and Kenneth K. Tanaka, eds., *Approaching the Land of Bliss: Religious Practice in the Cult of Amitābha* (Honolulu: University of Hawai'i Press, 2004).

13. Alan Sponberg and Helen Hardacre, eds., *Maitreya, the Future Buddha* (Cambridge: Cambridge University Press, 1988).

14. Zhiru Ng, *The Making of a Savior Bodhisattva: Dizang in Medieval China* (Honolulu: University of Hawai'i Press, 2007).

15. See Yü 2001.

16. Ibid.

17. See Jan Fontein, *The Pilgrimage of Sudhana: A Study of Gandavyūha Illustrations in China, Japan, and Java* (Den Haag: Mouton, 1967).

18. See Yü 2001, pp. 353–406.

19. This sutra has been translated into English by Bunnō Katō as *The Sutra of the Lotus Flower of the Wonderful Law*, in Bunnō Katō et al., trans., *The Threefold Lotus Sutra* (Tokyo: Kosei Publishing, 1975); by Leon Hurvitz as *The Scripture of the Lotus Blossom of the Fine Dharma (The Lotus Sūtra)*, translated from the Chinese of Kumārajīva (New York: Columbia University Press, 1976); and by Burton Watson as *The Lotus Sutra* (New York: Columbia University Press, 1993).

20. Miyeko Murase, "Kuan-yin as Savior of Men: Illustrations of the Twenty-fifth Chapter of the Lotus Sutra in Chinese Painting," *Artibus Asiae* 33.1–2 (1971): 39–73.

21. See Yü 2001, pp. 37–39.

22. Ibid., pp. 158–176. See also Robert F. Campany, "The Real Presence," *History of Religions* 32 (1993): 233–272; and Robert F. Campany, "The Earliest Tales of Bodhisattva Guanshiyin," in *Religions of China in Practice*, ed. Donald S. Lopez (Princeton: Princeton University Press, 1996), pp. 82–96.

23. See Yü 2001, pp. 80, 91, and passim. The most popular *dhāraṇī* connected with the name of Guanyin is the *Dabei zhou* (Great Compassion *Dhāraṇī*); see Maria Dorothea Reis-Habito, *Die Dhāraṇī des grossen Erbarmens des Bodhisattva Avalokiteśvara mit tausend Handen und Augen: Übersetzung und Untersuchung ihrer textlichen Grundlage sowie Erforschung ihres Kultes in China* (Nettetal: Steyler Verlag, 1993); and Maria Dorothea Reis-Habito, "The Great Compassion Dhāraṇī," in Henrik Hjort Sørensen, *The Esoteric Buddhist Tradition* (Copenhagen: Seminar for Buddhist Studies, 1994), pp. 31–50.

24. See Yü 2001, pp. 263–292. Another popular representation of Avalokiteśvara was that as the Eleven-headed Guanyin.

25. See Yü 2001, pp. 293–352.

26. See Edward H. Schafer, *The Divine Woman: Dragon Ladies and Rain Maidens in T'ang Literature* (Berkeley: University of California Press, 1973).

27. Yü 2001, pp. 407–413, rejects this hypothesis as Avalokiteśvara did not replace the famous named Chinese goddesses, such as the Queen Mother of the West (Xiwangmu). Barend ter Haar discusses Guanyin as a rain goddess in the Jiangnan area in his "Buddhist Inspired Options: Aspects of Religious Life in the Lower Yangzi Region from 1100 to 1340," *T'oung Pao* 87 (2001): 108–110.

28. This is the case for Linshui furen, a goddess widely venerated in Fujian for her rain-making powers. Her legend can be traced back to the tale of the dragon-slaying girl Li Ji in Gan Bao's *Soushen ji* (*In Search of the Supernatural*). See n. 133.

29. The Jade Emperor is the highest deity in the popular Chinese pantheon. Many Chinese legends about Guanyin, including *The Precious Scroll of Incense*

Mountain and *The Precious Scroll of Good-in-Talent and Dragon Daughter*, are set in a world in which native Chinese deities mingle freely with Buddhist divinities. The Jade Emperor heads a bureaucracy of gods, whom he may dispatch to the world of men.

30. See Yü 2001, pp. 419–438. A late precious scroll on this topic, *Tilan baojuan*, is reproduced in Zhang Xishun et al., eds., *Baojuan chuji* (Taiyuan: Shanxi renmin chubanshe, 1994), vol. 23. It is available in my Dutch translation, in *Prinses Miaoshan en andere Chinese legenden van Guanyin, de bodhisattva van barmhartigheid* (Amsterdam: Atlas, 2000), pp. 181–196.

One of the plays popular with *dan* (male performers of female roles) on the Beijing Opera stage of premodern times was *Trying to Seduce Mulian* (*Xi Mulian*), in which Guanyin tests the resolve of the Buddhist saint Maudgalyāyana (Mulian) by trying to seduce him in the shape of a beautiful girl. See Colin P. Mackerras, *The Rise of Peking Opera, 1770–1870* (Oxford: Oxford University Press, 1972), p. 256.

In some folktales of a more recent date, Guanyin also uses her charms as a young girl to seduce men to come up with the donations needed for the completion of a major bridge.

31. See Yü 2001, pp. 247–242. The White-robed Guanyin is often venerated for her power to grant children to childless couples, and in Ming and Qing images she is often depicted with a baby in her arms or lap.

The strong association of the White-robed Guanyin with Hangzhou and the strong link to the same city of the legend of the White Snake make one wonder whether both images could derive from an earlier local veneration of a rain-giving dragon-lady. The Guanyin of the Upper Tianzhu Monastery was especially renowned "for its response to prayers for rain" (ter Haar 2001, p. 108). In later centuries the iconography of the White-robed Guanyin and the White Snake (Madam White) is at times strikingly similar. For a modern folktale in which the White Snake is clearly portrayed as a substitute for the White-robed Guanyin, see Xu Hualong, "*Baishe zhuan* de qianxing yishi," *Minsu quyi* 72 (1991): 225, where he discusses "Weituo Thrice Tries to Seduce Madam White" (*Weituo sanxi Bainiang*).

32. See Yü 2001, pp. 438–448. Practically everybody in China in recent centuries, whether Buddhist or not, would be acquainted with the image and powers of the White-robed Guanyin from her frequent appearance in plays and novels, most notably the sixteenth-century vernacular novel *Journey to the West* (*Xiyou ji*).

In the new religions of the Ming and Qing dynasties, the White-robed Guanyin would often be identified with the Eternal Mother or considered to be a manifestation of the Eternal Mother. On Guanyin in these new religions, see Yü 2001, pp. 449–486.

33. Dudbridge 2004, pp. 5–14. The inscription, in the calligraphy of Cai Jing (d. 1126), was installed later in the year 1100, and reinstalled in the summer of 1308. A critical edition of the Chinese text of this inscription is provided in Dudbridge 2004, pp. 119–132. A complete English translation is offered by Yü 2001, pp. 495–504.

34. Dudbridge 2004, pp. 14–20.

35. Guanyin's visit to the Underworld is first mentioned in the *Life of the Mahāsattva Guanyin* (*Guanyin dashi zhuan*), a text associated with the name of the woman painter and calligrapher Guan Daosheng (1262–1319), whose husband was the famous painter and calligrapher Zhao Mengfu (1254–1322). This text is translated and studied by Dudbridge 2004, pp. 41–47; a translation may also be found in Wilt L. Idema and Beata Grant, *The Red Brush: Writing Women of Imperial China* (Cambridge: Harvard University Asia Center, 2004), pp. 311–313.

36. Dudbridge 2004, pp. 48–49.

37. A photographic reproduction of this edition can be found in Yoshioka Yoshitoyo, *Dōkyō kenkyū*, vol. 4 (Tokyo: Gogatsu Shobō, 1989), pp. 243–307. All references are based on this edition. This reproduction is followed by a typeset edition of a printing of the shorter version in a printed edition of 1871 (pp. 317–360) and a detailed comparison of the textual differences between the two versions. Dudbridge 2004, p. 51, notes the existence of at least two later editions of the elaborate version, one from Mt. Putuo.

38. My translation of the shorter version of *The Precious Scroll of Incense Mountain* is based on the 1872 edition, as reproduced in Zhang Xishun et al., eds., *Baojuan chuji*, vol. 26, pp. 453–552, and vol. 27, pp. 1–115. All references are based on this edition. As the blocks for printing this edition have been tampered with in one important passage, I have also consulted the 1931 printing of the text by the Xihu huikong jingfang at Hangzhou and the 1914 lithographic edition of the text by the Wenyi shuju of Shanghai, both at the Harvard-Yenching Library (Patrick Hanan Collection). For a listing of the known editions of *The Precious Scroll of Incense Mountain*, see Che Xilun, comp., *Zhongguo baojuan zonglu* (Taibei: Zhongyang yanjiu yuan Zhongguo wenzhe yanjiusuo choubeichu, 1998), pp. 160–161; or Che Xilun, comp., *Zhongguo baojuan zongmu* (Beijing: Beijing Yanshan chubanshe, 2000), pp. 307–309. From this listing it would appear that the earliest known edition of the shorter version is the one of 1868 from Hangzhou.

An extensive summary of the contents of *The Precious Scroll of Incense Mountain* may be found in David L. Overmyer, *Precious Volumes: An Introduction to Chinese Sectarian Scriptures from the Sixteenth and Seventeenth Centuries* (Cambridge: Harvard University Asia Center, 1999), pp. 40–44. Yü 2004 discusses the precious scroll briefly on pp. 317–320. I have provided a Dutch translation of the shorter version in Idema 2000b, pp. 63–180.

39. *Hangzhou Shang-Tianzhu Jiangsi zhi* (in *Wulin zhanggu congpian*, vol. 193), 3.2b and 10b, quoted in Lai Ruihe, "Miaoshan chuanshuo de liangzhong xin ziliao," *Zhongwai wenxue* 9.2 (1980): 123. Also see Dudbridge 2004, pp. 50, 52–53. These findings had also already been incorporated in the Chinese version of his 1978 publication: Du Deqiao (Glen Dudbridge), *Miaoshan chuanshuo—Guanyin pusa yuanqi kao* (Taibei: Juliu tushu gongsi, 1990).

40. The most detailed study of precious scrolls in English is Overmyer 1999. As his subtitle makes clear, he is primarily interested in the so-called sectarian scriptures of the sixteenth and seventeenth centuries, which form the bulk of the preserved *baojuan* texts from that period. Overmyer discusses the "pre-sectarian" precious scrolls on pp. 34–47. Descriptions in novels of the six-

teenth and seventeenth centuries make it clear, however, that pious Buddhist tales continued to be performed by nuns, either at the house of their female patrons or at their own convents. By the nineteenth century, "precious scroll" had become the general designation for relatively short prosimetric renditions of religious tales, whether Buddhist or Daoist in origin. These nineteenth-century texts are often divided into two *juan* ("scrolls" or chapters). The shorter version of *The Precious Scroll of Incense Mountain* follows this convention. One of the most important Chinese scholars in *baojuan* studies is Che Xilun. He has collected most of his articles on precious scrolls in his *Zhongguo baojuan yanjiu lunji* (Taibei: Xuehai chubanshe, 1997) and *Xinyang, jiaohua, yule: Zhongguo baojuan yanjiu ji qita* (Taibei: Xuesheng shuju, 2002). All contemporary scholarship on precious scrolls is heavily indebted to the pioneering work of Sawada Mizuho, *Hōken no kenkyū*, rev. ed. (Tokyo: Kokusho kankokai, 1975).

41. Neil Schmid, "*Yuanqi*: Medieval Buddhist Narratives from Dunhuang" (Ph.D. thesis, University of Pennsylvania, 2002); Neil Schmid, "Tun-huang Literature," in Victor Mair, ed., *The Columbia History of Chinese Literature* (New York: Columbia University Press, 2001), pp. 982–987.

42. Meng Yuanlao, *Dongjing meng Hua lu (wai sizhong)* (Beijing: Zhonghua shuju, 1962), p. 459. The names of the eleven performers listed in this category suggest they claimed a religious status of some kind.

43. *Riben Lunwangsi micang Shuihu*, ann. Sheng Ruiyu (Wuhan: Wuhan daxue chubanshe, 1994), p. 34.

44. Wilt L. Idema, "Evil Parents and Filial Offspring: Some Comments on the *Xiangshan Baojuan* and Related Texts," *Studies in Central and East-Asian Religions* 12–13 (2001–2002): 7–8. For the *shihua* characteristics of the *Lushan Yuangong hua*, see my "Emperor and General: Some Comments on the Formal and Thematic Continuities between the Vernacular Stories from Dunhuang and the Vernacular Stories from Later Dynasties," in *The Harmony and Prosperity of Civilizations: Selected Papers of the Beijing Forum (2004)* (Beijing: Beijing daxue chubanshe, 2005), pp. 124–125. *Lushan Yuangong hua* has been translated into English by Tansen Sen and Victor Mair as "The Tale of Master Yuan of Mount Lu," in Victor Mair, Nancy S. Steinhard, and Paul R. Goldin, eds., *Hawai'i Reader in Traditional Chinese Culture* (Honolulu: University of Hawai'i Press, 2005), pp. 304–339. *Da Tang Sanzang qujing shihua* has been translated into English by Charles J. Wivell as "The Story of How the Monk Tripitaka of the Great Country of the T'ang Brought Back the Sutras," in Victor Mair, ed., *The Columbia Book of Traditional Chinese Literature* (New York: Columbia University Press, 1994), pp. 1181–1207.

45. Quanzhen (Complete Truth) Daoism originated in twelfth-century northern China, becoming a widespread movement in the thirteenth century. Eventually it would become the major form of monastic Daoism. Early Quanzhen teaching stressed the ephemerality of life and the need for an immediate conversion. Those who had not yet been "reborn" were called "walking skeletons." When Miaoshan is brought back to the capital from the White Sparrow Convent to be executed and the palace ladies try to talk sense into her, she too compares unenlightened people to walking skeletons (*Guanshiyin pusa benxing jing*, pp. 62b–63a, in Yoshioka 1989). For the popularity of the theme of the

skeleton in Quanzhen preaching, see my "Skulls and Skeletons in Art and on Stage," in Leonard Blussé and Harriet Zurndorfer, eds., *Conflict and Accommodation in Early Modern East Asia: Essays in Honour of Erik Zürcher* (Leiden: E. J. Brill, 1993), pp. 191–215.

46. Han Bingfang argues for the authorship of Puming in his "Guanshiyin xinyang yu Miaoshan de chuanshuo: jian ti woguo zuizao yibu baojuan *Xiangshan baojuan* de dansheng," *Shijie zongjiao yanjiu*, no. 2 (2004): 54–61.

47. To this day *The Precious Scroll of Incense Mountain* is recited by female pilgrims visiting the Upper Tianzhu Monastery at Hangzhou.

48. A more detailed discussion of the differences between the two versions is provided in Idema 2001–2002, pp. 5–15.

49. Dudbridge 2004, pp. 89–95.

50. Ibid., pp. 95–98.

51. Scholars who have written on the meaning of the legend of Miaoshan (Glen Dudbridge, P. Steven Sangren, Yü Chün-fang) usually treat the various surviving texts as records of a single legend and do not focus on the particular characteristics of the story as told in one particular text. My discussion here will be focused on one particular text, *The Precious Scroll of Incense Mountain*. As this text contains elements that are absent from other versions of the legend, I do not make any claims for the validity of my findings beyond the interpretation of this single text.

52. Philadelphia: University of Pennsylvania Press, 1991.

53. Cazelles 1991, p. 43.

54. Ibid., pp. 33–34.

55. Ibid., p. 26.

56. Ibid., p. 50.

57. Ibid., p. 43.

58. For a discussion of the conflict between religious vocation and common sense as depicted in precious scrolls, see Beata Grant, "Patterns of Female Religious Experience in Qing Dynasty Popular Literature," *Journal of Chinese Religions* 23 (1995): 35–37.

59. "But the common people of street and ward praised her: / 'Rare is a princess with such a heart for the Way!'" (*Xiangshan baojuan*, I, p. 34a, in Zhang 1994). The 1773 version here has four more lines: "But the common people of street and ward praised her: / 'Rare is a princess with such a heart for the way! / She does not desire pleasures and good times / And does not yet know even where she will be able to settle.' / The people who burned incense and lit candles were without number / And the smoke of their incense mingled with the clouds across the street" (*Guanshiyin pusa benxing jing*, p. 41a, in Yoshioka 1989).

60. Dudbridge 1978, p. 50.

61. *Guanshiyin pusa benxing jing*, p. 51b.

62. *Xiangshan baojuan*, I, p. 1b, in Zhang 1994.

63. Cazelles 1991, p. 74.

64. In Renate Blumenfeld-Kosinski and Timea Szell, eds., *Images of Sainthood in Medieval Europe* (Ithaca: Cornell University Press, 1991), pp. 268–287.

65. Robertson 1991, p. 281.

66. Ibid., pp. 282–283.

67. Beata Grant, "The Spiritual Saga of Woman Huang: From Pollution to Purification," in David Johnson, ed., *Ritual Opera, Operatic Ritual* (Berkeley: Chinese Popular Culture Project, 1989), pp. 224–311. Also see Emily M. Ahern, "The Power and Pollution of Chinese Women," in Margery Wolf and Roxane Witke, eds., *Women in Chinese Society* (Stanford: Stanford University Press, 1975), pp. 193–214.

68. The exorcistic and healing powers of blood (and the color red) in Chinese culture need no further elaboration. A brief summary of the subject is provided in Jo Riley, *Chinese Theatre and the Actor in Performance* (Cambridge: Cambridge University Press, 1997), pp. 180–186.

69. Dudbridge 1978, pp. 39–43.

70. Ibid., p. 96; Yu Junfang (Yü Chün-fang), "Baojuan wenxue zhongde Guanuin yu minjian xinyang," in Lin Ru, ed., *Minjian xinyang yu Zhongguo wenhua guoji yantaohui lunwenji* (Taipei: Hanxue yanjiu zhongxin, 1994), pp. 346–349. F. Wang-Toutain notes that Avalokiteśvara was venerated as a bodhisattva who saved one from hell from a very early time, predating the introduction of Kṣitigarbha (Dizang) from the sixth century onward. See her *Le bodhisattva Kṣitigarbha en Chine du Ve au XIIIe siècle* (Paris: Presses de l'École Française d'Extrême Orient, 1998), p. 8. From the tenth century onward, Guanyin is depicted in art as a guide of souls, leading them, as an assistant of Amitābha, to his Pure Land of the Western paradise. In Ming and Qing times, Guanyin may also be portrayed as a protectress of children in hell.

71. Cazelles 1991, p. 43.

72. Ibid., p. 52.

73. Ibid., p. 63.

74. The expression *zigong* (child palace), here translated as "side palace," is glossed by all dictionaries as "the womb, the uterus." My translation is based on the analogy with expressions such as *ziyuan* (side hall) and *ziku* (subwine-shops). In the subsequent verse section I translate the same term as "cell."

75. *Xiangshan baojuan*, II, p. 11b, in Zhang 1994.

76. From its very introduction into China, Buddhism had to face the criticism that its teachings and practices were in conflict with filial piety (*xiao*), the foundational virtue of Confucianism. Buddhism eventually developed its own discourse on filial piety, arguing that only its monastics, if provided with suitable donations, were able to save the souls of one's ancestors from the tortures of the hells. The legend of Miaoshan, who saves her father from his disease, is often compared to the legend of the monk Mulian, who descends to the deepest hells to save his mother as the legends of a filial son and daughter. See Kenneth K. S. Ch'en, *The Chinese Transformation of Buddhism* (Princeton: Princeton University Press, 1973), pp. 14–50.

77. The later novelistic rendition of the legend as the *Complete Tale of Guanyin of the Southern Seas* (*Nanhai Guanyin quanzhuan*) of ca. 1600 stresses this by having the two sons-in-law rebel against their imperial father-in-law at their earliest opportunity (Dudbridge 2004, pp. 61–62). However, in *The Precious Scroll of Incense Mountain* the inherent insufficiency of uxorilocal marriage is not stressed beyond the fact that Miaoshan's two older sisters refuse to give up their eyes and hands for their father.

78. Cf. P. Steven Sangren, "Myths, Gods, and Family Relations," in Meir Shahar and Robert P. Weller, eds., *Unruly Gods: Divinity and Society in China* (Honolulu: University of Hawai'i Press, 1996), p. 164: "conflict results from Miaoshan's desire to *leave* home to be a nun and her father's desire to use her to obtain an uxorilocal son-in-law to continue his line."

79. A foul-smelling, wasting disease (such as leprosy) as a punishment for a heinous sin, often of a sexual nature, is also a common motif in medieval French romance literature.

80. Miaoshan's act brings together the theme of the bodhisattva donating his body to aid suffering creatures, which is quite popular in *jātaka* tales, and the Chinese belief in the medicinal properties of human flesh, especially the flesh of close relatives. Miaoshan's act has often been interpreted as providing the charter for the practice of *gegu* in Ming and Qing China (filial sons and filial daughters-in-law slicing off part of their thigh or liver to feed it to an ailing parent). See Reiko Ohnuma, "The Gift of the Body and the Gift of the Dharma," *History of Religions* 37.4 (1998): 321–359; Chün-fang Yü, "The Cult of Kuan-yin in Ming-Ch'ing China: A Case of Confucianization of Buddhism?" in Irene Bloom and Joshua A. Fogel, eds., *Meeting of Minds: Intellectual and Religious Interaction in East Asian Traditions of Thought* (New York: Columbia University Press, 1997), pp. 151–165; Yü 2001, pp. 338–347.

81. Stanford: Stanford University Press, 1996.

82. Johnson and Price-Williams, 1996, p. 194.

83. Stanford: Stanford University Press, 1998.

84. Cole 1998, p. 41.

85. Ibid., p. 177, stresses that the sins of Mulian's mother that condemn her to hell are sexual in nature. The sexual nature of the sin of the mother is explicit in the legend of Chenxiang, which in many ways may be seen as a non-Buddhist counterpart to the legend of Mulian. Chenxiang's mother is Third Daughter of the God of Mt. Hua, who falls in love with a student and forces him to have sex with her. When her elder brother hears about the affair, he imprisons his younger sister under the mountain. When Chenxiang, who is raised by his father, grows up and learns about his mother's fate, he sets out to learn magical skills, then defeats his uncle, and finally frees his mother by splitting the mountain with his axe.

86. Gary Seaman, "Ethnographic Film from the Field to the Classroom: Methodological and Practical Considerations in the Collection and Dissemination of Film Records of Popular Religion in China," *Chinoperl Papers* 7 (1977): 106–135, takes as his starting point his own ethnographic movie recording of the performance of this ritual in Taiwan. Also see Gary Seaman, "The Sexual Politics of Karmic Retribution," in Emily Martin Ahern and Hill Gates, eds., *The Anthropology of Taiwan Society* (Stanford: Stanford University Press, 1981), pp. 391–396.

87. The earliest fully developed treatments of the legend of Mulian saving his mother from hell are the various versions of the legend discovered among the Dunhuang manuscripts and dating from the ninth and tenth centuries. In later centuries the legend was widely popular in a great variety of performative genres. This body of literature and its religious meaning have attracted considerable scholarship from the 1990s onward.

88. Cole 1998, p. 74.

89. For an English translation and detailed discussion of the *Blood-Bowl Sutra*, see Cole 1998, pp. 197–217.

90. In precious scrolls on pious women, the heroine often immediately renounces all worldly desires as soon as she is informed of the inherent sinfulness of her female body. See Dudbridge 2004, pp. 103–105, quoting from *The Precious Scroll of Liu Xiang* (*Liu Xiang baojuan*). The *Blood-Bowl Sutra* also enjoyed considerable popularity in Japan. See, for instance, D. Max Moerman, *Localizing Paradise: Kunabo Pilgrimage and the Religious Landscape of Premodern Japan* (Cambridge: Harvard University Asia Center, 2005), pp. 221–231.

91. Discussions of Miaoshan's refusal to marry usually relate this to the fact that women resent being forced to leave their family, feeling abandoned by their parents. P. Steven Sangren, "Separations, Autonomy, and Recognition in the Production of Gender Differences: Reflections from Considerations of Myths and Laments," in Charles Stafford, ed., *Living with Separation in China: Anthropological Accounts* (London: RoutledgeCurzon, 2003), pp. 60–61, argues that Miaoshan desires recognition by her father as an autonomous human being. However, *The Precious Scroll of Incense Mountain* stresses King Miaozhuang's love for his daughter, who is offered all the pleasures of marriage without having to leave the family. No wonder her sisters eagerly take up this exceptional offer. Miaoshan's opposition, however, is not to an eventual transferral to another family, but to the human condition as such, especially the female condition.

92. Yü 2001, pp. 333–338.

93. In canonical stories of bodhisattvas sacrificing all or part of their body for the benefit of others, this usually prefigures the gift of the Dharma by the Buddha to a later reincarnation of the beneficiaries. The body of the bodhisattva in these tales stands as a metaphor for the body of the Dharma. See Ohnuma 1998, pp. 323–359. In *The Precious Scroll of Incense Mountain*, enlightenment follows in the same existence upon the ingestion of the medicine of the body parts of the bodhisattva: Guanyin is bodhisattva and Buddha at the same time.

94. Yu Junfang 1994 argues that the legend of Miaoshan changes the Buddhist theme of sacrificing one's body for the sake of the Dharma, for the sake of all living beings, or for the sake of a stranger or even an animal into the Chinese theme of sacrificing one's body for the sake of a parent or parent-in-law.

95. *Bulletin of the School of Oriental and African Studies* 54 (1996): 268–295.

96. Henricks 1996, p. 283. Henricks's article is only one of the many attempts to reconstruct and interpret the original myth of Shun. The Chinese scholar Yuan Ke has stressed the antagonism between Shun and his younger brother Xiang (Elephant), and has seen in the legend of Shun a reflection of earlier southern myths on the taming of elephants. Whalen Lai, in his "Unmasking the Filial Sage-King Shun: Oedipus at Anyang," *History of Religions* 35 (1995): 163–184, also focuses on the conflict between Shun and his brother and notes that Xiang tries to make Shun's wives his own. "The major incest taboo is not mother and son . . . but brother and sister-in-law" (p. 174). He also points out that at this stage Shun's mother is "not a central figure" (p. 167).

97. New critical and annotated editions of both texts may be found in Huang Zheng and Zhang Yongquan, ann., *Dunhuang bianwen jiaozhu* (Peking: Zhonghua shuju, 1997), pp. 200–211, 1024–1070. For a short discussion of the *Shunzi bian* and its sources, see e.g., Cheng Yizhong, "*Shunzibian* yu Shunzi gushi de yanhua," in Liu Cunren et al., eds., *Qingzhu Pan Shichan xiansheng jiuzhi huadan Dunhuangxue tekan* (Taipei: Wenjin chubanshe, 1996), pp. 89–99. The text is preserved in two fragments, one of which was copied in 949. Cheng Yizhong argues in favor of an early Tang date of composition. Qu Jinliang, in his *Dunhuang fojiao wenxue yanjiu* (Taipei: Wenjin chubanshe, 1995), pp. 213–216, following the suggestion of Xie Haiping, argues on very flimsy evidence in favor of the even earlier date of the fifth and sixth centuries, even while showing that all references to *bian(wen)* as text or performance date only from the eighth century and later. It may therefore be safer to treat the text as a work of the eighth or ninth century.

Cheng Yizong notes that whereas earlier versions of the legend all have Shun married to the daughters of Yao at the beginning of the narrative, now the marriage is postponed to the very end. This implies that the possibility of a conflict between Shun and his brother over Shun's wives has been removed. Liu Shouhua, "Shilun Dunhuang bianwen *Shunzi zhixiao gushi* di xingtai yanbian," *Huazhong shifan daxue xuebao*, no. 4 (1991): 72–77, sees the growing importance of the role of the stepmother as one of the major changes introduced by the *Shunzi bian*.

98. Arthur Waley, *Ballads and Stories from Tun-huang* (London: George Allen and Unwin, 1960), pp. 66–67, translated the essential sentence in this respect as "Though like other men's their heads are black and their faces are white, this land of Chi does produce people with the hearts of pigs or dogs," and remarks in a note, "The text of this sentence is certainly corrupt." On the basis of the currently available editions of the emended text, this sentence should be translated "When he saw how black my hair was and how white my face, he had the desires of a pig or dog."

99. It may be noted that Shun, too, when emerging from the well at his neighbor's place, meets with his deceased mother, who directs him to Mt. Li. Miaoshan upon her return from the Underworld is met not by her father but by the God of the Big White (the Morning Star) in the guise of an old man who directs her to Incense Mountain.

100. In the rituals of the Siege and Destruction of Hell as performed on Taiwan, the soul of the deceased is freed from the prison of Hell. The Hell from which the deceased is freed "is not just the Inferno in general, but either the special hell for those who died a violent death...or the Blood Lake Hell...for women who, through miscarriage or abortion, polluted the earth with their blood....[T]he bereaved families consider this rite, in which they actively participate, as one of the most meaningful of the entire service" (Kristofer Schipper, "Mu-lien Plays in Taoist Liturgical Context," in David Johnson, ed., *Ritual Opera, Operatic Ritual* [Berkeley: Chinese Popular Culture Project, 1989], p. 137). Schipper starts his discussion of the ritual with a reference to the story of "Zhengbo ke Duan yu Yan," cautiously suggesting the possibility that it may be the source of later practices and beliefs ("Whether or not one

wishes to consider this as the source of later popular ideas on the subject, it certainly provides evidence of upper-class beliefs and practices related to visiting parents in the Underworld"; p. 127).

101. Cole 1998, pp. 234–235.

102. Museum of Fine Arts Boston, *Selected Masterpieces of Asian Art* (Boston: Museum of Fine Arts, 1992), pp. 166–167, plate 151.

103. A very early example of a painting of Guanyin accompanied by Shancai and Longnü may be provided by a late-Heian-period (twelfth century) painting in the same Boston Museum of Fine Arts. It is titled "Bodhisattva of Compassion with Magic Jewel and Wheel." On this Japanese painting Guanyin is said to be accompanied by Shancai and by "Kichijô-ten, goddess of wealth and beauty, who also carries a flaming jewel" (ibid., p. 35, plate 21). As early Japanese Buddhist paintings often followed Chinese examples, a sinologist is tempted to interpret Kichijô-ten as Longnü who offers her pearl to the bodhisattva.

104. Katō 1975, pp. 212–214. This story has been taken up in many recent discussions of Buddhism and gender, as the story stands at the intersection of the widely held belief in Buddhist circles that one has to be reborn as a man in order to be able to achieve final enlightenment and the equally Buddhist standpoint that gender distinctions are as empty as all other distinctions of the rational mind.

105. Thomas Cleary, trans., *Entry into the Realm of Reality. The Text. The Gandavyuha, the Final Book of the Avatamsaka Sutra* (Boston: Shambala, 1989), pp. 151–156.

106. Fontein 1967, pp. 23–77.

107. For a detailed discussion of this "novel" and its relation to other contemporary vernacular prose hagiographies, and the sixteenth-century novel *Journey to the West* (*Xiyou ji*), see Dudbridge 2004, pp. 57–67. Du Deqiao 1990, pp. 171–212, presents a photographic reproduction of a fully illustrated late-Ming edition of the novel.

108. *Nanhai Guanyin quanzhuan*, in *Guanyin pusa quanshu* (Shenyang: Chunfeng wenyi chubanshe, 1987), pp. 38–41.

109. Dudbridge 2004, p. 63.

110. Chün-fang Yü, "Images of Kuan-yin in Chinese Folk Literature," *Chinese Studies* 8.1 (1990): 235–236.

111. I have used the text as reproduced in Zhang 1994, vol. 27, pp. 115–172. All quotations are from this edition. The text of this woodblock edition was established by Yanbo diaotu (the Angler of the Misty Waves), while the costs of the printing were borne by a certain Zhou Hongyuan. The date of the printing is given as 1912 by Li Shiyu in his *Baojuan zonglu* (Peking: Zhonghua shuju, 1961), p. 43. The text itself offers hardly any clue for a more precise dating of its composition. It still uses "Huguang" (p. 1a) as the designation of a province, even though that province was split up into the two provinces of Hubei and Hunan in 1664. However, the term remained in common use. For a brief discussion of this precious scroll, see Yü 2001, pp. 442–443.

112. Huang Long zhenren is one of the deities venerated by the Xiantian sect. He has an important part in the *Guanyin jidu benyuan zhenjing*, a precious scroll that once again recounts the legend of Miaoshan, this time as a first-

person narrative by the protagonist. After Miaoshan has been strangled at her royal father's orders, Huang Long zhenren takes her to see the female deity Yaochi Jinmu (the Metal Mother of the Jaspis Pond); he next is her guide on her tour through the Ten Courts of Hell. See Che Xilun, "Ming Qing minjian zongjiao di ji zhong baojuan," in Che 1997, p. 110. For a more extensive discussion of the *Guanyin jidu benyuan zhenjing*, see Dudbridge 2004, pp. 83–87. The *Guanyin jidu benyuan zhenjing* is occasionally reprinted under the title *Xiangshan baojuan*.

Another indication of a sectarian background of *The Precious Scroll of Good-in-Talent and Dragon Girl* may be found in the description of meditation techniques on pp. 22a–23a, which has a strong Daoist coloring. One may also note that Guanyin is referred to as "Mother Guanyin" (*Guanyin mu*) on p. 1b, pointing to an identification of the bodhisattva with the Eternal Mother of sectarian belief.

113. The *Lotus Sutra* already mentions that Avalokiteśvara will save one from snakes.

114. For a short discussion of this legend see Yü 1990, pp. 236–237; and Yü 2001, pp. 443–447. For a more detailed treatment of this tale, see Sawada Mizuho, *Chūgoku dōbutsu dan* (Tokyo: Kōbundō, 1978), pp. 211–235; Wilt L. Idema, "Guanyin's Parrot: A Chinese Buddhist Animal Tale and Its International Context," in Alfred Cadonna, ed., *India, Tibet, China: Genesis and Aspects of Traditional Narrative* (Firenze: Leo S. Olschki, 1999), pp. 103–150; and Wilt L. Idema, "The Filial Parrot in Qing Dynasty Dress: A Short Discussion of the *Yingge baojuan* [Precious Scroll of the Parrot]," *Journal of Chinese Religions* 30 (2002): 77–96.

115. Some folktales on the relation of Guanyin to Mt. Putuo relate that Guanyin took possession of the island only after subduing its original deity, a huge snake.

116. Antii Aarne, *The Types of the Folktale: A Classification and Bibliography. Antti Aarne's Verzeichnis der Märchentypen*, transl. and enl. Stith Thompson 2nd rev. (Helsinki: Suomalainen Tiedeakatemia, 1973), p. 56, no. 155; Nai-tung Ting, *A Type Index of Chinese Folktales in the Oral Tradition and Major Works of Non-religious Classical Literature* (Helsinki: Suomalainen Tiedeakatemia, 1978), p. 34, no. 155.

117. Zheng Zhenduo, "Zhongshan lang gushi de yanbian," in his *Zhongguo wenxue yanjiu* (Hong Kong: Guwen shuju, 1961), 3: 1123–1124. Also see "Ondank is 's wereld loon," in Ton Dekker et al., eds., *Van Aladdin tot Zwaan kleef aan. Lexicon van sprookjes: ontstaan, ontwikkeling, variaties* (Nijmegen: SUN, 1997), pp. 266–272.

118. For the Chinese text see Lu Ji, ed., *Gujin shuohai* (Shanghai: Shanghai wenyi chubanshe, 1989, reprint of 1909 edition), no continuous pagination. It has been translated into English by James R. Hightower as "The Wolf of Chung-shan," in Cyril Birch, ed., *Anthology of Chinese Literature*, vol. 2: *From the Fourteenth Century to the Present Day* (New York: Grove Press, 1972), pp. 46–52. Hua-yuan Li Mowry, "The Wolf of Chung-shan," *Tamkang Review* 11.2 (1980–1981): pp. 139–159, discusses the Indian origin of the story, its analogues in Western literature, and the Chinese dramatic adaptations.

119. Cf. Madeline K. Spring, *Animal Allegories in T'ang China* (New Haven:

American Oriental Society, 1993); and Wilt L. Idema, "Dierenverhaal en dierenfabel in de traditionele Chinese letterkunde," in Wilt L. Idema et al., eds., *Mijn naam is haas: Dierenverhalen in verschillende culturen* (Baarn: Ambo, 1993), pp. 222–237.

120. J.-A. Dubois, *Le Pantcha-Tantra, ou les cinq ruses: Fables du Brahme Vichnou-Sarma* (Paris: Merlin, 1826), pp. 49–55, "Le Brahme, le Crocodile, l'Arbre, la Vache et le Renard." This tale does not occur in the Sanskrit versions of the *Pañcatantra*, but a related version is found in Persian versions of this work.

121. Wilt L. Idema, *The Dramatic Oeuvre of Chu Yu-tun, 1379–1439* (Leiden: E. J. Brill, 1985), pp. 94–108.

122. For a translation and discussion of this poem, see Tanaka Kenji, *Gafu sankyoku* (Tokyo: Chikuma shobo). 1983, pp. 251–268. The plaint of the buffalo has been a common theme in Chinese literature ever since the Song dynasty, when growing numbers of people came to stress the sinfulness of slaughtering oxen and buffaloes and of eating beef. This movement was not initially tied to Buddhism, as Buddhism stressed the sinfulness of killing any living being and refused to make distinctions between different kinds of animals in this respect. See Vincent Goossaert, *L'interdit du boeuf en Chine: Agriculture, éthique et sacrifice* (Paris: Collège de France, Institut des Hautes Études Chinoises, 2005), esp. pp. 132–134, 186–190, 201–203.

123. Fu Xihua, *Mingdai zaju quanmu* (Beijing: Zuojia chubanshe, 1958), p. 86. Wang Jiusi's play has been translated repeatedly: by Wilt L. Idema as "De klucht van de wolf uit Zhongshan," *Maatstaf* 20.4 (1972): 145–161; by James I. Crump as "The Wolf of Chungshan," *Renditions* 7 (1977): 29–38; and by William Dolby as "Wolf of Mount Zhong," in his *Eight Chinese Plays from the Thirteenth Century to the Present* (London: Paul Elek, 1978), pp. 93–102.

124. Sarah Allen, *The Way of Water and Sprouts of Virtue* (Albany: State University of New York Press, 1997), pp. 4–5.

125. Idema 1993b, pp. 197–201. Also see Yi Ruofen, "*Kulou huanxi*—Zhongguo wenxue yu tuxiang zhong de shengming yishi," *Zhongguo wenzhe yanjiusuo jikan* 26 (2005): 73–125.

126. Idema 1993b, pp. 201–214.

127. In Zhang 1994, vol. 27, p. 17.

128. Judith Magee Boltz, "Singing to the Spirits of the Dead: A Taoist Ritual of Salvation," in Bell Yung, Evelyn S. Rawski, and Rubie S. Watson, eds., *Harmony and Counterpoint: Ritual Music in Chinese Context* (Stanford: Stanford University Press, 1996), pp. 209–210, 223–224; Francois Picard, "Le chant du squelette (*Kulou ge*)" (unpublished paper).

129. Vivienne Lo, "The Legend of the Lady of Linshui," *Journal of Chinese Religions* 21 (1993): 86.

130. *Shancai longnü bajuan*, p. 7a–b (in Zhang 1994, vol. 27). "His hole of passion has not yet been opened" means he has not yet felt any sexual attraction. "Misty flowers" is a common euphemism for courtesans and prostitutes.

131. "Hunger" has been a euphemism for female sexual desire ever since the Book of Odes. See Edward L. Shaughnessy, "How the Poetess Came to Burn the Royal Chamber," in his *Before Confucius: Studies in the Creation of*

the Chinese Classics (Albany: State University of New York Press, 1997), pp. 221–238.

132. A seventeenth-century source, Gu Fu's *Pingsheng zhuangguan* (Shanghai: Shanghai renmin meishu chubanshe, 1962), 8:48b, credits the Song-dynasty painter Li Song (active ca. 1190–1230) with a painting titled "Kulou yi che tu" (Skeleton pulling a cart).

133. Gan Bao, *Soushen ji*, coll. and ann. Wang Shaoying (Peking: Zhonghua shuju, 1979), pp. 231–232. Gan Bao notes that the ballad of the feats of Li Ji was still current in his time. Gan Bao's *Soushen ji* has been translated into English by Kenneth DeWoskin and J. I. Crump, Jr., as *In Search of the Supernatural: The Written Record* (Stanford: Stanford University Press, 1996). Their translation of the tale of Li Ji is found on pp. 230–231.

The widespread veneration of snake gods in Fujian is documented by Xu Xiaowang in his *Fujian minjian xinyang yuanliu* (Fuzhou: Fujian jiaoyu chubanshe, 1993), pp. 28–48.

134. In Song times and later, the basic elements of the tale of Li Ji were also elaborated in the legend of Linshui furen. One of the many themes of that rich legend too is the subjugation of rampant female sexuality in the shape of a (white) snake. See Brigitte Berthier, *La Dame-du-bord-de-l'eau* (Nanterre: Société d'ethnologie, 1988). The current legend describes the deity as an incarnation of a drop of blood of the bodhisattva Guanyin. Historically, the process may well have been the reverse: the female Guanyin, especially the bodhisattva clad in white, most likely is a transformation of earlier and local Chinese goddesses who by slaying a snake paradoxically embodied the victory of culture over nature, of female self-restraint over female self-assertion, of patriarchal power over competing forms of cohabitation.

Chapter 1: *The Precious Scroll of Incense Mountain*, Part 1

1. The Upper Tianzhu Monastery in Hangzhou was a Tiantai monastery. Such monasteries in the twelfth to fourteenth centuries featured a "hall of penance/repentance" or "hall of contemplation" that was dedicated to the practice of extended ritual penance and *samādhi* retreats. The Chinese word used here to refer to such a hall is *qitang*, which more literally might be translated as "term hall." See Dan Stevenson, "The 'Hall for the Sixteen Contemplations' as a Distinctive Institution for Pure Land Practice in Tiantai Monasteries of the Song (960–1279)," in Kalpakam Sankarnarayan, Rabindra Panth, and Ichigo Ogawa, eds., *Buddhism in Global Perspective* (Mumbai: Somaiya Publications, 2004), pp. 147–204.

2. The Three Vehicles refer to the way of the *śrāvaka* (a personal disciple of the Buddha), the *pratyeka-buddha* (someone who achieves enlightenment on his own but does not teach), and the bodhisattva, which are discussed at length in chapters 2 and 3 of the *Lotus Sutra*, where they are contrasted to the One [Buddha] Vehicle preached by that sutra, which is presented as the true and ultimate teaching. The Sudden and Gradual refer to the way of sudden and gradual approaches to enlightenment. All are means by which sentient beings may be "ferried" across the sea of suffering to the realm of the deathless.

3. More precisely, "venerate her by presenting ritual offerings."

4. Performers of narrative in China may punctuate their story by beating a piece of dry hard wood on the table in front of them. A wooden ruler would be a ready-made piece of wood for such purposes.

5. This is a somewhat simplified quote from chapter 25 of the *Lotus Sutra*. My translation here is adapted from Katō 1975, pp. 319–321.

6. The emperor's love of hunting, the wanton killing of living beings, is most likely mentioned as a cause of the emperor's lack of a son.

7. The Six Palaces refers to the Inner Palace, where the palace women are housed, guarded, and served by eunuchs.

8. The Three Lights are the sun, the moon, and the planets and stars.

9. A sign not only of beauty but of intelligence and wisdom.

10. The Trayastriṁśāh Heaven (the Heaven of the Thirty-three) is the second of the six heavens of form, and the home of Indra, who rules here, assisted by thirty-two other gods. It is located atop Mt. Sumeru, the mountain at the center of our universe.

11. The Daluo Heaven is the highest heaven in Daoist cosmology, the abode of immortals.

12. The Golden Immortal is the Buddha.

13. The characters *mi* and *le* combine to form Mile, the Chinese transcription of Maitreya, the buddha of the future. The "land of joy [and peace]" here refers to the Western Pure Land of Amitābha.

14. The three worlds are the worlds of desire, the worlds of form, and the worlds beyond desire and form.

15. To show his respect and awe.

16. The *ulumbara* flower blossoms only once every three thousand years.

17. In China, a pregnancy is said to last ten months, counting from the month in which the baby is conceived to the month in which the baby is delivered. Ten months is therefore the normal term of a pregnancy.

18. "The seven jewels" is a standard expression for all kind of jewels and gems.

19. Traditionally the day was divided in twelve hours (twice the length of the modern hour). The hour of *si* corresponds to 9–11 a.m.

20. *Maṇi* means pearl.

21. All buddhas past and present are said to be recognizable by a particular set of thirty-two auspicious bodily marks.

22. "A good friend" is a religious counselor.

23. "Earth-prison" (or earth's prison) is a perhaps overly literal translation of *diyu*, which usually is rendered as hell(s). In the most common conception below the earth are eighteen earth-prisons, where sinners suffer long periods of terrible torture before being allowed to be reborn in the mode that has been assigned to them by the ten judges (Ten Kings) of the Underworld.

24. Mt. Sumeru, the mountain at the center of our universe.

25. Amitābha.

26. The translation of this line is a guess.

27. "Birth and death" is the Chinese translation of the concept of *saṁsāra*, the endless cycle of transmigration (including its long periods of punishment in

the hells), as sustained by the production of karma by our thoughts, words, and deeds. Because of our positive and negative attachments, we are bound to suffer in each of our lives, and create negative karma. The prospects are even bleaker for women as the blood they shed in menstruation and childbirth pollutes the gods and creates evil karma.

28. In view of the many sins human beings tend to commit, it is rare to be reborn as a human being immediately upon one's death. Only as a human being, however, can one reach final enlightenment.

29. The Gate of Emptiness is one of the conventional designations of Buddhism, as it teaches the emptiness of all phenomena.

30. King Yama is the chief of the ten judges (Ten Kings) in the Underworld.

31. A kalpa is the immeasurably long period between the origin of a world system and its destruction (after which eventually a new world system will come into being on the basis of the remaining karma).

32. The word used here for fruit (*zi*) is the same as the one used for son (*zi*).

33. The night was divided into five "watches" of equal length. The fifth watch was the last watch of the night, and roughly corresponded to the hour of *yin* (3–5 a.m.). Each hour was subdivided into eight "notches" marking a period corresponding to fifteen minutes.

34. The Three Purities are the highest divinities in the Daoist pantheon.

35. "Jade leaves" and "golden branches" are common metaphors for members of the imperial family.

36. Chang'e is the beautiful goddess of the moon.

37. That is, he should have passed the competitive metropolitan examinations with the highest ranking.

38. "The One Man" is a designation for the emperor.

39. "Impermanence" is a euphemism for death. In Chinese popular religion it also is the name of two messengers of the Underworld, one very tall and one very short, who come and arrest the soul at the moment of death.

40. The six roads refer to the six modes of rebirth: as a ghost in one of the hells, as a hungry ghost, as an animal, as an *asura* (titan), as a human being, and as *deva* (a god or denizen of one of the lower heavens, still subject to transmigration). Only rebirth as a human being allows one an opportunity to achieve buddhahood.

41. The three pathways refer to the hells of fire, the hells of blood, and the hells of swords (where every leaf of grass is as sharp as a sword).

42. The Buddha is often referred to as the Great Physician, and his teaching as the medicine that cures suffering.

43. The jade hare inhabits the moon; the golden crow inhabits the sun.

44. The King of Emptiness refers to the Buddha.

45. The "right fruit" refers to the final, complete nirvana of buddhahood.

46. The Lotus Flower Congregation here probably refers to those who are reborn in the Pure Land of Amitābha. The longer version writes "Dragon Flower Congregation," which refers to the assembly that will be formed by Maitreya when he appears in the human world.

47. The five kinds of vision are human vision, the vision of a *deva* (attainable by man in meditation), *arhat*-vision, bodhisattva-vision, and Buddha-vision

or omniscience. The six supernatural powers are the instantaneous view of anything anywhere, the ability to hear any sound anywhere, the ability to know the thoughts of all other minds, the ability to know all former existences of self and others, the power to be anywhere and do anything at will, and the consciousness of the waning of vicious propensities. The term "three bodies" refers to the threefold body or nature of the Buddha: the Buddha-body in its essential nature; his body of bliss, which he received for his own enjoyment; and his body of transformation, by which he can appear in any form. The four wisdoms are the variously defined four forms of wisdom of the Buddha. *Bodhi* refers to the superior wisdom leading to enlightenment.

48. Forbearance is one of the six bodhisattva perfections.

49. The gall is believed to be the seat of bravery.

50. An allusion to the parable of the burning house found in chapter 3 of the *Lotus Sutra*.

51. The three pathways are the three lower forms of rebirths; the eight dangers are the eight conditions in which it is difficult to see the Buddha or hear the Dharma.

52. The production of silks and woolens involves the taking of lives (of silkworms) or of hurting living beings (by robbing sheep of their fleece).

53. *Tathāgata* literally translates as "the thus come one." One of the explanations for this term is "one who comes as do all other buddhas," and the term is often used as a synonym for Buddha.

54. Brahma and Indra are the highest deities in the traditional Indian pantheon.

55. Māra is the highest ruler of the realms of desire. In a famous episode in the life of Śākyamuni, Māra tried to prevent him from achieving definitive enlightenment by tempting him with all the pleasures of the world. When Māra's own efforts failed, his three daughters tried to seduce Śākyamuni with their physical charms, also without success.

56. The Pure Land refers to the Western Paradise of Amitābha.

57. The Tuṣita Heaven is the abode of Maitreya, the buddha of the future.

58. The toad is yet another denizen of the moon.

59. "Ocean storehouse of the dragon palace" refers to the vast collection of Mahayana sutras that was legendarily stored in the palace of the Dragon King below the ocean and partially recovered by Nāgārjuna when he stayed there for ninety days.

60. The cold palace is that section of the inner palace that houses women who have fallen out of favor with the emperor.

61. Many Chinese stories include a scene in which a young maiden finds a husband by throwing a ball into a crowd of suitors and marrying the one who catches the ball, but there is no indication at all that this ever was social practice.

62. The marks of a Buddha.

63. The simple dress of a layperson.

64. The *Odes* and the *Documents* are two of the Five Classics, which are studied in Confucianism as the repositories of eternal norms.

65. The Buddhas of the past, present, and future.

66. Buddhist apologetics argue consistently that the traditional Chinese ancestral sacrifices may be an expression of the filial feelings of the surviving descendants but are of no benefit to the deceased at all and actually harm all concerned because they involve the slaughter of animals. The only way to create merit that may also benefit the deceased, according to these Buddhist preachers, is by good works, first of all donations to the Buddhist clergy.

67. The highest truth experienced in meditation is beyond words.

68. The Three Jewels are the Buddha, the Dharma, and the *saṅgha*.

69. "A person who is born again [for one final time]" is a person who will achieve final enlightenment in the present life.

70. Here the 1773 edition has a long diatribe against the luxurious style of living of ecclesiastical authorities:

Jabbering on, you never yet once have said you are delighted,
Mumbling phrases you only tell me the Way is much hardship.
But when seated, you're sitting on embroidered cushions,
Resting at night, you're covered by an embroidered blanket.
No work with worms: your gown is a gift of your students,
You don't have fields: your food is provided by donors.
As soon as the drum is once sounded you get your gruel,
At the time of the meal, you wait in your room for the bell.
I don't have a heart that craves for such wealth and status,
But you have the guts to tell me to return to the palace!

71. The six harmonies of the monastic community are bodily unity in form of worship, oral unity in chanting, mental unity in faith, moral unity in observing the precepts, doctrinal unity in views and explanations, and economic unity in community of goods, deeds, studies, or charity. The five virtues here probably refer to the five virtues required in a confessor at the confessional ending of the annual summer retreat: freedom from predilections, anger, and fear, and the ability to detect deception and discern those who would shirk confession.

72. The nuns of the western sector are primarily engaged in meditation, while the nuns of the eastern section take care of the administration of the convent.

73. This line means that the princess is willing to endure the sufferings of a *preta* or hungry ghost, whose mouth bursts out in flames when he tries to eat.

74. The Six Nails are the gods of the days that have the element *ding* (nail; able-bodied male) in the two-character designation in the cycle of sixty.

75. The Six Scales are the gods of the days that have the element *jia* (scale; armor) in the two-character designation in the cycle of sixty.

76. The Three Officials are the (Daoist) gods of heaven, earth, and (subterraneous) water.

77. The Five Mountains are China's five holy mountains of the east (Mt. Tai), the west (Mt. Hua), the north, the south, and the center.

78. The precept-gods are the gods who protect the precepts of the Buddhist *saṅgha*. While nuns are expected to keep 348 precepts, the round number of 500 is often used to refer to the totality of their precepts.

79. The 1773 version of the text here has six more lines describing the fearsome appearance of the government troops.

80. The 1773 version of the text here includes twelve lines providing a comical description of the panic among the nuns:

The flames rose up to heaven, a storm roaring thunderously,
Mules brayed, horses whinnied, gods and ghosts were scared.
The octogenarian nuns in the eastern hall did a *salto mortale*,
The abbess in her abbatical quarters had no place to escape.
The rectrix and the librarian bored their heads into the wall,
The precentrix and the secretary dim-wittedly beat their breast;
The repairs supervisor and the manager kowtowed frantically,
The lineal teacher and the preacher had lost spirit and mettle.
The guest prefect and the inspectrix and the superintendent
Hanged themselves from the rafters—not even a shadow was left.
The elderly nuns advanced in years were all scared to death,
The acolytes who were still in their teens wept without end.

81. This refers to the Buddha, as preaching the *Lotus Sutra* on Mt. Gṛdhrakūta.

82. A *cakravartin* or "wheel-turning king" is a universal monarch.

Chapter 2: *The Precious Scroll of Incense Mountain*, Part 2

1. The Yellow Springs is the traditional Chinese designation for the world of the dead below the earth.

2. Later in the text we are informed that the body of Marvelous Goodness is hung with paper coins.

3. The horse is a common metaphor for the human will, and the buffalo often is used as an image of human nature.

4. The 1773 version of the text here includes a ten-line passage describing the mourning of the whole cosmos as manifested by a continuous drizzle.

5. In the 1773 version these four lines clearly refer to the emperor, and it is he who orders the postponement of execution.

6. That is, they will scatter in all directions at the earliest opportunity.

7. The metal wind is the wind of autumn, as the element metal is associated with fall.

8. While crossing a river on a ferry, a man dropped his sword in the water. He then made a cut in the side of the boat to mark where he had lost the sword.

9. The two passages between brackets had been struck from the blocks in the edition on which this translation is based, probably because their praise of the pleasures of sex was considered too explicit. They have been restored on the basis of other editions of the text.

10. The expression *zigong* (child palace) is glossed by all dictionaries as "the womb, the uterus." My translation is based on the analogy with expressions such as *ziyuan* (side hall) and *ziku* (subwineshops). In the subsequent verse section I translate the same term as "cell."

11. In Daoist mysticism, the process of achieving insight is often compared to the process of melting and refining ore and metals to turn cinnabar into gold.

12. The 1773 version here has six lines in which the emperor orders that following execution the body may not be buried but has to be destroyed utterly:

Take her to the execution ground, have her beheaded,
Then quickly select three thousand horsemen with bows.
Tie her corpse to the general's pillar, and then make sure
That volleys of arrows pulverize it into clouds of dust.
Don't bury her skeleton in the earth, or any of the bones,
But have them trampled by the horses till nothing is left.

13. The 1773 version here has the following two lines:

He first tried to behead her with a knife, but it broke into pieces,
He then tried to behead her with a sword, but that broke into two.

14. *Samādhi* refers to concentrated meditation, resulting in enlightenment.

15. In Chinese popular Buddhism, *yakṣas* are hideous demons. They are often equated with the horse-faced and ox-headed demons who guard and torture the sinners in the hells.

16. Paper money that has not been properly burnt to ashes and therefore is of no use in the Underworld.

17. The six pathways refer to the six levels of rebirth: as a ghost in hell, a hungry ghost, an animal, an *asura*, a human being, or a god.

18. The bodhisattva Kṣitigarbha is believed to be the highest overlord of the underworld. He is venerated as a savior who rescues sinners from hell.

19. Grannie Meng operates a teashop in the underworld and offers a cup of tea to every soul. After swallowing Grannie's tea, the soul forgets everything about his or her life on earth.

20. The three karmas refer to the sins created by one's deeds, words, and thoughts. The five precepts forbid killing, stealing, committing adultery, lying, and drinking alcohol. Lay Buddhists are asked to vow to maintain the five precepts.

21. "Keeping the fast" (*chi zhai*) might more literally be translated as "maintaining ritual purity," but Buddhist piety strongly emphasizes the need to stick to a vegetarian diet (including an abstinence from alcohol and strong spices), and the specific meaning of this expression in precious scrolls is maintaining a vegetarian diet.

22. The three paths are the paths of misery, illusion, and mortality.

23. This translation is very tentative!

24. The Metal Star of the Great White (the planet Venus) is also identified with Indra. In Chinese popular narratives he is often dispatched to help the main protagonist of the story when that person in confronted with great problems. The god may take on any shape he likes when he manifests himself.

25. The *Sutra of Countless Ways* is not an existing sutra. It suggests the limitless ways in which the god may help human beings in need of assistance.

26. Both the lion and the elephant-king are metaphors for the Buddha.

27. Starting from the Song dynasty (960–1276), upper-class Chinese women started to bind their feet, and in Ming and Qing times, the practice had spread throughout Chinese society. Bound feet were very unsuited for walking long distances. Ironically, Guanyin in her female form is always depicted with unbound, natural feet, even while she is praised for her feminine beauty.

28. *Prajñā* refers to the highest form of wisdom, the principal means for attaining nirvana.

29. This is probably a reference to the comic description of the panic in the convent, which was omitted from this version of the text. See ch. 1, note 80.

30. The precise nature of the *kāmalā*-disease is not clear. It has been suggested that it might refer to leprosy.

31. The emperor is unable to show his respect by placing his palms together before his breast and can only raise his deformed fists.

32. The "country of Joy" refers to the Pure Land of Amitābha.

33. The name of the historical Buddha was Gautama Siddhartha.

34. The Medicine King and the Medicine Chief are both mentioned in the *Lotus Sutra*. These bodhisattvas are widely revered for their miraculous cures.

35. The Chinese language does not make a distinction between singular and plural and between male and female gender in nouns and pronouns as many Indo-European languages do. So it is not clear whether the monk needs an arm and an eye or the arms and eyes, and he is also not specific as to the gender of the "one without anger."

36. The *kalaviṅka* is a bird that is found only in paradise.

37. The Flower Store Realm is the Flower Store Realm of the Buddha Vairocana as described in the opening chapter of the *Avatamsaka Sūtra*.

38. *Huiguang fanzhao* (the returning light shines on itself) not translated.

39. When a certain Bian He had found a rock containing a fine piece of jade, he offered it to the king of Chu, who thought he was cheating him and ordered one of Bian He's kneecaps removed. When Bian He later offered the rock to the king's successor, he too thought that Bian He tried to cheat him, and ordered his other kneecap removed. After this king too had died, Bian He once again presented his rock. This time the new king insisted that his jade cutters open the rock, which was indeed found to contain a fine piece of jade.

40. The three roots are desire, hate, and stupidity. Once one has understood their true nature, one is saved.

41. The last line refers to the cremation of the corpse.

42. Sir Moon Parasol (Yuegai) is mentioned in chapter 13 of the *Vimalakīrti-nirdeśa sūtra* as a young prince who inquires about the "offering of the Law," that is, the teachings of the Buddha. The Sanskrit form of "Moon Parasol" had been reconstructed on the basis of the Chinese translation as Candracchattra, but the Sanskrit text of the *Vimalakīrti-nirdeśa sūtra* discovered in 1999 in Lhasa actually writes Somaccatra. The *Vimalakīrti-nirdeśa sūtra* was extremely popular in China and has been repeatedly translated into English; see, for example, Charles Luk, *The Vimalakirti Nirdesa Sutra* (Berkeley: Shambala, 1972); and Burton Watson, *The Vimalakirti Sutra* (New York: Columbia University Press, 1997).

43. The phrase "extraordinary excellence" (*qite*) is used to characterize the the glorified body of Amitābha perceived in the course of meditative visualization.

44. Guanyin here lists the various Daoist-inspired spiritual, physical, and sexual techniques associated, rightly or wrongly, with the sects and new religions of Ming and Qing China. She also criticizes their exclusive social organization.

45. Ratnagarbha is the buddha who, many eons ago, announced his future buddhahood to the later Gautama Siddhartha.

46. Stories that supposedly took place in the final decades of the Tang dynasty first link Guanyin to Mt. Putuo, a little island off the Chinese coast near Ningbo, which was named after Potalaka, the mountain abode of Guanyin in the *Garland Sutra*. "Manifest Dew" looks like the title of a reign-period, but no reign-period of this name is known from the Tang dynasty.

47. The basic meaning of *mahāsattva* is "a great man," and as such is often used as designation of a bodhisattva or buddha. In popular religious texts the term often is a designation of Guanyin.

Chapter 3: *The Precious Scroll of Good-in-Talent and Dragon Girl*

1. This line is a rephrasing of a line from the Book of Odes, III, iii, II, 7, "Yi." See James Legge, trans., *The Chinese Classics*, vol. 4: *The She King or the Book of Poetry* (repr. Taipei: Wenshizhe chubanshe, 1971), p. 515: "You ought to be equally free from shame before the light which shines in."

2. The mountain here refers to Mt. Putuo, named after Mt. Potalaka, home of Guanyin in the *Flower Garland Sutra*.

3. The Buddha is said to employ expedient means (*fangbian*; Skt. *upāya-kauśalya*) in teaching his disciples according to their capacities for enlightenment. From there, the expression has obtained the more general meaning of compassionate assistance.

4. Jinzha was the oldest son of general Li Jing, the guardian of the gate of heaven. The best known of his offspring was his youngest son, Nezha. The latter's epic battles with his father are detailed in the hundred-chapter novel *Creation of the Gods* (*Fengshen yanyi*) of the early seventeenth century. In the present text, Jinzha would appear to have taken over the role of Weituo, a fierce martial protector of Buddhism, who is often depicted accompanying Guanyin in full martial gear.

5. Jiedi-gods are deities who protect Buddhism.

6. The actual word used here in the original is "Buddha," not "bodhisattva." In popular Buddhism, the distinction between the two terms tends to blur.

7. The speaker here is the court astrologer or diviner. Years, months, days, and hours are counted by assigning them a two-character combination from the list of sixty two-character combinations that are formed by combining the ten single characters constituting the "heavenly stems" and the twelve single characters constituting the "earthly branches." On the basis of the eight characters of birth, a skilled diviner can predict the future of a child. Penglai and Yingzhou are floating islands in the Eastern Ocean that are inhabited by immortal beings.

8. The Star of the Ground is the first star of the Big Dipper (Ursa Major), in charge of the virtue of yang. In physiognomy it refers to the nose. The Cowherd (also known as the Buffalo Star) is the Chinese name for the star Altair.

9. The Five Mounts are the five holy mountains of the four directions and the center. In Chinese physiognomy the term refers to the five sense organs. The Four Conduits refer to the four major rivers of ancient China (Yellow River, Yangzi, Huai, and Ji), which were also revered as deities. In physiognomy the term refers to the ears, the eyes, the mouth, and the nose.

10. Chinese physiognomy divides both the head and the body into three sections, which have to be equal to ensure a good fortune. Long earlobes are said to be an indicator of good fortune.

11. The phoenix is the king of birds; it will alight only on the parasol tree.

12. The turtle is believed to live to a very old age.

13. The gate with its vermilion steps refers to the imperial court.

14. The peaches of immortality of the Queen Mother of the West, the ruler of all female immortals, ripen only once every three thousand years. When they do, she invites all immortals and deities to her garden atop Mt. Kunlun to eat these special peaches.

15. Chen Lian apparently has kept to a vegetarian diet, which also includes abstinence from such things as onions and garlic.

16. "Misty flowers" is a common euphemism for courtesans and prostitutes.

17. In Chinese the words for "talent" (*cai*) and "riches" (*cai*) have the same pronunciation. As Shancai may also be understood to mean "Good-in-Riches," Shancai was also venerated as a god of wealth.

18. The three paths are the three paths of rebirth: as human, animal, or hungry ghost.

19. "Little monk" is also a common euphemism for the penis.

20. The bodhisattva Kṣitigarbha, who has vowed to release all living beings from suffering, is widely revered as the highest deity of the Underworld.

21. Zhuang Zhou (ca. 369 BCE–ca. 286 BCE) is credited with the authorship of the Daoist classic *Master Zhuang* (*Zhuangzi*). The Zhou dynasty reigned from the eleventh century BCE to 256 BCE. The Western Zhou actually refers to the early centuries of the Zhou dynasty. Zhuang Zhou lived during the Eastern Zhou, when the Zhou dynasty resided at Luoyang and had lost most of its power.

22. "Grand Superior" is an abbreviated form of Grand Superior Old Lord (Taishang laojun), one of the titles of the deified Old Master (Laozi).

23. Outside the magistrate's office a drum was placed, to be beaten by those who wanted to lodge a complaint.

24. The Ancestral Teacher of Pure Yang is Lü Dongbin, one of the popular group of the Eight Immortals. He is usually depicted as a young man carrying a sword.

25. In the Daoist-inspired language of Internal Alchemy mysticism, cinnabar is the main ingredient of the elixir of life, the highest Truth.

26. Insight into emptiness dawns when one realizes that the image of the Buddha produced in meditative visualization "does not come from anywhere and does not go anywhere" and that it "comes thusly and goes thusly."

27. The term "layered tower" refers to the spine.

28. Qian and Kun are the names of trigrams, the first symbolizing pure yang, the second symbolizing pure yin.

29. The Three Teachings are Confucianism, Daoism, and Buddhism.

30. A fully realized Buddha is said to have a body that is sixteen feet tall.

31. The crane is a symbol for the hermit, while the Phoenix Pond refers to the imperial palace.

32. In the *Book of Changes*, an unbroken line (yang) in one of its sixty-four hexagrams is called a nine, while a broken (yin) line is called a six.

33. In fuller accounts of this legend, the preaching parrot convinces the hunters of the evil of their ways and converts them to Buddhism.

34. Bodhidharma is a sixth-century Indian monk of legendary fame, who is credited with the transmission of Chan Buddhism to China.

35. The term "six roots" refers to the six senses: mouth, nose, ears, eyes, body, and mind.

36. The term "Yellow Court" refers to the spleen. According to the teachings of Internal Alchemy, this is where the elixir is formed.

37. All human beings, even the most inveterate sinners, share the Buddha-nature. As soon as we open ourselves to this natural light, we may become enlightened.

38. Pictures of this scene, showing Guanyin standing on the head of a whale and Good-in-Talent standing on a lotus flower, are common.

39. Note that Good-in-Talent's mother as a matter of course has been condemned to hell, just like Mulian's mother.

Glossary

ao 鰲
Baiyi Guanyin 白衣觀音
Baode 寶德
baojuan 寶卷
Bian He 卞和
bian(wen) 變文
bingchen 丙辰
bingyin 丙寅
cai (riches) 財
cai (talent) 才
Cai Jing 蔡京
Chang'e 嫦娥
chen 辰
Chen Debao 陳德寶
Chen Lian 陳連
Chenxiang 沉香
chi zhai 持齋
Chu 楚
Da Muqianlian mingjian jiumu bianwen 大目乾連冥間救母變文
Da Tang Sanzang qujing shihua 大唐三臧取經詩話
da yinyuan 大音緣
Dabei zhou 大悲咒
dan 旦
daoqing 道情
Daoxuan 道宣
Dashizhi 大勢至
ding 丁
dingyou 丁酉
diyu 地獄
Dizang 地臧
dizi 弟子
(Master) Dongguo 東郭
duimian fuqi 對面夫妻
Dulou fu 髑髏賦
e tongzi 惡童子
en 恩
fangbian 方便
Fengshen yanyi 封神演義
Gan Bao 干寶
gegu 割股
Guan Daosheng 管道昇
Guanshiyin 觀世音
Guanshiyin pusa benxing jing 觀世音菩薩本行經
Guanshiyin pusa benxing jing jianji 觀世音菩薩本行經簡集
Guanyin 觀音
Guanyin dashi zhuan 觀音大士傳
Guanyin jidu benyuan zhenjing 觀音濟度本願真經
Guanyin jing 觀音經
Guanyin mu 觀音姥
Guanzizai 觀自在
Gujin shuohai 古今說海
Guwen guanzhi 古文觀止
(Lady) Han 韓
Hangzhou Shang-Tianzhu Jiangsi zhi 杭州上天竺講寺志
Honglou meng 紅樓夢
Huaizhou 懷晝
Huang Long zhenren 黃龍真人
huangsha ping 黃沙瓶
Huayan jing 華嚴經

Huguang 湖廣
Huiguang fanzhao 迴光返照
jia 甲
jiashen 甲申
(Lord) Jian 簡
Jiang Zhiqi 蔣之奇
jiachen 甲辰
Jiedi 揭諦
jimao 己卯
Jinzha 金吒
juan 卷
Kang Hai 康海
kule aiyin xuyao xiangxiang 苦樂哀音須要相像
Kun 坤
Laozi 老子
le 樂
Li Ji 李寄
Li Jing 李靖
Linshui furen 臨水夫人
Liu Qin 劉欽
Liu Xiang baojuan 劉香寶卷
long 龍
Longnü 龍女
Lü Dongbin 呂洞賓
Lu Zhishen 魯智深
Lushan Yuangong hua 廬山遠公話
Ma Zhongxi 馬中錫
Magu dongtian 麻姑洞天
Malang fu 馬郎婦
mao 卯
Miaoshan 妙善
Miaoshu 妙書
Miaoyin 妙音
Miaozhuang 妙莊
Mile 彌勒
Mulian 目連
Namo Guanshiyin pusa 南無觀世音菩薩
Nanhai Guanyin 南海觀音
Nanhai Guanyin quanzhuan 南海觀音全傳
Nezha 哪吒
nianhua 年畫
Penglai 蓬萊
Po Qie 婆伽
Pudu 普渡
Pumen jing 普門經
Puming 普明
Putuo 普陀
Putuoshan 普陀山
Qian 乾
qitang 期堂
qite 奇特
Quanzhen 全真
(millionaire) Ren 任
shan tongzi 善童子
Shancai 善才
Shancai longnü baojuan 善才龍女寶卷
shen 神
shihua 詩話
Shuihu zhuan 水滸傳
Shun 舜
Shunzi bian 舜子變
si 巳
Soushen ji 搜神記
Taishang laojun 太上老君
Tanchang yinyuan 彈唱音緣
Tianshang jin niuxing 天上金牛星
Tianzhu 天竺
Tilan baojuan 提籃寶卷
Tilan Guanyin 提籃觀音
Wang Jiusi 王九思
Weituo 韋馱
Weituo sanxi Bainiang 韋馱三戲白娘
wuji 戊己
Wulin jiushi 武林舊事
Xi Mulian 戲目連
Xiang 象
Xiangshan baojuan 香山寶卷
Xiangshan si 香山寺
Xiangshan zhuan 香山傳
Xiantian 先天
xiao 孝
Xie Haiping 謝海平
Xinglin 興林
Xiwangmu 西王母
Xiyou ji 西遊記
Xu Zhi 許智
Xuanzang 玄奘
Xuepen jing 血盆經
Yanbo diaotu 煙波釣徒
Yao 堯

Yao Shouzhong 姚守中
Yaochi Jinmu 瑤池金母
yaojing 妖精
(nobleman) Ye 葉
yin 寅
Yingge baojuan 鶯哥寶卷
Yingge xiaoyi zhuan 鶯哥孝義傳
Yingzhou 瀛洲
yinyuan 因緣
yisi 乙巳
Yiyang 宜陽
yiyou 乙酉
you 酉
Yuan Ke 袁珂
Yuegai 月蓋
Zhang Gongchen 張拱辰
Zhang Heng 張衡
Zhao Mengfu 趙孟頫
zhaocai tongzi 招財童子
Zhengbo ke Duan yu Yan 鄭伯克斷於鄢
Zhongshan lang zhuan 中山狼傳
Zhou Hongyuan 周洪源
Zhou Mi 周密
(nobleman) Zhu 朱
Zhu Youdun 朱有燉
Zhuangzi 莊子
zigong 子宮
ziku 子庫
ziyuan 子院
zouyu 騶虞
Zuozhuan 左傳

Bibliography

Aarne, Antti Amatus. 1973. *The Types of the Folktale: A Classification and Bibliography. Antii Aarne's Verzeichnis der Märchentypen*, trans. and enl. Stith Thompson, 2nd rev. Helsinki: Suomalainen Tiedeakatemia.

Ahern, Emily M. 1975. "The Power and Pollution of Chinese Women." In Margery Wolf and Roxane Witke, eds., *Women in Chinese Society*, pp. 193–214. Stanford: Stanford University Press.

Allen, Sarah. 1997. *The Way of Water and Sprouts of Virtue*. Albany: State University of New York Press.

Berthier, Brigitte. 1988. *La Dame-du-bord-de-l'eau*. Nanterre: Société d'ethnologie.

Birch, Cyril, ed. 1972. *Anthology of Chinese Literature*. Vol. 2: *From the Fourteenth Century to the Present Day*. New York: Grove Press.

Boltz, Judith Magee. 1996. "Singing to the Spirits of the Dead: A Taoist Ritual of Salvation." In Bell Yung, Evelyn S. Rawski, and Rubie S. Watson, eds., *Harmony and Counterpoint: Ritual Music in Chinese Context*, pp. 177–225. Stanford: Stanford University Press.

Campany, Robert F. 1993. "The Real Presence." *History of Religions* 32:233–272.

———. 1996. "The Earliest Tales of Bodhisattva Guanshiyin." In Donald S. Lopez, ed., *Religions of China in Practice*, pp. 82–96. Princeton: Princeton University Press.

Cazelles, Brigitte. 1991. *The Lady as Saint: A Collection of French Hagiographic Romances of the Thirteenth Century*. Philadelphia: University of Pennsylvania Press.

Che Xilun 車錫倫. 1997. *Zhongguo baojuan yanjiu lunji* 中國寶卷研究論集. Taibei: Xuehai chubanshe.

———, comp. 1998. *Zhongguo baojuan zongmu* 中國寶卷總目. Taibei: Zhongyang yanjiu yuan Zhongguo wenzhe yanjiusuo choubeichu.

———, comp. 2000. *Zhongguo baojuan zongmu*. Beijing: Beijing Yanshan chubanshe.

———. 2002. *Xinyang, jiaohua, yule: Zhongguo baojuan yanjiu ji qita* 信仰教化娛樂中國寶卷研究及其他. Taibei: Xuesheng shuju.

Ch'en, Kenneth. 1964. *Buddhism in China: A Historical Survey*. Princeton: Princeton University Press.

———. 1973. *The Chinese Transformation of Buddhism*. Princeton: Princeton University Press.

Cheng Yizhong 程毅中. 1996. "*Shunzibian* yu Shunzi gushi de yanhua" 舜子變與舜子故事的變化. In Liu Cunren 柳存仁 et al., eds. *Qingzhu Pan Shichan xiansheng jiuzhi huadan Dunhuangxue tekan* 慶祝番石禪先生九秩華誕敦煌學特刊, pp. 89–99. Taipei: Wenjin chubanshe.

Cleary, Thomas, trans. 1989. *Entry into the Realm of Reality. The Text. The Gandavyuha, the Final Book of the Avatamsaka Sutra.* Boston: Shambala.

Cole, Alan. 1998. *Mothers and Sons in Chinese Buddhism*. Stanford: Stanford University Press.

Crump, James I., Jr., trans. 1977. "The Wolf of Chungshan." *Renditions* 7:29–38.

Dekker, Ton, et al., eds. 1997. *Van Aladdin tot Zwaan kleef aan. Lexicon van sprookjes: ontstaan, ontwikkeling, variaties*. Nijmegen: SUN.

DeWoskin, Kenneth, and J. I. Crump, Jr., trans. 1996. *In Search of the Supernatural: The Written Record*. Stanford: Stanford University Press.

Dolby, William, trans. 1978. "Wolf of Mount Zhong." In his *Eight Chinese Plays from the Thirteenth Century to the Present*, pp. 93–102. London: Paul Elek.

Du Deqiao 杜德橋 (Glen Dudbridge). 1990. *Miaoshan chuanshuo—Guanyin pusa yuanqi kao* 妙善傳說觀音菩薩緣起考. Taibei: Juliu tushu gongsi.

Dubois, J.-A. 1826. *Le Pantcha-Tantra, ou les cinq ruses: Fables du Brahme Vichnou-Sarma*. Paris: Merlin.

Dudbridge, Glen. 1978. *The Legend of Miaoshan*. Oxford: Ithaca Press.

———. 1982. "Miaoshan on Stone: Two Early Inscriptions." *Harvard Journal of Asiatic Studies* 42.2:589–614.

———. 2004. *The Legend of Miaoshan*. Oxford Oriental Monographs. Oxford: Oxford University Press.

Fontein, Jan. 1967. *The Pilgrimage of Sudhana: A Study of Gandavyūha Illustrations in China, Japan, and Java*. Den Haag: Mouton.

Fu Xihua 傅惜華. 1958. *Mingdai zaju quanmu* 明代雜劇全目. Beijing: Zuojia chubanshe.

Gan Bao 干寶. 1979. *Soushen ji* 搜神記, coll. and ann. Wang Shaoying 王紹楹. Peking: Zhonghua shuju.

Goossaert, Vincent. 2005. *L'interdit du boeuf en Chine: Agriculture, éthique et sacrifice.* Paris: Collège de France, Institut des Hautes Études Chinoises.

Grant, Beata. 1989. "The Spiritual Saga of Woman Huang: From Pollution to Purification." In David Johnson, ed., *Ritual Opera, Operatic Ritual*, pp. 224–311. Berkeley: Chinese Popular Culture Project.

———. 1995. "Patterns of Female Religious Experience in Qing Dynasty Popular Literature." *Journal of Chinese Religions* 23:29–58.

Gu Fu 顧復. 1962. *Pingsheng zhuangguan* 平生狀觀. Shanghai: Shanghai renmin meishu chubanshe.

Guanyin pusa quanshu 觀音菩薩全書. 1987. Shenyang: Chunfeng wenyi chubanshe.

van Gulik, Robert H. 1955. *Hayagriva: The Mantrayanic Aspect of Horse-Cult in China and Japan*. Leiden: E. J. Brill.

ter Haar, Barend. 2001. "Buddhist Inspired Options: Aspects of Religious Life in the Lower Yangzi Region from 1100 to 1340." *T'oung Pao* 87:92–152.

Han Bingfang 韓秉方. 2004. "Guanshiyin xinyang yu Miaoshan de chuanshuo: jian ji woguo zuizao yibu baojuan *Xiangshan baojuan* de dansheng" 觀世音信仰與妙善的傳說: 兼及我國最早一部寶卷香山寶卷的誕生. *Shijie zongjiao yanjiu*, no. 2:54–61.

Henricks, Robert G. 1996. "The Three-bodied Shun and the Completion of Creation." *Bulletin of the School of Oriental and African Studies* 54:268–295.

Hightower, James R. 1972. "The Wolf of Chung-shan." In Cyril Birch, ed., *Anthology of Chinese Literature.* Vol. 2: *From the Fourteenth Century to the Present Day*, pp. 46–52. New York: Grove Press.

Huang Zheng 黃征 and Zhang Yongquan 張涌泉, ann. 1997. *Dunhuang bianwen jiaozhu* 敦煌變文校注. Peking: Zhonghua shuju.

Hurvitz, Leon, trans. 1976. *Saddharmapundārika, the Scripture of the Lotus Blossom of the Fine Dharma*. Translated from the Chinese of Kumārajīva. New York: Columbia University Press.

Idema, Wilt L., trans. 1972. "De klucht van de wolf uit Zhongshan." *Maatstaf* 20.4:145–161.

———. 1985. *The Dramatic Oeuvre of Chu Yu-tun, 1379–1439*. Leiden: E. J. Brill.

———. 1993a. "Dierenverhaal en dierenfabel in de traditionele Chinese letterkunde." In W. L. Idema et al., eds., *Mijn naam is haas: Dierenverhalen in verschillende culturen*, pp. 222–237. Baarn: Ambo.

———. 1993b. "Skulls and Skeletons in Art and on Stage." In Leonard Blussé and Harriet Zurndorfer, eds., *Conflict and Accommodation in Early Modern East Asia: Essays in Honour of Erik Zürcher*, pp. 191–215. Leiden: E. J. Brill.

———. 1999. "Guanyin's Parrot: A Chinese Buddhist Animal Tale and Its International Context." In Alfred Cadonna, ed., *India, Tibet, China: Genesis and Aspects of Traditional Narrative*, pp. 103–150. Firenze: Leo S. Olschki.

———. 2000a. "Guanyin's Acolytes." In Jan A. M. de Meyer and Peter M. Engelfriet, eds., *Linked Faiths: Essays on Chinese Religions and Traditional Culture in Honour of Kristofer Schipper*, pp. 205–226. Leiden: E. J. Brill.

———, trans. 2000b. *Prinses Miaoshan en andere Chinese legenden van Guanyin, de bodhisattva van barmhartigheid*. Amsterdam: Atlas.

———. 2001–2002. "Evil Parents and Filial Offspring: Some Comments on the *Xiangshan Baojuan* and Related Texts." *Studies in Central and East-Asian Religions* 12–13:1–40.

———. 2002. "The Filial Parrot in Qing Dynasty Dress: A Short Discussion of the *Yingge baojuan* [Precious Scroll of the Parrot]." *Journal of Chinese Religions* 30:77–96.

———. 2005. "Emperor and General: Some Comments on the Formal and Thematic Continuities between the Vernacular Stories from Dunhuang and the Vernacular Stories from Later Dynasties." In *The Harmony and Prosperity of Civilizations: Selected Papers of the Beijing Forum (2004)*, pp. 114–127. Beijing: Beijing daxue chubanshe.

———, and Beata Grant. 2004. *The Red Brush: Writing Women of Imperial China*. Cambridge: Harvard University Asia Center.

Johnson, Allen W., and Douglass Price-Williams, eds. 1996. *Oedipus Ubiquitous: The Family Complex in World Folk Literature*. Stanford: Stanford University Press.

Karetzky, Patricia Eichenbaum. 2004. *Guanyin*. Hong Kong: Oxford University Press.

Katō, Bunnō, et al., trans. 1975. *The Threefold Lotus Sutra*. Tokyo: Kosei Publishing.

Lai Ruihe 賴瑞和. 1980. "Miaoshan chuanshuo de liangzhong xin ziliao" 妙善傳說的兩種新資料. *Zhongwai wenxue* 9.2:116–126.

Lai, Whalen. 1995. "Unmasking the Filial Sage-King Shun: Oedipus at Anyang." *History of Religions* 35:163–184.

Legge, James, trans. 1971. *The Chinese Classics*. Vol. 4: *The She King or The Book of Poetry*. Repr. Taipei: Wenshizhe chubanshe.

Li Miao 李淼, comp. 2001. *Guanyin pusa baojuan* 觀音菩薩寶卷. Changchun: Jilin renmin chubanshe.

Li Shiyu 李世瑜. 1961. *Baojuan zonglu* 寶卷綜錄. Peking: Zhonghua shuju.

Liu Shouhua 留守華. 1991. "Shilun Dunhuang bianwen *Shunzi zhixiao gushi* di xingtai yanbian" 試論敦煌變文舜子至孝故事的形態衍變. *Huazhong shifan daxue xuebao*, no. 4:72–77.

Lo, Vivienne. 1993. "The Legend of the Lady of Linshui." *Journal of Chinese Religions* 21:69–96.

Lu Ji 陸楫, ed. 1989. *Gujin shuohai* 古今說海. Reprint of 1909 edition. Shanghai: Shanghai wenyi chubanshe.

Luk, Charles, trans. 1972. *The Vimalakirti Nirdesa Sutra*. Berkeley: Shambala.

Mackerras, Colin P. 1972. *The Rise of Peking Opera, 1770–1870*. Oxford: Oxford University Press.

Meng Yuanlao 孟元老. 1962. *Dongjing meng Hua lu (wai sizhong)* 東京夢華錄外四種. Beijing: Zhonghua shuju.

Moerman, D. Max. 2005. *Localizing Paradise: Kunabo Pilgrimage and the Religious Landscape of Premodern Japan*. Cambridge: Harvard University Asia Center.

Mowry, Hua-yuan Li. 1980–1981. "The Wolf of Chung-shan." *Tamkang Review* 11.2:139–159.

Murase, Miyeko. 1971. "Kuan-yin as Savior of Men: Illustrations of the Twenty-fifth Chapter of the Lotus Sutra in Chinese Painting." *Artibus Asiae* 33.1–2:39–73.

Museum of Fine Arts Boston. 1992. *Selected Masterpieces of Asian Art*. Boston: Museum of Fine Arts.

Ng, Zhiru. 2007. *The Making of a Savior Bodhisattva: Dizang in Medieval China*. Honolulu: University of Hawai'i Press.

Ohnuma, Reiko. 1998. "The Gift of the Body and the Gift of the Dharma." *History of Religions* 37.4:321–359.

———. 2007. *Head, Eyes, Flesh, and Blood: Giving Away the Body in Indian Buddhist Literature*. New York: Columbia University Press.

Overmyer, David L. 1999. *Precious Volumes: An Introduction to Chinese Sectarian Scriptures from the Sixteenth and Seventeenth Centuries*. Cambridge: Harvard University Asia Center.

Payne, Richard, and Kenneth K. Tanaka, eds. 2004. *Approaching the Land of Bliss: Religious Practice in the Cult of Amitābha*. Honolulu: University of Hawai'i Press.

Picard, Francois. N.d. "Le chant du squelette (*Kulou ge*)." Unpublished paper.

Po, Sung-nien, and David Johnson. 1992. *Domestic Deities and Auspicious Emblems: The Iconography of Everyday Life in Village China. Popular Prints and Papercuts from the Collection of Po Sung-nien*. Berkeley: Chinese Popular Culture Project.

Qu Jinliang 曲金良. 1995. *Dunhuang fojiao wenxue yanjiu* 敦煌佛教文學研究. Taipei: Wenjin chubanshe.

Reis-Habito, Maria Dorothea. 1993. *Die Dhāraṇī des grossen Erbarmens des Bodhisattva Avalokiteśvara mit tausend Handen und Augen. Übersetzung und Untersuchung ihrer textlichen Grundlage sowie Erforschung ihres Kultes in China*. Nettetal: Steyler Verlag.

———. 1994. "The Great Compassion Dhāraṇī." In Henrik Hjort Sørensen, *The Esoteric Buddhist Tradition*, pp. 31–50. Copenhagen: Seminar for Buddhist Studies.

Riben Lunwangsi micang Shuihu 日本輪王寺密藏水滸. 1994. Ann. Sheng Ruiyu 盛瑞裕. Wuhan: Wuhan daxue chubanshe.

Riley, Jo. 1997. *Chinese Theatre and the Actor in Performance*. Cambridge: Cambridge University Press.

Robertson, Elizabeth. 1991. "The Corporeality of Female Sanctity in *The Life of Saint Margaret*." In Renate Blumenfeld-Kosinski and Timea Szell, eds., *Images of Sainthood in Medieval Europe*, pp. 268–287. Ithaca: Cornell University Press.

Sangren, P. Steven. 1996. "Myths, Gods, and Family Relations." In Meir Shahar and Robert P. Weller, eds., *Unruly Gods: Divinity and Society in China*, pp. 150–183. Honolulu: University of Hawai'i Press.

———. 2003. "Separations, Autonomy, and Recognition in the Production of Gender Differences: Reflections from Considerations of Myths and Laments." In Charles Stafford, ed., *Living with Separation in China: Anthropological Accounts*, pp. 53–84. London: RoutledgeCurzon.

Sawada Mizuho 澤田瑞穗. 1975. *Hōken no kenkyū* 寶卷の研究. Rev. ed. Tokyo: Kokusho kankokai.

———. 1978. *Chūgoku dōbutsu dan* 中國の動物談. Tokyo: Kōbundō.

Schafer, Edward H. 1973. *The Divine Woman: Dragon Ladies and Rain Maidens in T'ang Literature*. Berkeley: University of California Press.

Schipper, Kristofer. 1989. "Mu-lien Plays in Taoist Liturgical Context." In David Johnson, ed., *Ritual Opera, Operatic Ritual*, pp. 126–154. Berkeley: Chinese Popular Culture Project.

Schmid, Neil. 2001. "Tun-huang Literature." In Victor Mair, ed., *The Columbia History of Chinese Literature*, pp. 982–987. New York: Columbia University Press.

———. 2002. "*Yuanqi:* Medieval Buddhist Narratives from Dunhuang." Ph.D. thesis, University of Pennsylvania.

Seaman, Gary. 1977. "Ethnographic Film from the Field to the Classroom: Methodological and Practical Considerations in the Collection and Dissemination of Film Records of Popular Religion in China." *Chinoperl Papers* 7:106–135.

———. 1981. "The Sexual Politics of Karmic Retribution." In Emily Martin

Ahern and Hill Gates, eds., *The Anthropology of Taiwan Society*, pp. 391–396. Stanford: Stanford University Press.

Sen, Tansen, and Victor Mair, trans. 2005. "The Tale of Master Yuan of Mount Lu." In Victor Mair, Nancy S. Steinhard, and Paul R. Goldin, eds., *Hawai'i Reader in Traditional Chinese Culture*, pp. 304–339. Honolulu: University of Hawai'i Press.

Shaughnessy, Edward L. 1997. "How the Poetess Came to Burn the Royal Chamber." In his *Before Confucius: Studies in the Creation of the Chinese Classics*, pp. 221–238. Albany: State University of New York Press.

Sponberg, Alan, and Helen Hardacre, eds. 1988. *Maitreya, the Future Buddha*. Cambridge: Cambridge University Press.

Spring, Madeline K. 1993. *Animal Allegories in T'ang China*. New Haven: American Oriental Society.

Stein, Rolf A. 1986. "Avalokiteśvara/Kouan-yin, un exemple de transformation d'un dieu en déesse." *Cahiers d'Extrême Asie*, pp. 17–80.

Stevenson, Dan. 2004. "The 'Hall for the Sixteen Contemplations' as a Distinctive Institution for Pure Land Practice in Tiantai Monasteries of the Song (960–1279)." In Kalpakam Sankarnayaran, Rabindra Panth, and Ichigo Ogawa, eds., *Buddhism in Global Perspective*, pp. 147–204. Mumbai: Somaiya Publications.

Tanaka Kenji 田中謙二. 1983. *Gafu sankyoku* 樂府散曲. Tokyo: Chikuma shobo.

Teiser, Stephen F. 1994. *The Scripture on the Ten Kings and the Making of Purgatory in Medieval Chinese Buddhism*. Honolulu: University of Hawai'i Press.

Ting, Nai-tung. 1978. *A Type Index of Chinese Folktales in the Oral Tradition and Major Works of Non-religious Classical Literature*. Helsinki: Suomalainen Tiedeakatemia.

Waley, Arthur. 1960. *Ballads and Stories from Tun-huang*. London: George Allen and Unwin.

Wang-Toutain, F. 1998. *Le bodhisattva Kṣitigarbha en Chine du Ve au XIIIe siècle*. Paris: Presses de l'École Française d'Extrême Orient.

Wang Shucun 王樹村, comp. 1995. *Guanyin baitu* 觀音百圖. Guangzhou: Lingnan yishu chubanshe.

Watson, Burton, trans. 1993. *The Lotus Sutra*. New York: Columbia University Press.

———, trans. 1997. *The Vimalakirti Sutra*. New York: Columbia University Press.

Wivell, Charles J., trans. 1994. "The Story of How the Monk Tripitaka of the Great Country of the T'ang Brought Back the Sūtras." In Victor Mair, ed., *The Columbia Book of Traditional Chinese Literature*, pp. 1181–1207. New York: Columbia University Press.

Xiangshan baojuan 香山寶卷. 1914. Shanghai: Wenyi shuju.

Xiangshan baojuan. 1931. Hangzhou: Xihu huikong jingfang.

Xu Hualong 徐華龍. 1991. "*Baishe zhuan* de qianxing yishi" 白蛇傳中的潛性意識. *Minsu quyi* 72:203–225.

Xu Xiaowang 徐曉望. 1993. *Fujian minjian xinyang yuanliu* 福建民間信仰源流. Fuzhou: Fujian jiaoyu chubanshe.

Yan Suhui 顏素慧. 2001. *Guanyin xiaobaike* 觀音小百科. Taibei: Yushushe.

Yi Ruofen 衣若芬. 2005. "*Kulou huanxi—*Zhongguo wenxue yu tuxiang zhong de shengming yishi" 骷髏幻戲—中國文學與圖象中的生命意識. *Zhongguo wenzhe yanjiusuo jikan* 26:73–125.

Yoshioka Yoshitoyo 吉岡義豐. 1989. *Dōkyō kenkyū* 道教研究. Vol. 4. Tokyo: Gogatsu Shobō.

Yü, Chün-fang. 1990. "Images of Kuan-yin in Chinese Folk Literature." *Chinese Studies* 8.1:221–285.

———. 1997. "The Cult of Kuan-yin in Ming-Ch'ing China: A Case of Confucianization of Buddhism?" In Irene Bloom and Joshua A. Fogel, eds., *Meeting of Minds: Intellectual and Religious Interaction in East Asian Traditions of Thought*, pp. 151–165. New York: Columbia University Press.

———. 2001. *Kuan-yin: The Chinese Transformation of Avalokiteśvara*. New York: Columbia University Press.

Yu Junfang (Yü Chün-fang). 1994. "Baojuan wenxue zhongde Guanyin yu minjian xinyang 寶卷文學中旳觀音與民間信仰." In Lin Ru 林如, ed., *Minjian xinyang yu Zhongguo wenhua guoji yantaohui lunwenji* 民間信仰與中國文化國際研討會論文集, pp. 333–351. Taipei: Hanxue yanjiu zhongxin.

Zhang Xishun 張希舜 et al., eds. 1994. *Baojuan chuji* 寶卷初集. 40 vols. Taiyuan: Shanxi renmin chubanshe.

Zheng Zhenduo 鄭振鐸. 1961. "Zhongshan lang gushi de yanbian" 中山狼故事旳演變. In his *Zhongguo wenxue yanjiu* 中國文學研究, 3:1123–1124. Hong Kong: Guwen shuju.

Zürcher, Erik. 1959. *The Buddhist Conquest of China: The Spread and Adaptation of Buddhism in Early Medieval China*. 2 vols. Leiden: E. J. Brill.

About the Author

Wilt L. Idema (Ph.D. Leiden University 1974) teaches Chinese literature at Harvard University. His main area of research is Chinese vernacular literature of the later imperial dynasties, including fiction, drama, and narrative ballads. His numerous publications on these subjects include both studies and translations. In recent years he has become increasingly interested in the interactions between popular literature and popular religion, and in women's literature. His more recent publications in English include *A Guide to Chinese Literature* (with Lloyd Haft; University of Michigan Center for Chinese Studies, 1997), *The Red Brush: Writing Women of Imperial China* (with Beata Grant; Harvard University Asia Center, 2004), and *Meng Jiangnü Brings Down the Great Wall: Ten Versions of a Chinese Legend* (University of Washington Press, 2008).

Kuroda Institute
Studies in East Asian Buddhism

Studies in Ch'an and Hua-yen
Robert M. Gimello and Peter N. Gregory, editors

Dôgen Studies
William R. LaFleur, editor

The Northern School and the Formation of Early Ch'an Buddhism
John R. McRae

Traditions of Meditation in Chinese Buddhism
Peter N. Gregory, editor

Sudden and Gradual: Approaches to Enlightenment in Chinese Thought
Peter N. Gregory, editor

Buddhist Hermeneutics
Donald S. Lopez, Jr., editor

Paths to Liberation: The Marga and Its Transformations in Buddhist Thought
Robert E. Buswell, Jr., and Robert M. Gimello, editors

Sôtô Zen in Medieval Japan
William M. Bodiford

The Scripture on the Ten Kings *and the Making of Purgatory in Medieval Chinese Buddhism*
Stephen F. Teiser

The Eminent Monk: Buddhist Ideals in Medieval Chinese Hagiography
John Kieschnick

Re-Visioning "Kamakura" Buddhism
Richard K. Payne, editor

Original Enlightenment and the Transformation of Medieval Japanese Buddhism
Jacqueline I. Stone

Buddhism in the Sung
Peter N. Gregory and Daniel A. Getz, Jr., editors

Coming to Terms with Chinese Buddhism: A Reading of The Treasure Store Treatise
Robert H. Sharf

Ryôgen and Mount Hiei: Japanese Tendai in the Tenth Century
Paul Groner

Tsung-mi and the Sinification of Buddhism
Peter N. Gregory

Approaching the Land of Bliss: Religious Praxis in the Cult of Amitabha
Richard K. Payne and Kenneth K. Tanaka, editors

Going Forth: Visions of Buddhist Vinaya
William M. Bodiford, editor

Burning for the Buddha: Self-Immolation in Chinese Buddhism
James A. Benn

The Buddhist Dead: Practices, Discourses, Representations
Bryan J. Cuevas and Jacqueline I. Stone, editors

The Making of a Savior Bodhisattva: Dizang in Medieval China
Zhiru